English Teachers –
the Unofficial Guide

English teaching has always courted controversy. Its centrality to the curriculum has meant that our view of English is intimately bound up with our view of education and society itself.

Bethan Marshall traces the competing traditions of English teaching and considers their relevance to the current debate through an analysis of English teachers' views about themselves and their subject. The findings are based on a highly original research method in which teachers were asked to respond to and comment upon five different descriptions of their approaches to English teaching.

English Teachers – the Unofficial Guide:

- contextualises current debates about English teaching within the subject's contested history;
- provides a vehicle for teachers to reflect on their own practice and locate themselves within the debate;
- opens up the debate on assessment practices within English teaching.

This fascinating book reveals the complexities of the teachers' views of their subject. It will be an essential read for Postgraduate Certificate in Education students, secondary English teachers and academics interested in the English curriculum debate.

Bethan Marshall taught English in London comprehensives for several years before taking up her current post as a lecturer in education at King's College London. A frequent commentator on educational policy, she writes regularly for the broadsheets as well as the *Times Educational Supplement*.

English Teachers –
the Unofficial Guide
Researching the philosophies
of English teachers

Bethan Marshall

London and New York

For Richard, Myfanwy and Angharad

First published 2000
by RoutledgeFalmer
11 New Fetter Lane, London EC4P 4EE

Simultaneously published in the USA and Canada
by RoutledgeFalmer
29 West 35th Street, New York, NY 10001

RoutledgeFalmer is an imprint of the Taylor & Francis Group

© 2000 Bethan Marshall

Typeset in Goudy by
The Running Head Limited, Cambridge
Printed and bound in Great Britain by MPG Books, Bodmin

British Library Cataloguing in Publication Data
A catalogue record for this book is available from the British Library

Library of Congress Cataloging-in-Publication Data
Marshall, Bethan, 1958–
English teachers: the unofficial guide: researching the
philosophies of English teachers
Bethan Marshall.
    p. cm.
Includes bibliographical references and index.
1. English philology–Study and teaching–Great Britain.
2. English teachers–Great Britain–Attitudes. I. Title.
PE68.G5 M37   2000
428′.0071′041—dc21   00–042203

ISBN 0–415–24077–8 (hbk)
ISBN 0–415–24078–6 (pbk)

Contents

Figures and tables

Figures

Tables

Acknowledgements

At the risk of sounding like an overwrought actor on Oscar night, I would like to thank the following people without whom this book would not have been possible. I have to begin with my colleagues Diane Reay and Dylan Wiliam, who have guided and encouraged me throughout. Their keen minds and diverse contributions to this research have been invaluable, and without them I doubt whether the enterprise would have ever been completed. I must thank too those who have read, proof-read and commented on sections of this book, in particular Brian Street and Elizabeth Catherwood. Their marginal notes have forced me to clarify my thoughts and examine my analysis. I am most grateful also to Tony Burgess, Brian Cox, Chris Davies, Terry Furlong, Kit Thomas and Anne Turvey, all of whom gave up their time to read this work in its various states of readiness. They have provided me with valuable insight and much needed support.

So too have all those who have allowed me to bore them as I grappled with some of the finer points of the argument. The list is too long to recount here and it would be invidious to select any one in particular. Next come the legion of English teachers who filled in the Rough Guide, along with those who, unwittingly, helped me in its creation by being so vociferous in their views that I could not help but form an opinion of their philosophy. I must thank also Tom Paulin, whose scholarship pervades this work and who is the English teacher everyone should have. I would like to thank also Anna Clarkson, my editor, and her assistant, Rachel Larman.

Last but by no means least I need to thank my family who have tolerated my hours at the computer with remarkable forbearance. Myfanwy and Angharad not only lent me their coloured pencils to code the responses but also helped me to keep a sense of perspective. And Richard, also an English teacher, has, by turns, read, argued, kept quiet, been bored, encouraged and cajoled throughout. It is to him that I owe the greatest debt.

In Chapter 6 official acknowledgement is made to the Joint Matriculation Board for allowing access to confidential material. The JMB does not necessarily accept the views expressed in this chapter.

Introduction

When I began this research I faced a dilemma. All my academic training fitted me for research in the humanities. The way I wrote, the way I thought, the way I analysed all suited a very different purpose from the one on which I was about to embark – research in the social sciences. Although my desire to find the implicit subject philosophies of English teachers was the question of a social scientist, the tools that I felt I had for discovering them lay more with the art of criticism than anything else. Given, however, that I came from the same subject discipline as the object of my gaze, I began to wonder whether this potential weakness might not be turned into a strength. I had already undertaken research (Marshall and Brindley, 1998) – which will be discussed in chapter 5 – that suggested English teachers shared some of my misgivings about more conventional forms of data collection. And so I began to explore the ways in which I could develop a research instrument that would allow the English teachers I was researching, as well as myself, to use the skills we all possessed – those of analysing and critiquing a text.

The end result of this process was the Rough Guide to English Teachers (see after p. 56), a small booklet which contained descriptions of five different kinds of English teachers. Those surveyed were asked to respond by analysing the texts I had provided. By almost literally characterising their philosophies in this way, and by demanding textual analysis as a way of validating them, I had developed a research instrument which paid heed to its audience. The book is an account of the origins of these philosophies, found in chapters 1 and 2; the development of the instrument, in chapter 3; the responses of teachers to both its form and content, in chapters 4 and 5; and finally, in chapter 6 the suggestion of a possible use that might be made of such information beyond the simple desire to know what kind of English teacher one is.

As this list implies, the formation of the research instrument itself was inseparable from the other task I had posed myself in creating it – that of defining the implicit subject philosophies of English teachers. Many of the more recent attempts to explore subject philosophies have either simply set themselves up in opposition to their perception of the prevailing hegemony, or have been written too near in time to the many curriculum changes that have taken place. This has made it harder fully to take into account the impact that these changes have had on teachers' philosophies. My own attempt at researching these views is, in part, an attempt to rectify this gap. The battles over the curriculum in the last ten years, which will be explored in greater depth in the first chapter, have forced English teachers to define and redefine their subject philosophies in the light of the policy demands made on them.

My task was made no easier by the curious conundrum that is English teaching. It is a subject which is apparently so amorphous that it eludes definition and yet it is sufficiently hard edged to provoke bitter controversy. When discussing the nature of English teaching a certain vagueness often comes over those endeavouring to define it. Some simply capitulate. Paddy Creber in his book *Thinking through English* admits that 'English is an untidy subject!' (Creber, 1990: 5), though the exclamation mark suggests that he does not view this as a wholly negative state of affairs. Peter Medway goes further by trying to pinpoint some of the reasons for this untidiness. He writes:

> In any study of a general phenomenon . . . There is particular interest in a deviant case. In the history of school subjects and of the processes by which they emerged, were sustained, flourished or failed to flourish, adapted or failed to adapt, the case of English in England and Wales provides such a special instance. The first way in which English is special is that certain characteristics generally attributable to academic subjects are notably lacking. The most obvious example is that English does not comprise a body of facts and concepts to be communicated.
>
> (Medway, 1990: 1)

In the same volume as Medway, Stephen Ball, another frequent commentator on English teaching – though, unusually in this field, not a former practitioner – develops the theme further by considering some of the implications of that lack of definition. Along with his two co-authors, Ball points out that 'since the beginnings of mass public education in England and Wales, the teaching of English has been a focus of keen political interest and political control' (Ball, Kenny and Gardiner, 1990: 47). They go on to add: 'Concomitantly, English teaching, the definition of what is to count as English, has been a matter of struggle and conflict between contending interests' (ibid.: 47). The title of the volume, *Bringing English to Order*, is intended to reflect the desire of governments to 'discipline practitioners and rectify "unacceptable" deviations from that version of English which best suits the interests of dominant political elites' (ibid.: 47).

In his book *English and Englishness* Doyle elaborates on the reason for such unwanted attention by observing the centrality of English to the way in which we view education:

> English came to occupy a strategically central role . . . within the national education system . . . from the 1920s, the ensemble of pedagogic practices and knowledges began to be reordered around a 'modern' curriculum centred upon English.
>
> (Doyle, 1989: 39)

Of course it is the subject's very lack of definition that allows it to be so fiercely contested. It enables everyone to have their 'version of English'. Some more recent policy makers have acknowledged that there are different views. Both the Cox Report (DES and WO, 1989) and, to a lesser extent, the Bullock Report, which preceded it (DES, 1975) outlined different versions of the subject. However, the Literacy Hour (DfEE, 1998) and the latest attempt to redefine English for a new curriculum document (DfEE, 1999a) do not acknowledge these differences and present a non-problematised view. This only adds to the need for further debate. For these conflicting views of English continue to reverberate both publicly and politically.

This then is the canvas against which the philosophies in the Rough Guide are drawn. To extend the metaphor for a moment, the process is also something of a self-portrait both in its form and content. It is an insider's account. But to return to a more literary vein, I am an English teacher, and throughout this research I have drawn on my knowledge and understanding of the issues and the people involved. My use of empathy, personal writing and close reading of the text – as well as my consideration of the audience and the social and historical context of the debate – are all practices which English teachers seek to foster to a greater or lesser extent. In this way I have written the subject discipline into the very heart of this research, into the research design, into the very fabric of the analysis. I offer a narrative of sorts, complete with characters, setting, conflict and a kind of resolution. I even build in the critics' response. Let us turn then to chapter 1.

1 The battle for the curriculum

The last ten years have seen unprecedented public debate about what constitutes English teaching. Many views on the subject, often vociferously expressed, are not held by teachers themselves, but they add to the general noise of controversy. Indeed they are often articulated to counteract the perceived practices of English teachers. Writing on the eve of the National Curriculum, which was to prompt so much of the discussion, James Britton and Nancy Martin (1989) pointed out that the opinions of English teachers themselves have often been only marginal to the debate.

Yet there is a sense in which the profession only started to focus on the question of what kind of English teacher a person was when, in 1990, the Conservative government required all English teachers to teach to the same script. This is not to say that debate had not existed before. Others had noted that English was a contested subject. John Dixon, in his influential *Growth through English* (1975, first published in 1967), had identified three views of the subject which he called 'cultural heritage', 'skills' and 'personal growth'. The 1975 *A Language for Life: Report of the Committee of Inquiry*, commonly called the Bullock Report, based on the results of a questionnaire, also identifies 'personal growth' and 'skills' along with 'English as an instrument of social change' (DES, 1975: para. 1.3). These two previous attempts most closely echo those of Professor Brian Cox and his working party. For it was this group, which reported in 1989, that brought these differences into the public domain.

English for Ages 5–16, known as the Cox Report, identified five 'views of English teaching: personal growth, cross curricular, adult needs, cultural heritage and cultural analysis' (DES and WO, 1989: paras 2.20–27). The choice of the word *view* is significant in that Cox and his working party were not necessarily attributing these views to English teachers themselves. Rather, they were suggesting that these views needed to be identified before they got on with the complex task of writing an English curriculum, for their audience lay not only within the profession but outside it as well, in the form of politicians and the electorate, to whom Cox and his committee had to sell the idea. In his book about the writing of the curriculum Cox comments, for example, 'Mr Baker was not entirely wrong in wanting a simple, forceful document for parents, though he failed to understand that some difficult issues – the teaching of grammar or Standard English, for example – need careful and detailed explanation' (Cox, 1991: 22). On the other hand, he writes, 'I feared that many readers, prejudiced by the supposed right wing commitment of the group, would misread the report, and take it for granted that we were opposed to all the innovations of recent years' (ibid.: 23).

The fact that he felt compelled, unlike any of the other subject writers, to indicate that there were different views of the subject is in itself indicative of the complexity of the subject and the controversy it attracts. In his book Cox makes clear his chief purposes in laying bare the different approaches to the English curriculum: 'This list is of vital importance, for it gives a broad approach to the curriculum which can unite the profession' (ibid.: 21). He is adamant, however, that the views 'were not to be seen as sharply distinguishable, and certainly not mutually exclusive' (DES and WO, 1989: para. 2.20 and Cox, 1991: 21).

Others disagreed. In a detailed analysis of the five Cox models, as they became known, Jay Snow argued that ' "cultural heritage" view and "personal growth" have been historically intertwined in a project to deploy English as a means of managing, through humanising, the mass populations of industrial society' (Snow, 1991: 26). Snow went on to add that while Cox implied a passivity in 'cultural analysis' and 'adult needs', he advocated 'an active understanding that involves experience in their own control over "the processes by which meanings are conveyed" ' (ibid.: 26). If this were done, he argued, ' "cultural analysis" should replace "personal growth" as the starting point for the rationale for English, informing all aspects of our work' (ibid.: 26).

Similarly, Ken Jones argued in *English and the National Curriculum: Cox's revolution* (Jones, 1992) that the attempt to present a balanced view ignored the way in which 'cultural analysis' actively opposed a 'cultural heritage' view of the curriculum. Interestingly, neither of Jones' nor Snow's articles actually questioned Cox's five models; rather, both critiqued the first four and situated themselves firmly in the last category. As Snow wrote,

> Helping our students to use language and literature for critical analysis, and providing them with the linguistic resources necessary for access to the discourse of power, can enable them to reflect on their position as subjects and to participate in setting the agenda for social change.
> (Snow, 1991: 26)

While not referring to the Cox models, the agenda is perhaps most clearly stated in Terry Eagleton's article in the same edition of *English in Education*. The article had started life as a keynote speech to the National Association for the Teaching of English's 1991 annual conference. In it Eagleton issued the following challenge:

> The radical project, then, turns out to be the traditional one. English studies appeared on the scene as a form of critical deconstruction – as the enemy within; and what we on the left seek to do is to return to that moment and stay faithful to it in fresh ways.
>
> (Eagleton, 1991: 9)

Nevertheless, because the Cox views of the curriculum had allowed for different readings, and because the document included little actual prescribed content, there was room to approach it in a number of different ways, and it was generally welcomed. The document contained no prescribed canon of literature, only that Shakespeare and some pre-twentieth-century literature should be taught. It also allowed for a critical or historical reading of 'Some of the works which have been most influential in shaping and refining the English language' (DES and WO, 1990: 31). Standard English and grammar, which Cox had been careful to discuss in his report, were to be taught in the context of knowledge about language, which allowed for critical language awareness. The report had noted, for example, that while standard English was a 'dialect', it was nevertheless 'the native language of a certain social group', as well the language of 'commerce and the professions' (ibid.: paras 4.5, 4.9 and 4.11).

It is also possible that what Snow described as 'the primacy of Cox's "personal growth" model' (Snow, 1991: 26) had found favour among the English teachers themselves. The working party had included a quotation from the famous Plowden Report of 1967 (DES and WO, 1967). 'At the heart of the educational process lies the child. No advances in policy, no acquisitions of new equipment have their desired effect unless they are in harmony with the nature of the child' (cited in DES and WO, 1989). Cox comments: 'the inclusion of this quotation attracted considerable good will' (Cox, 1991: 23–4).

Andrew Goodwyn, in an article in *English in Education*, two years after the introduction of the curriculum, writes,

> The reaction to Cox's final report was generally positive; organisations such as NATE [National Association for the Teaching of English] welcomed it in broad terms, and teachers in schools seemed relieved by the report's contents and supportive of Cox's ideas. So

Cox seemed to have considerable evidence of his assertions; perhaps he is right about the happy coexistence of five apparently disparate and even oppositional views.

(Goodwyn, 1992: 4–5)

Unlike Snow and Jones, however, Goodwyn asked how many of these views were actually held by English teachers themselves. In what he describes as research 'which is by no means complete', and 'offering some tentative conclusions' (ibid.: 5), he discusses a survey of 46 respondents teaching English in a range of schools and sixth form colleges. He divided the results of his survey into personal priorities and current influence. Personal growth emerged most strongly as the 'most important model for the majority of teachers' (ibid.: 5) and it was also 'perceived as the most influential' (ibid.). Cultural analysis he felt, however, was 'making its mark' (ibid.: 5) and emerged as the second in the list of personal priorities. Significantly, however, few English teachers saw this as a 'current influence' (ibid.: 5).

Goodwyn interprets the discrepancy between these two positions as an indication that there is still ambiguity over the role of media studies and its place within English teaching. What is more likely is that those who were most sympathetic to 'cultural analysis' saw little or no encouragement for this position in the way the government's policies were drawn up. The rewriting of the National Curriculum for English, by David Pascall and his working party, had just begun, and changes to assessment at key stage 3 had been announced in the summer of 1992, following previous alterations the year before. It is possible that the group who identified with a 'cultural analysis' position would be most alive to the political implications of government policy and would interpret 'current influence' in a way that understood external as well as internal influences on English teachers.

The other Cox models fared less well in Goodwyn's survey. The vast majority of teachers 'rejected having the chief responsibility for cross-curricular English'. 'Cultural heritage is seen as relatively unimportant now and over 80 per cent felt that it was more important for pupils to know about a range of texts than the conventional canon' (ibid.: 7). And finally, 'They placed adult needs last on their list of personal priorities and last as a current influence on English teaching' (ibid.: 8).

Goodwyn's conclusions attempt to make sense of the evidence of his survey. What they do not do is challenge the efficacy of the models of English. They only record that, despite their presence on Cox's list, few if any English teachers hold them. His central question, then, is how to resolve the differences between the predominant personal growth model and that of emerging cultural analysis. 'My view', he concludes, 'is that these models are developing into a composite of both' (ibid.: 9). He charts three important influences: the rise of media education, knowledge about language, and the study of literature, which 'becomes part of culture in a broad not canonical way'. All these areas of study, he contends, can be interpreted as providing scope for personal growth and cultural analysis.

In an article for the *British Educational Research Journal* entitled 'English Teacher Ideologies: An empirical study', Chris Davies takes a different approach. Noting in passing that the five categories of English teacher, as identified by Cox, have their antecedents in the Bullock Report of 1975, he comments that it is more likely

> that both Bullock and Cox present classifications of views derived from published literature on the subject (going all the way back to Newbolt, and thus further back to Arnold, in the instance of Bullock), and from submissions written specially for the respective committees by professionals whose expertise lies in their capacity to express the kind of systematic theories about the subject that practising teachers might literally have no time for.
>
> (Davies, 1992: 195)

He comments that, until the introduction of the National Curriculum, 'English teachers have tended to assert their freedom from rigid curriculum structures, their professional autonomy, quite explicitly' (ibid.: 193), and goes on to argue that the 'National Curriculum does not appear to have wholly removed this sense of independence' (ibid.). Therefore, he contends,

> It appears worthwhile to ask questions about the nature of English teachers' beliefs and convictions regarding their subject, because it is likely that on occasions teachers exercise their autonomy . . . under some degree of influence from their subject ideologies.
>
> (ibid.: 195)

Unlike Goodwyn, who had sought ways of integrating a personal growth model with one of cultural analysis, Davies' work concentrated on four main areas in which 'the overall subject field became apparent', adding that 'these were of particular interest, in that each area represented a distinct instance of attitudinal opposition within the subject' (ibid.: 198). His four areas considered the role of literature within English, the personal as opposed to the political dimension of English, the tension between educating taste and valuing popular culture, and the value placed on Standard English. This gave him two broad hypothetical categories: mainstream/conservative and innovatory/radical.

Like Goodwyn, he surveyed teachers by means of a questionnaire to test this hypothesis and discovered that 'the opposition between a mainstream conservative ideology and an innovatory/radical ideology was shown to be the dominant dimension among the set of statements included in the questionnaire' (ibid.: 201). In his book *What Is English Teaching?* (Davies, 1996) he elaborates on his 1992 paper, calling these two groups liberal humanists and cultural theorists. He cautions, however, that 'these teachers tended to eschew strong or extreme positions . . . there was generally little enthusiasm for any heavy statements about any aspect of the subject, modern or traditional' (Davies, 1996: 27).

These two broad categories are found again in Peter Griffiths' book *English at the Core* (Griffiths, 1992). While he does not refer to them directly they are implicit within his analysis of classroom practice and his appeal for a different approach in the light of the National Curriculum. Identifying the dominant influence of personal growth as a model of English teaching, he argues that

> It is important for teachers to have an increased awareness of the effects and the effectiveness of the discourse which earns them their daily bread. So long as they believe that their activities are essentially neutral as social practices, they will continue to produce powerful social results all unawares.
>
> (ibid.: 18)

He goes on to assert that this broadly liberal approach, which favours 'personal development as an all-sufficient pedagogy, cannot be sufficient against this new populism' (ibid.: 18) as typified by the back to basics campaign of the Conservative government. He develops the point by commenting that it is

> Insufficiently effective, I think, because personal growth has frequently (though not invariably) tended to be construed as individual in an atomistic sense – as a developmental process which can be helped or hindered by classroom material and classroom conversation, but in which the social dimension is often weak and occasionally negligible . . . What English teachers might profitably attempt to do is to work with a much more dialogic and social model of language and learning, and personal growth, and one which fully recognises the constraints of the institutional nexus of the school, the curriculum and the state.
>
> (ibid.: 18)

In many respects this is an echo of Terry Eagleton's call to English teachers on the left to be 'the enemy within' (Eagleton, 1991: 9). But it also
reflects the tension between Davies' two broad categories of the mainstream and radical English teacher, while describing it differently. For
Griffiths the key factor is less the attitude to the subject itself than the
way the teachers position themselves and their pupils in relation to the
institution and society in which they both find themselves. It is from this
that all else follows.

In his article Snow, however, identified ways in which these two
oppositional agendas (that of the mainstream, personal growth model,
and the radical or innovative) may coalesce around the notion of 'social
transformation' (Snow, 1991). Unlike Goodwyn, who seeks to resolve
them, he writes of this possibility more as a warning. As we have seen, for
Snow, Cox's description of 'cultural analysis' has too passive a ring. Preferring, therefore, to describe it as 'critical literacy' he argues, with Eagleton,
that 'literature can be a means of exploring "difference and otherness in
terms of both class and gender"' (ibid.: 22). And he looks to the work of
Paulo Freire to extend the concept:

> Literacy becomes a meaningful construct to the degree that it is viewed
> as a set of practices that functions to either empower or disempower
> people. In this larger sense, literacy must be analysed according to
> whether it promotes democratic and emancipatory change.
>
> (cited in Snow, ibid.: 22)

Yet, he suggests,

> There are dangers in a notion of social change which emphasises a
> plan for 'society as a whole'. If the project of Arnold and Newbolt
> was to create a particular kind of society through the educational
> production of individuals as subjects, it is possible that critical
> literacy might involve a similar subjugation to 'the overall goals of
> national reconstruction' . . . Critical literacy, like progressivism, offers
> a model of social change which requires the educational production
> of particular forms of subjectivity – the individual discovering as true
> an identity determined by the 'plan for society as a whole'.
>
> (ibid.: 23)

All these articles and research were carried out, however, before the Pascall
revisions to the National Curriculum. Where Cox had found some form
of consensus, albeit around two readings of his five views, which broadly
either ignored or critiqued the other three, the Pascall curriculum (DfE

and WO, 1993) united English teachers in opposition to it. The resolution that Goodwyn looked for and Snow guarded against was found in opposition to further government reforms. And it is worth at this point pausing to record them.

In 1991, with Kenneth Clarke as Secretary of State for Education, the government had commissioned Warwick University to examine the effects of the National Curriculum on primary English. In that same year the government had suppressed the publication of the Language in the National Curriculum project materials. The project was headed by the linguist Professor Ronald Carter, who had been given the brief of providing materials for teachers to improve their own knowledge about language and the teaching of it. Carter's work and the LINC materials he and his team had produced were dismissed as being 'unsuitable' (Eggar, cited in Cox, 1995: 17). Professor Christopher Brumfit of Southampton University (who later directed the report on grammar teaching published in June 1996) was moved at the time, in *The Oxford Companion to the English Language*, to describe the suppression of the publication as 'an act of direct political censorship' (Brumfit, 1992: 269).

In 1992 John Patten, the new Secretary of State for Education, decided that the English curriculum needed revising. *National Curriculum English: The case for revising the order* (NCC, 1992) was said to have been based on the interim report of the Warwick group which demonstrated that there was an urgent case for revision, particularly 'in the teaching of initial reading'. The research was not published at the time and it is hardly surprising, for Patten's whole 'case' rested on the fieldwork of half the spring term in 1992. Only sixteen key stage 1 (infant) and five key stage 2 (junior) classrooms had been visited. The researchers had interviewed eleven teachers at key stage 1, three at key stage 2 and looked at the school documents in four schools (three infant and one junior). They described their findings as 'very tentative' (cited in Cox, 1995: 44). Both Bridie Raban-Risby (1995), head of the Warwick team, and Urzula Clark (1994) subsequently wrote about the way they felt their findings were misused. Raban-Risby's balanced account of the actual findings belies the ways they were represented at the time. Clark, in an intensely personal account, describes the whole process as 'working in a dark ever receding tunnel' (Clark, 1994: 31), adding, 'As far as I am aware the project team was not consulted about the document [the case for revising the order] prior to its publication, or given any indication of how its work might be used in preparing its case' (ibid.: 36).

Despite this and in the face of overwhelming opposition from teachers and academics, which would have been even greater had they known the 'very tentative' basis on which it rested, in September 1992 John Patten ordered the revision. The report was eventually published in 1994 (Raban, Clark and McIntyre, 1994), too late for anyone to compare its findings with the way they had been represented. But the summer of 1992 had seen a concerted campaign to undermine the Cox curriculum. Brian Griffiths had described it in a leaked letter to the *Sunday Times* as 'imprecise and woolly' (cited in Cox, 1995: 56). The psychologist Martin Turner, a leading campaigner for teaching reading solely through the use of phonics and who later, in a *Guardian* article, described Cox as a disciple of the 'anarchist' Gramsci, claimed that it had been influenced by 'fads' and 'fashions' (ibid.: 36). In a speech to his local constituency John Patten implied that the whole curriculum was influenced by 'soft headed' (ibid.: 57) and progressive approaches to the teaching of English which were undermining standards. In the words of Duncan Graham, head of the NCC until 1991, the perception was that 'Cox had, against all the odds, gone native' (Graham, 1996: 176).

As for the curriculum itself, the working party to revise the orders was headed up by David Pascall and included Martin Turner. No attempt at consensus was made. Only one view predominated. Joan Clanchy, head of the North London Collegiate, an independent girls' school, resigned. In her letter of resignation to John Patten she complained that 'the dominant aim has become a curriculum designed for tests and the result is a model of English teaching which is barren and anti-intellectual' (cited in Cox, 1995: 38). And, in an article for the *Times Educational Supplement*, she described the lack of debate, objecting to 'only being given Centre for Policy Studies pamphlets to read by way of homework' (ibid.: 38). NATE's *Made Tongue Tied by Authority: New orders for English? A response by the National Association for the Teaching of English to the review of the statutory order for English* (published in November 1992), which included an article by Brian Cox, made no impact on government policy.

Mary Bousted describes the influence of the Centre for Policy Studies in her article 'When Will They Ever Learn?' (Bousted, 1993) and looks in particular at the paper written by John Marenbon, *English Our English*, who was at the time responsible for the controversial key stage 3 testing arrangements in English. In it he acknowledges the personal growth model but virtually dismisses it as an irrelevance by arguing that

> It is doubtless valuable that children should grow emotionally, that they should learn to tolerate the views of others and to engage in critical thinking. But these – and many others of the ambitious aims often proposed for English – are virtues which are slowly acquired in the course of acquiring particular intellectual skills and areas of knowledge. Time given to a vague and generalised attempt to gain such virtues is time lost to the specific and rigorous studies which alone

will foster them. English could be one of these studies, were it to pursue the simple and well defined aims of teaching children to write and speak standard English correctly and in initiating their acquaintance with the literary heritage of the language.

(Marenbon, 1987: 18)

The influence of this paper on the initial Pascall curriculum, published in April 1993, is evident, although Marenbon himself later attempted to withdraw from the fray and distance himself from the ensuing battles in papers such as 'English, the Government and the Curriculum' (Marenbon, 1994). In this, presented at a conference at the University of East Anglia, he attempts to suggest minimal state intervention while attempting to re-characterise his views as '"conservative pluralism"' (ibid.: 9). Some in his audience, however, were still left unconvinced that any real change had taken place. John Dixon, writing about Marenbon's paper, was moved to write: 'As he continued with his own speech, I realised that he had little or no conception of what most of us meant by English teaching' (Dixon, 1994: 3).

To return to Pascall: Standard English is unambiguously described as being 'characterised by the correct use of vocabulary and grammar' (DfE and WO, 1993: 9). That the model of writing emphasised technical accuracy over expression is evident in the way the strands and statements of attainment were presented. All but one – composition, a slightly old fashioned term in itself – refer to some form of technical skill. Reading, for the first time, contained a literary canon to be taught. 'Pupils should read a range of high quality literature and be introduced to texts of central importance to the literary heritage' (ibid.: 27). It omitted all references to media studies, information technology and knowledge about language.

This belief in a curriculum as a transmitter of values, through an unproblematic notion of 'literary heritage', ran completely contrary to the two predominant models of English teaching. Faced with such an overtly right-wing curriculum most English teachers were no longer able to see 'that their activities [were] essentially neutral as social practices' (Griffiths, 1992: 18), and so they joined the cultural theorists in opposition, having been forced to realise 'the constraints of the institutional nexus of the school, the curriculum and the state' (ibid.: 18). In particular, as we shall see in chapters 2 and 5, they lent their support to the boycott of the National Curriculum tests.

And this opposition meant that almost all English teachers became, whether consciously or not, 'the enemy within'. The way Brian Cox himself is perceived is significant in understanding the extent to which the Pascall curriculum brought this about. Not only, as we have seen, did Martin Turner describe him as a disciple of the 'anarchist' Gramsci, Melanie

Phillips, in her book *All Must Have Prizes* (1997), also sees Cox as having betrayed his previous position as author of the Black Papers. Seeing his book, *The Battle for the Curriculum*, as 'the final betrayal of the stand Cox had once made on behalf of children against those detached and super-cilious ideologues whose measure he had once so devastatingly taken' (Phillips, 1997: 156–7), she goes on to argue that 'His proposals for English, though watered down, remain the bedrock of the English curriculum and continue to be used as a justification of the New Literacy culture' (ibid.: 157). The champion of personal growth had apparently become a cultural analyst.

The 'slimmed down' Dearing curriculum in Easter 1995, following in the wake of two years of industrial dispute over the testing regime of the National (see chapter 6), was, however, based on the Pascall rather than the Cox curriculum. The canon remained, as did echoes of the rationale behind it. 'Pupils should be introduced to major works of literature from the English literary heritage' (DfEE and WO, 1995: 20). Any twentieth-century writers should be 'high quality' with 'well established reputations' (ibid.: 20).

Standard English also received far greater prominence than in the Cox curriculum. Each one of the attainment targets now included a section labelled Standard English and Language Study; the definition of Standard English no longer included references to its status as a dialect or identification with social class. Rather, it simply states: 'Standard English is distinguished from other forms of English by its vocabulary, and by its rules and conventions of grammar, spelling and punctuation' (ibid.: 3).

What really marks out the difference between the Dearing curriculum and the Cox curriculum, however, is its overriding tone. Born out of a need to compromise, Dearing takes a pragmatic approach to the controversies that raged throughout the three years of industrial dispute. While flawed, the Cox curriculum situates itself firmly within a liberal arts tradition. At the end of his autobiography Cox nails his colours to the mast. As he looks to the challenge facing schools, he writes:

> Behind all these arguments about resources and organisation lies the question of how far we retain the faith of Matthew Arnold in the civilising power of the Humanities. My life-long enthusiasm for teaching literature testifies to my own commitment. I still hold to the words that I wrote in 1968 at the end of our editorial for the tenth anniversary of *Critical Quarterly*: 'Great literature helps to keep alive our most subtle and delicate feelings, our capacity for wonder, and our faith in human individuality'.
>
> (Cox, 1992: 268)

And he continues to campaign for this vision. *Literacy Is not Enough*, a collection of essays edited by Brian Cox, was compiled, in part, as a response to the Labour government's National Literacy Strategy (DfEE, 1998). The book was aimed at those who seek to reduce reading and writing to a set of skills, to remind them that words are more than marks on a page to be decoded; that language is a way of creating meaning and a tool of the imagination. In the foreword Cox argues that the reaction against 'the progressive Utopianism of the 1960s . . . has gone too far', adding 'Most English teachers believe that the study of English language and literature contributes to personal growth [and] the development of a creative imagination' (Cox, 1998: ix). While welcoming such initiatives as the National Year of Reading and the Labour government's 'determination to improve basic standards of literacy' he hopes that they 'will acknowledge that its policy of teaching reading is too prescriptive, authoritarian and mechanistic' (ibid.: ix).

At the time of writing this book, draft proposals for extending the literacy strategy into the secondary sector are circulating. They have already had two distinct incarnations. In the summer of 1999 the Qualifications and Curriculum Authority sent out draft proposals for schemes of work at key stage 3 (QCA, 1999a). It seems that these were intended to show how the plethora of requirements for the literacy strategy could be incorporated into the secondary curriculum. They outlined a variety of activities including work on novels, poetry, the media, drama and language. While unobjectionable in themselves the general tenor of the work focused heavily on the analytical skills pupils were intended to acquire, and this gave all the schemes a somewhat dry flavour. This is never clearer than when the range of writing tasks are considered. According to their own breakdown of the range of activities to be undertaken by pupils over the three years of key stage 3 the ratio of analytical tasks to creative or imaginative ones is roughly five to one.

They will, it appears, never see the light of day. For in January 2000, David Blunkett formally announced the introduction of the Literacy Hour into year 7, with the addition of another literacy test to be sat at the end of that year. This will be taken for the first time in 2001. Accompanying Blunkett's announcement have been further draft proposals, five to date (DfEE, 2000), which, like the Literacy Hour, set out those areas of knowledge and skills (at word, sentence and text level) that children must acquire. Given the somewhat minimalist nature of these lists in their present form, they are in one sense less prescriptive than the previous incarnation. Teachers will be free to incorporate them in whatever form they choose. And they are of course non-statutory. Yet their very existence makes them an issue with which English teachers must deal and this inevitably makes them harder to ignore. Their concentration on the technical aspects of English make them closer in tone to sections of the Pascall curriculum.

There is, however, more evidence of Cox's original approach in the new *English: National Curriculum for England* (DfEE, 1999a), although the relationship between this document and the National Literacy Strategy (NLS) in both the primary and now secondary sector is never fully explored. There is evidence of the influence of the NLS on the curriculum document, particularly in those sections on writing which again focus on the technical. Yet the language of the new curriculum does have more of the resonance of the Cox report and includes non-statutory comments in the margin which significantly soften the tone. Next to the section on reading at key stages 2 it wants pupils to read 'enthusiastically', and at key stages 3 and 4, for example, it suggests:

> Reading: during key stages 3 and 4 pupils read a wide range of texts independently, both for pleasure and for study. They become enthusiastic, discriminating and responsive readers, understanding layers of meaning and appreciating what they read at a critical level.
>
> (DfEE, 1999a: 34)

Even here, however, the legacy of the Pascall curriculum remains, although this is a particularly – and perhaps significantly – English phenomenon and does not apply to any other country in the United Kingdom. Until the autumn of 1999, English teachers were led to believe that the statutory list of pre-twentieth-century writers was to appear as guidance only in the new curriculum. Those who attended consultation meetings were clear that this was the intention, and media coverage over the summer confirmed this impression. But as the new school year dawned a press release announced that the politicians had reconsidered over the holidays, and the canon was back, with the minor concession that the list would include writers up to 1914.

This move tilts the balance of secondary English, in England alone, back into the past, focusing on an island culture, despite the more welcome gestures to a more inclusive curriculum in the Curriculum 2000 document as a whole (DfEE, 1999b). It makes no reference to numerous nineteenth-century writers from America nor to poets like Tagore from the Indian subcontinent, who, on occasion, wrote in English. Pupils are still required to study two Shakespeare plays, two major writers before 1914 and four major poets. They are also required to study twentieth-century fiction and poetry along with texts from other countries and, for the first time, non-fiction. But the statutory weight lies with British heritage, with an unacknowledged nod in the direction of the Irish. That a Labour government, so committed to modernity and the future, should feel the need to insist on a literary canon in the twenty-first century, is yet again a testimony not only to their tendency to prescribe the detail of the curriculum, but to the controversy that English attracts.

2　A brief history of English

While the last ten years seemed to have spawned particularly public controversy, the subject itself, even the need for a subject called English, has always been fiercely contested. Truly to understand the contemporary debate it is necessary to delve back into the past and explore, albeit briefly, the growth of English.

Accounts to date have tended to give a chronological and thus linear narrative (see Matthieson, 1975, and Paulson, 1998). Yet it is easier, perhaps, to understand the current positions if we view the development of English as a series of competing traditions. Without wishing to traduce the complexity of the history we are about to examine it is perhaps worth beginning by summarising those traditions, in Figure 1, before going on to consider them in more detail.

Matthew Arnold

Cox's appeal to Matthew Arnold at the end of his biography is testimony to the latter's enduring influence over English as a subject. And no discussion of its origins is complete without a look at the philosophy of Matthew Arnold, who argued vociferously for the inclusion of English in the newly introduced elementary school system. In essence he looked to the study of literature to replace, in the state sector, that which classical education provided for the public school – culture and civilisation. His position has made many uneasy. To begin with he never questioned the class distinctions inherent in his position, allowing one curriculum for the elite and another for the masses (Matthieson, 1975). More importantly, the force of his argument came from the perceived threat of the masses if they were not civilised (Williams, 1961; Ball, Kenny and Gardiner, 1990). Such inherent elitism has, however, obscured the extent of his oppositional stance where education was concerned. This arose, in part, from his role as a school inspector.

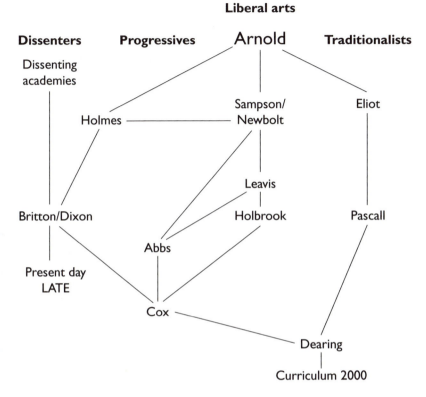

Liberal arts

Dissenters   **Progressives**   Arnold   **Traditionalists**

Dissenting academies

Holmes ——————— Sampson/Newbolt   Eliot

Leavis

Britton/Dixon   Holbrook   Pascall

Abbs

Present day LATE

Cox

Dearing

Curriculum 2000

Figure 1   Traditions within English

Almost from the beginning of government involvement in education, the need for an inspectorate was recognised, and in 1851 Matthew Arnold, the poet and critic, became one of Her Majesty's Inspectors, just twelve years after the state had begun to control elementary provision for some children. He eventually retired in 1886, having campaigned throughout his career for the place of English in the school curriculum and, in particular, for the teaching of poetry.

In his introduction to the 1948 edition of *Culture and Anarchy*, John Dover Wilson contextualises some of the frustrations that prompted Arnold to write his best-known prose work, in a way that, while different from the current arguments about school inspections, league tables, and testing arrangements, sounds very familiar. He describes the way the first ten years of the inspectorate were run under 'the guiding hand' of Kay-Shuttleworth, who sent out inspectors 'as apostles of culture' (Dover Wilson, 1948: xiii). This philosophy continued until 1862, when,

> On the recommendation of the Newcastle Commission, in the sup-
> posed interests of 'sound cheap elementary instruction', and under
> the aegis of the brilliant but commercially minded Robert Lowe, the
> cabinet minister then responsible for education, the notorious Re-
> vised Code was promulgated which shackled the elementary schools
> for a generation with the mechanical system of 'payment by results',
> and entirely changed the character of the inspectors' duties. Hitherto
> Arnold had inspected schools which he entered, as the guide, phi-
> losopher and friend of the teacher; henceforward he became the ex-
> aminer of children in the three Rs at an annual judgement day.
>
> (Dover Wilson, 1948: iv)

The language which Dover Wilson himself chooses echoes much of
Arnold's own writing. His juxtaposition of 'culture' with that of a 'mechanical system'; the contrast between a 'philosopher and friend' with an
'examiner . . . at an annual judgement day': both reflect, in heightened
terms, opposing traditions of education. The emotive quality of Dover
Wilson's language, written nearly a century later, demonstrates the force
of the Arnoldian inheritance.

Arnold clearly had less confidence than some of his twentieth-century
successors that a mechanistic, market-driven inspectorate would help to
create the kind of education service he desired. And he used his position
as one of Her Majesty's Inspectors vigorously to oppose what he saw as the
philistinism of the system. Matthew Arnold was just over half way through
his career as one of Her Majesty's Inspectors when he wrote *Culture and
Anarchy* in 1869. Railing against the philistinism he saw all around him,
he wrote:

> Faith in machinery is, I said, our besetting danger; often in machinery
> most absurdly disproportioned to the end which this machinery, if it
> is to do any good at all, is to serve; but always in machinery, as if it
> had a value in and for itself.
>
> (Arnold, 1948: 48)

His frustration is clear. What is interesting is the way he applied this
mistrust of what he saw as the prevailing mechanistic thinking of his day
to a view of education. The kinds of classrooms he saw are caricatured in
Dickens' *Hard Times*, written fifteen years before. Here Dickens portrays
the bleak spectacle of children crammed with facts but with little
opportunity for the imagination to roam. The names Gradgrind and
Choakumchild speak volumes. For Arnold such an education encouraged
passivity where he wanted to see creativity. While acknowledging that

much of the education children receive will of necessity be mechanical, he argues: 'But whatever introduces any sort of creative activity to relieve the passive reception of knowledge is valuable' (Arnold, 1979: 97). He adds that subjects should be taught in a 'less mechanical and more interesting manner' so that they can 'call forth pleasurable activity' (ibid.: 98).

As interesting is the way in which his views on the benefits of art caused him to question the prevailing orthodoxies of examination. In language that would resonate with many English teachers today, his view of the subject led him to question the assessment system that was used to examine both pupils' knowledge and teacher performance. Teachers, he argued, would simply learn to coach their charges through examination hoops in order to survive the inspection, and little education would be derived from the process. For, as he wrote in 1867,

> And as it is now found possible by ingenious preparation to get children through the Revised Code examination in reading, writing and ciphering, without their really knowing how to read, write or cipher, so it will with practice, no doubt, be found possible to get three fourths of the one fifth of the children over six through the examination in grammar, geography, and history, without their really knowing any one of these three matters.
>
> (ibid.: 96)

Instead, he argued, 'More free play for the Inspector and more free play for the teacher is what is wanted' (ibid.: 96). Two years later he saw no change. 'All test examinations . . .', he complained, 'may be said to narrow reading upon a certain given point, and to make it mechanical' (ibid.: 95). He felt that the inspections had become governed by 'a narrowing system of test examinations' when there were 'organisations wanting to be guided by us into the best ways of learning and teaching' (ibid.: 95). He went on to warn of the dangers of teaching to the test when the stakes were high, for the school grant depended on the pupils' success in the test.

> It tends to make instruction mechanical and to set a bar to duly extending it . . . [and] must inevitably concentrate the teachers' attention on producing this minimum and not simply on the good instruction of the school. The danger to be guarded against is the mistake of assuming these two – the producing of the minimum successfully and the good instruction of the school – as if they were identical.
>
> (ibid.: 95)

In some senses Arnold's legacy, his desire to use culture to oppose the mechanistic, is the progenitor of competing traditions in the fight to establish English on the curriculum.

Liberal arts

Newbolt

The first and most obvious inheritor of the Arnoldian legacy is Newbolt, and it is through him that Arnold's project was partially realised. The Newbolt Report of 1921 (Departmental Committee of the Board of Education, 1921) firmly established English as the core subject on the curriculum, and its writers did so by using Arnold's argument that literature has civilising powers. As with Arnold, the first part of the report is spent explaining why the teaching of classics is no longer an option, and why mechanistic exercises are inappropriate if the full humanising force of art is to be felt. The writers of the report turn to the teaching of English, linking the expression of the language with the art it can produce, to provide what they were looking for. English, the writers of the report argue,

> In its full sense connotes not merely acquaintance with a certain number of terms, or the power of spelling these terms correctly and arranging them without gross mistakes. It connotes the discovery of the world by the first and most direct way open to us, and the discovery of ourselves in our native environment . . . For the writing of English is essentially an art, and the effect of English literature, in education, is the effect of art upon the development of the human character.
>
> (Departmental Committee of the Board of Education,
> 1921: ch. 1, para. 14)

They go on to add that it must be taught as a 'fine art' (ibid., ch. 1, para. 14). As with Arnold, however, the legacy of Newbolt is problematic. Like Arnold, the committee were arguing for English to combat the threat of the masses. The country had just emerged from the ravages of the First World War and Russia had not long ago experienced a revolution. The report owes much to the work of George Sampson, a member of the committee. In his influential *English for the English*, published in the same year, he wrote: 'Deny to working class children any common share in the immaterial and presently they will grow into the men who demand with menaces a communism of the material' (Sampson, 1952: xv). Add to this his comment that 'A poor, intelligent boy who is compelled to come to

school has a clear right to have his language cleansed and purified' (ibid.:
27), and the whole book seems insufferably elitist.

Yet it would be a mistake to read it only in this superficial way, for
underpinning Sampson's work is a more democratic urge. For Sampson
the main reason for introducing English into schools is to create unity:
'There is no class in the country that does not need a full education in
English. Possibly a common basis for education might do much to miti-
gate the class antagonism' (ibid.: 44). He goes on to add, 'If we want that
class antagonism to be mitigated, we must abandon our system of class
education and find some sort of education common to all schools of all
classes', and concludes, 'The one common basis for a common culture is a
common tongue' (ibid.: 45).

This then was the rationale behind the Newbolt Report also. As a
stated aim it too is problematic. Doyle (1989) points out that

> The sense of 'Englishness' that English came to signify was apparently
> so free of any narrow patriotism or overtly nationalist or imperialist
> politics that any debate about the meaning of the term itself was
> deemed unnecessary until quite recently.
>
> (ibid.: 40)

I will return to this theme later. What is important to note is that for the
writers of the Newbolt Report, English was to allow for the personal
growth of the child through an encounter with art. Like Arnold this
position is intimately connected with a view that places culture and the
mechnistic in opposition. And like Arnold again, the mechanistic was to
be found in the workplace and industry. As Sampson argued,

> I am prepared to maintain, and indeed, do maintain, without any
> reservations or perhapses, that it is the purpose of education, not to
> prepare children *for* their occupations, but to prepare children *against*
> their occupations.
>
> (Sampson, 1952: 11)

The Cambridge school

The prevailing dominance of Sampson's view is to be seen in Goodwyn's
(1992) findings, which show so little support for the idea of English preparing children for the world of work. But this dominance owes as much
to the work of F. R. Leavis as it does to Sampson and Newbolt, for it was
Leavis who next inherited the mantle of Arnold's vision. Ball, Kenny and
Gardiner (1990) add caution to the idea that schools of thought affect
classroom practice on anything more than a limited scale, but even they
recognise the influence of Leavis and his disciples. Newbolt had identified

the shortcomings of non-specialist teachers, but rather than demanding specialist training as such, simply required English teachers to be a special breed. As Protherough, Atkinson and Fawcett (1991: 13) point out, this latter view still predominates within the profession. Newbolt also laid a special burden on university departments to produce those capable of teaching English, and it is this challenge that Leavis adopted.

Leavis shares many of the concerns of his predecessors. As Abbs (1982) comments:

> In new and worsening cultural circumstances, the Cambridge school gave powerful currency to the notion that the teacher, critic and artist had no choice but to oppose the destructive, seemingly inexorable drift of industrial civilisation.
>
> (ibid.: 12)

The zeal with which Leavis pursued this aim was no less single minded. He sought to bring about change by the creation of an 'educated class' (Doyle, 1989: 97) which was to be characterised by its ability to respond to literature and above all to discriminate high from low or popular culture. Ball lists 'some of his catch phrases' which include 'sensitive, imaginative, perceptive, sympathetic, creative, reflective and responsive' (Ball, Kenny and Gardiner, 1990: 54). It was through Leavis that the Great Tradition, a list of canonical texts which embodied his philosophy of pre-industrialised consciousness, took hold.

Leavis' influence spread through the work of those like Denys Thompson, who edited the journal *The Use of English*, and Frank Whitehead, his successor and author of *The Disappearing Dais* (1966). Significantly, at the beginning of this book, Whitehead quotes Dewey who, as we shall see, was central to the progressive movement. Others also developed Leavis further. While Leavis had his eyes firmly on the elite, David Holbrook, another of Leavis' former students and prominent member of NATE, extended Leavis' cultural mission to pupils in the secondary modern schools in works such as *English for Maturity* (1961) and *English for the Rejected* (1964). If the Cambridge school was all about literature, Holbrook, while still espousing the virtues of discrimination, suggested the importance of the pupils' own creativity.

Progressive education

In so doing Holbrook also echoes the concerns of those that are often characterised as the Progressive movement. As with Leavis, its origins lie in the previous century and beyond. Yet English as a school subject is intimately connected with progressive education. Critics of progressive education, such as Melanie Phillips (1997), trace it back to Rousseau, because he argued for the innocence of the child, and therefore promulgated the notion of child-centred education. Seen in this light, personal growth, as a tenet of progressivism, becomes a call to allow the child to flower without interference. But this is a very partial reading.

Radicals like Godwin and Mary Wollstonecraft looked to education to challenge received orthodoxies. Tom Paulin (1998), in his biography of Hazlitt, and Andrew Motion (1998), in his biography of Keats, point to the influence of dissenting academies on both these writers. Motion describes the chief philosophy of Keats' school, which avoided the teaching of the classics, as 'distinctly progressive' (ibid.: 22). Commenting on other dissenting academies he adds that they were 'defiantly forward looking . . . they explored rational teaching methods that emphasised the value of doubt and questioning' (ibid.: 24). Arnold's pursuit of the notion of personal growth, albeit through aesthetic encounters, is in part testimony to the influence of such views of education. And so in turn traces of Arnold can be found in some of the later seminal texts of the progressive movement.

Holmes

It is at the turn of the century that the connection between English teaching and the progressive movement becomes clearer, however, with its stress on the potential and creativity of the child. This lies at the heart of Edmond Holmes' *What Is and What Might Be*. Written in 1911, Holmes' section headings, in themselves, echo Arnold's language. Part 1 is entitled 'What Is or The Path of Mechanical Obedience'. Part 2, where he elaborates the alternative, is called 'What Might Be or the Path of Self Realisation'. Like Arnold again his vision of the innate potential of the child leads him to question formal examinations. Throughout the book he criticises what he sees as controlling force of exams on Western education. He asks:

> How did the belief that a formal examination is a worthy end for the teacher and child to aim at, and an adequate test of success in teaching and in learning, come to establish itself in this country? And not only in this country, but in the whole Western world? . . . In every Western country that is 'up to date' . . . the examination system controls education, and in doing so arrests the self-development of the child, and therefore strangles his inward growth.
>
> (Holmes, 1911: 8)

For Holmes the examination system is intimately connected with a view of the passive child he wishes to oppose:

> Blind, passive, literal, unintelligent obedience is the basis on which the whole system of Western education has been reared . . . [The child] must become a tabula rasa before his teacher can begin to write on it. The vital part of him – call it what you will – must become clay before his teacher can begin to mould him.
>
> (ibid.: 50)

In such a system he describes the role of the teacher thus:

> His business is to drill the child into the mechanical production of quasi-material results; and his success in doing this will be gauged in due course by an 'examination' – a periodic test which is designed to measure, not the degree of growth which the child has made, but the industry of the teacher as indicated by the receptivity of the class.
>
> (ibid.: 51)

Dewey

Holmes' views on education are intimately connected with a critique of what he sees as the prevailing orthodoxies of his day. His stress on creativity and his mistrust of exams found their way into the Newbolt Report. It is, however, in Dewey's work that we see one of the clearest articulations of the way in which an attitude towards society will inevitably find expression in a philosophy of education. His book *Democracy and Education*, written in 1916, considers the notion that education was integral to the development of independent citizens.

He revisits these arguments in his later work, *Experience in Education*. Written in 1938 as a response to many of the criticisms levelled at the results of his previous book, he analyses where interpretation of his ideas may have gone wrong. This book is important because it allows for the possibility of the importance of tradition while at the same time insisting on independence of mind. For Dewey, tradition and 'traditional education' are not synonymous. And although he did not contribute directly towards the introduction of English as a subject, this subtle but significant difference is vital in understanding the difference between certain subsequent positions in its development.

The essence of Dewey's argument lies in the notion that any view of education has to consider *how* children learn as well as *what* they learn. He calls this the internal and external aspects of the educational experience. It is a view he contrasts with 'traditional education'. Like Holmes he sees 'the main purpose and objective' of traditional education as the preparation of

> The young for future responsibilities and for success in life, by means of acquisition of the organised bodies of information and prepared forms of skill which comprehend the material instruction. Since the subject matter as well as standards of proper conduct are handed down from the past, the attitude of the pupils must, upon the whole, be one of docility, receptivity, and obedience.
>
> (Dewey, 1966: 18)

He goes on to characterise progressive education as the antithesis of this model, but qualifies this by adding:

> Just because traditional education was a matter of routine in which plans and programs were handed down from the past, it does not follow that progressive education is a matter of planless improvisation . . . Revolt against the kind of organisation characteristic of the traditional school constitutes a demand for high organisation based upon ideas.
>
> (ibid.: 28–9)

The challenge is 'to discover and put into operation a principle of order and operation which follows from understanding what educative experience signifies' (ibid.: 29). He acknowledges, however,

> It is accordingly a much more difficult task to work out the kinds of materials, of methods, and of social relationships that are appropriate to the new education than is the case with traditional education.
>
> (ibid.: 29)

If the Newbolt Report of 1921 is read in the light of this latter endeavour, rather than as an attempt to impose Dewey's description of 'traditional education' (as it has sometimes been interpreted), it reads very differently. For as Matthieson (1975) indicates, Holmes was not the only progressive to influence the report. Both Sampson and Newbolt rejected the use of formal grammar teaching, preferring instead to see language taught in the context of children's writing. Newbolt defended the right of those who spoke in dialect, arguing that standard English was not 'superior' but should be taught alongside pupils' dialects so as not to disadvantage those who did not speak it (Departmental Committee of the Board of Education, 1921, ch. 3, para. 69).

The London school

The baton of progressive education, where English is concerned, passed to the London Association for the Teaching of English. Founded in 1947, it pre-dates its national sister organisation NATE, into which it was later absorbed, by sixteen years. Its influence on this latter organisation is noted by Ball. 'In swallowing up LATE in its organisation NATE had incorporated within itself a militant dissenting incubus' (Ball, 1985: 68). He goes on to describe the way in which key figures in this group were 'directly involved in moving NATE away from the pervasive influence of the Cambridge School' so that the '"Britton–Martin model of language" was established by the 1970s as NATE orthodoxy' (ibid.: 69). Through the work of LATE members such as John Dixon and Douglas Barnes, and of those at the Institute of Education, like James Britton and Harold Rosen, the focus of attention shifted away from growth through the study of the text towards the child learning through language. I will examine some of these figures in more detail in the next chapter. But to summarise, much of this work was based on a rediscovery of Vygotsky (in particular *Thought and Language*, 1986), whose research made explicit the connections between language and learning. This resonated with teachers who were confronted with ethnically diverse classrooms in which many languages were spoken. In addition these teachers were looking to ways of authenticating the child's experience.

The links with Dewey's child-centred approach are evident, as are the connections with earlier voices like Holmes who wanted to emphasise the need for self-expression. Their emphasis on language has, however, compelled some of their critics to recharacterise this group. Abbs (1982), who calls them the Socio-linguistic school, complains that they 'have shown little appreciation or even knowledge of the Cambridge Movement or the earlier Progressive movement' (Abbs, 1982: 17). He does, however, acknowledge the benefits to be derived from their emphasis on oracy, in the work of Andrew Wilkinson, believing it to be an element missing from previous models. He also finds helpful the way in which the focus on language emphasises the process of learning. Indeed, Abbs' summation of the beneficial effects of the London School make even clearer their connection with Dewey:

> The sociolinguists were out to demonstrate that the truth was not simply 'out there' to be imprinted on the passive mind of the child; but that it was made through individual attempts to actively formulate meaning.
>
> (ibid.: 19)

Their particular 'merit' is the way in which 'they keep principle and practice, abstract theory and practical implications closely tethered' (ibid.: 19). Abbs' main objection to this group is their very linguistic emphasis, which takes them away from the literary; and their propensity to be political, to use what he calls 'ideological weapons' (ibid.: 22). In a sense his quarrel exemplifies Ball, Kenny and Gardiner's (1990) description of the chief differences between the London and Cambridge schools:

> At the heart of the dispute between Cambridge and London, literature and language, there were not simply two views of the subject, but more profoundly and politically of importance, two conceptions of the 'good society', and of the nature of civilisation and citizenship.
>
> (ibid.: 59)

This, they argue, encourages the Cambridge school to look to the past to the pre-machine age; it encourages the London school to celebrate the present and look to the future. They point out, however, that while the former is capable of sentimentalising the past, the latter can romanticise its view of the present, and both these trends can lead to 'the subordination of the pupils' (ibid.: 59).

It is possibly for this reason that Ball, Kenny and Gardiner (1990) go on to define the development of what they describe as the 'radical version' of English. Instead of celebrating working-class culture, this view takes what might be deemed a more 'oppositional stance' to dominant versions of culture, rather than the 'alternative' (ibid.: 61) that the progressives sought to find. As Ball and his co-writers suggest, this oppositional stance 'amounts to what Aronowitz and Giroux call "critical literacy"' (ibid.: 61). It is useful, as Ball does, to quote their definition in full.

> Critical literacy responds to the cultural capital of a specific group or class and looks to ways in which it can be confirmed, and also at the ways in which the dominant society disconfirms students by either ignoring or denigrating the knowledge and experiences that characterise their everyday lives. The unit of analysis is social and the key concern is not with individual interests but with the individual and collective empowerment.
>
> (Aronowitz and Giroux, cited in Ball et al., 1990: 61)

For many London teachers this took the focus away from simply looking at class and towards considering race and gender.

The traditionalists

Yet it is not only the left who integrate their view of education into their view of society. As we have seen, Dewey made clear that the traditionalists are not without an opinion or even an agenda. In the 1998 King's College London Annual Lecture Nick Tate, Chief Executive of the Qualifications and Curriculum Authority, quoted T. S. Eliot. Eliot, in his essay, 'On Modern Education and the Classics', describes education as

> A subject which cannot be discussed in a void: our questions raise other questions, social, economic, financial, political. And the bearings are on more ultimate problems even than these: to know what we want in education we must know what we want in general, we must derive our theory of education from our theory of life.
>
> (Eliot, cited in Tate, 1998: 3–4)

In his lecture Tate propounded a liberal arts view of the curriculum; I will go on to discuss the difference between Tate's position and that of Eliot later. But for now it is important to recognise the subtle but important difference between the notion of encouraging discrimination as a way of bringing about transformation – a kind of liberation through education, with all the inherent elitism which that can imply – and the belief in education as a form of social control. As we have seen there is a conservatism inherent in the liberal arts position that sets the arts against the ravages of industrialism. Yet, although the language may often sound the same and at points become indiscernible, they do constitute different points of view. The liberal arts perspective still contains within it the significance of personal growth and self-expression in a way that traditionalism does not. For this group education is not an enabler but a corrective. It is worth looking again at Dewey's definition of the characteristics of traditional education. As we have seen, he described it as the

> Acquisition of the organised bodies of information and prepared forms of skill which comprehend the material instruction. Since the subject matter as well as standards of proper conduct are handed down from the past, the attitude of the pupils must, upon the whole, be one of docility, receptivity, and obedience.
>
> (Dewey, 1966: 18)

He connects 'prepared forms of skill' and 'subject matter' with 'standards of proper conduct'. And it is the specific elision of Standard English and standards in general, of linguistic and behavioural codes, that I wish to consider at this point. For this idea is played out against a national debate about declining standards in spoken and written English. Stephen Ball (1984) describes the 'panic' that attends such discussions, and Brian Street (1997) talks of 'Hobbesian fears'.

Almost from the beginning of public education, standards have apparently been falling. As Colin MacCabe points out in an edition of *Critical Quarterly* edited by Brian Cox, on Cox's curriculum, 'It is notorious that educational standards, and particularly literacy, seem to fall with such monotonous regularity from generation to generation that it is a wonder that anybody reads at all' (MacCabe, 1990: 7). To give a sample of the kind of report to which he refers, in 1912 a head teacher wrote to *The Times* complaining that reading standards were falling because parents no longer read to their children and too much time was spent listening to the gramophone (cited in Cox, 1995: 37). In the same year the English Association wrote that 'It is a plain fact that the average girl or boy is unable to write English with a clearness or fluency or any degree of grammatical accuracy' (ibid.: 37). The Newbolt Report in 1921, quoting Boots Pure Drug Co., commented that 'The teaching of English in present day schools produces a very limited command of the English language' (Departmental Committee of the Board of Education, ch. 3, para. 7). In the same report all but a few employers complained that they had found difficulty in 'obtaining employees who can speak and write English clearly and correctly' (ibid., ch. 3, para. 77).

Seven years later little had changed. According to the Spens Report of 1938, 'It is a common and grave criticism that many pupils pass through grammar school without acquiring the capacity to express themselves in English' (cited in Cox, 1995: 38). The Norwood Report of 1943 claimed to have received 'strong evidence of the poor quality of English of Secondary School pupils . . . the evidence is such as to leave no doubt in our minds that we are confronted by a serious failure of secondary schools' (ibid.: 38).

But this fear of the moral consequences of falling standards was given its clearest articulation under the Conservative government of 1979–97. It was Norman Tebbit who remarked in an interview on the *Today* programme in 1985,

> If you allow standards to slip to the stage where good English is no better than bad English, where people can turn up filthy and nobody takes any notice of them at school – just as well as turning up clean – all those things tend to cause people to have no standards at all, and once you lose your standards then there's no imperative to stay out of crime.
>
> (Tebbit, cited in Graddol, Maybin, Mercer and Swann, 1991: A52)

Yet such a view was not only given credence by Tory ministers. John Rae, the former head teacher of Westminster School, while making the link less crudely causal, also sees an explicit connection between the permissive society and progressive teaching, in an article for the *Observer* in February 1982:

> The overthrow of grammar coincided with the acceptance of the equivalent of creative writing in social behaviour. As nice points of grammar were mockingly dismissed as pedantic and irrelevant, so was punctiliousness in such matters as honesty, responsibility, property, gratitude, apology and so on.
>
> (Rae, cited in ibid.: A52)

Brian Cox himself criticises Rae in his book *Cox on Cox*. Commenting on another article Rae had written, this time for the *Evening Standard*, Cox describes Rae's views on the fixity of language as 'mistaken' (Cox, 1991: 36). Norman Tebbit and John Rae may be said, however, to owe in part their analysis of falling standards, and the attendant dire moral consequences, to the description of the problem in the Black Papers. And yet these were the brain-child of the same Brian Cox, along with his colleague, Anthony Dyson. The first edition was written in 1969; two followed in 1970. All were a response to their perception of the ill-effects of progressive education in the sixties. They were also written in the wake of student unrest in London, Paris and the United States and the fear of anarchy which this provoked. Cox implies in his autobiography *The Great Betrayal* (Cox, 1992: 167) that the Manson murders at the end of 1969 also lent some of the observations of the Black Papers their apocalyptic feel. Several contributors – including Kingsley Amis and Rhodes Boyson, then a secondary head teacher, but subsequently a Conservative education minister under Thatcher – sounded warning notes very like those of Tebbit and Rae. Contributors to the later 1975 and 1977 editions (which Cox edited with Boyson), such as John Marks, later became prominent members of the right-wing think tank, The Centre for Policy Studies.

The Black Papers received considerable adverse publicity, not least as a result of Peter Shore's speech to the NUT conference on 8 April 1969. In it he accused the Black Papers of being racist, describing parts of it being 'reminiscent of Goebbels' and 'an attack on liberal ideas in education generally' (from the *TES* report of the speech, cited in Cox, 1992: 173). Yet they subsequently found expression in Callaghan's Ruskin College speech in October 1976 (Callaghan, 1996). Although he denied the connection in the speech, Callaghan had, as the Black Papers had done, sounded the death knell for progressive ideas in education, under the banner of declining standards. As Shore himself had predicted, 'We should be extremely foolish if we ignored [the Black Papers] or underestimated the impact it may make, because it is so ridiculously and outrageously behind the times' (cited in Cox, 1992: 173).

Brian Cox's own role in the Black Papers, however, and his subsequent position as champion of English teachers, can only be understood in the light of the difference between a view of education that enables and one that is corrective. He claims that his position, that of a 'moderate progressive' (ibid.: 146), has not substantially altered in thirty years of debating these issues. Rather, he believes that with the publishing of the Cox Report, 'I succeeded in persuading the profession that these were indeed my views' (ibid.: 187). These he states most fully in the conclusion of his autobiography. As we have seen, it is to Arnold he turns, commending 'the faith of Matthew Arnold in the civilising power of the Humanities', and the way in which 'Great literature helps to keep alive our most subtle and delicate feelings, our capacity for wonder, and our faith in human individuality' (ibid.: 268). It is his advocacy of these virtues that allows him to see himself as the 'moderate progressive' he describes; and again, as we have seen, there is a strand of Arnoldian thought that finds its way into the progressive movement.

In contrast neither Rae, nor Tebbit, Marks nor Boyson ever speak of 'our capacity for wonder', of 'faith' or 'subtle and delicate feelings'. Nevertheless, others with whom Cox had perhaps greater affinity, such as Richard Hoggart, often seen as something of a Leavisite, withdrew from the fray at the time. After the publication of the first Black Paper, Hoggart resigned from the editorial board of *Critical Quarterly*. Even in Cox's book, *The Great Betrayal*, while suggesting that 'If I edited the Black Paper now I might tone down the extreme language' (ibid.: 168), Cox lays much of the blame on the press for the misreading of his intentions. 'Most education journalists confined their attention to the extravagant elements and ignored the solid arguments' (ibid.: 168). While acknowledging that they no longer agree, Cox remains loyal to Boyson, describing his contribution to the second Black Paper as 'one of his best, and offers a balanced assessment which little accords with his present-day public image' (ibid.: 191–2). He goes on to defend him further, by writing: 'Dr Boyson's ideas about education have always been more complex than the usual caricatures allow' (ibid.: 178). It is possible that his own experience of press coverage has led him to this more sympathetic reading of Boyson's position. For certainly much press coverage did ignore the more progressive sections of the Black Papers, just as it traduced the subtlety of Cox's own proposals when writing the National Curriculum.

The belief in the morality of grammar teaching, which Cox so roundly criticises (as do his philosophical forbears, Arnold, Sampson and Newbolt), is usually linked with the desirability of teaching a canon of literature. As with linguistic skills, a canon represents 'organised bodies of information ... handed down from the past' (Dewey, 1966: 18). What has complicated the debate is the way in which this has become inextricably linked with cultural identity. Cox did not include a canon of literature in the 1989 curriculum, precisely because he wished to avoid the charge of equating the English curriculum with a sense of Englishness that would, he believed, exclude many of the pupils at which it was aimed.

Although there is a sense in which Sampson and Newbolt might be said to have been the originators of this point of view (as Doyle, 1989, to a degree suggests), their work, as we have seen was designed to produce a very different end. They sought an English curriculum as a way of avoiding the social exclusion of sectors of the community who they believed were being disenfranchised. It is to Eliot that we must look to see the emergence of a hegemonic view of culture that is dependent on excluding one definition of identity, or heritage, at the expense of another. And it is in the debates that still surround the legacy of his work that we still see the arguments articulated.

Throughout the summer months of 1996 a battle raged in the letters pages of the *London Review of Books* about the merits of the book *T. S. Eliot, Anti-Semitism and Literary Form* by Anthony Julius, or, to be more precise, about Tom Paulin's review of that book. For many the review disclosed nothing new. Eliot's anti-Semitism is well known, discussed and documented, yet for Paulin this missed the point of the book. In his subtly argued piece he demonstrates the need to review Eliot's work because of the centrality of his views in a cultural hegemony that he believes is too little questioned and still has enormous influence. As Paulin points out,

> Because Eliot has so dominated this century's poetry, and because his writings have been so central to critical practice and to English literature as an academic discipline, to subject him to this kind of investigation is to call a large part of our culture – root, branch and flower – into question.
>
> (Paulin, 1996a)

His suggestion is that at the heart of Eliot's views of culture, and the related sense of Englishness and national identity, lies his anti-Semitism. Discussing James Shapiro's study *Shakespeare and the Jews*, Paulin writes:

Anti-Semitism is closely linked with the formation of Englishness
... The immigrant writer (Eliot) felt that Englishness and anti-
Semitism were closely related, and he chose to echo sentiments which,
it's often alleged, were common among all classes in the country
then.

(ibid.)

Thus, for Paulin, the debate cannot be confined to whether or not we can
appreciate Eliot's poetry despite any repugnance at certain lines, some of
which he later omitted, such as the notorious lines in 'The Wasteland'. It
needs to be seen in the broader context of his legacy, which cannot be so
neatly contained in a discussion about aesthetic values.

And this legacy is seen most clearly and starkly in the battles over the
National Curriculum for English, particularly the Pascall curriculum. Again
in 1948, Eliot had himself seen the potential of a national curriculum for
creating a cultural hegemony. In 'Notes towards a Definition of Culture'
he wrote:

There is the question of what culture is, and the question whether
it is anything we can control or deliberately influence. These questions confront us whenever we devise a theory, or frame a policy, of
education.

(Eliot, 1975: 294)

His use of the word 'control' is in itself significant. It connotes a very
specific view of society, which needs controlling through schooling rather
than liberating through education. He expands this idea in the same essay
when he warns of the dangers of cultural disintegration, and looks to
education as a way of shoring the crumbling citadel. Edward Said, in his
book *Culture and Imperialism*, spells out the sub-text of such an approach:
'In time, culture comes to be associated, often aggressively, with the nation or the state; this differentiates "us" from "them", almost always with
some degree of xenophobia' (Said, 1993: xiii).

Not everyone who cites the influence of Eliot draws these conclusions.
Some have attempted to rescue him from the charge of xenophobia, and
wish to explore notions of national identity away from the right. Nick
Tate reopened the question of Englishness at the end of 1995. He used,
as a possible way into the debate, Eliot's definition of what might be
'embraced by the term culture':

It includes all the characteristics and interests of the people: Derby
Day, Henley regatta, Cowes, the twelfth of August, a cup final day,

the dog races, the pin table, the dart board, Wensleydale cheese, boiled cabbage cut into sections, beetroot in vinegar, nineteenth century Gothic churches and the music of Elgar. The reader can make up his own list.

(Eliot, 1975: 298)

And that is precisely what Tate did, including his own penchant for the Yorkshire Dales and puddings. While such an activity may seem like a harmless parlour game, Tate wants more than such lists afford him. He developed his ideas further in a speech given to the Association of Teachers and Lecturers in June 1996, entitled 'Why Learn?'. In it he raises the need for an inclusive culture which feeds a notion of citizenship:

We have ended up with the rather odd situation where people can be deeply sympathetic to other people's cultural traditions but disdainful towards their own. We fail to distinguish between 'national identity' and 'nationalism' and have virtually altogether abandoned the word patriotism. We fail to grasp that ideas are multiple, complex and fluid. It is perfectly possible to feel a strong sense of British identity alongside identity as a Jew, as a European, or even as a 'citizen of the planet'. It is equally possible to have a sense of British, or English identity which is inclusive and which gives the majority culture its due while respecting minority cultures.

(Tate, 1996)

What he goes on to argue for is a cultural pluralism with a sense of civic identity at its core. This he believes will create 'a sense of dignity and self esteem' (ibid.). Yet the speech is an exercise in failure, not because of what it attempts to achieve, but rather because of its inability to conceive of a tradition other than that in which Eliot worked.

The dilemma facing Tate is that a multicultural relativism cannot be the answer to his objective. Eliot's racism would have to be allowed as being a legitimate part of what it is to be 'us', 'we'. For, as Gauri Viswanathan argues in *Masks of Conquest: Literary study and British rule in India*, even if we take the more relativistic stance of multiculturalism within Eliot's tradition, and

broaden the curriculum to include the literature of other cultures . . . the relative tolerance of [this] position does not negate the possibility that even the most inclusionary curriculum can itself be part of the process of control.

(Viswanathan, 1989: 167)

In other words it may still be 'an instrument of hegemonic activity' (ibid.: 167).

Yet Paulin does present an alternative to 'the overwhelming, the stifling cultural authority which the Eliot oeuvre has acquired' by reasserting a tradition of republican democracy which fashions its conceits within the exclusivity and discrimination of dissent. This is the powerful vision with which Paulin challenges Eliot's own. Nor is he in any sense anti-traditional. The argument that Paulin provoked in the *London Review of Books* arises from clashing traditions. Like Dewey he looks to democratic engagement in society, that avoids a demand for 'obedience' but looks instead to Paine's *The Rights of Man*, Milton's 'Areopagitica' and MacDiarmid's 'A Drunk Man Looks at the Thistle'. This is no 'planless improvisation' but a 'revolt against the kind of organisation characteristic of the traditional school . . . based upon ideas' (Dewey, 1996: 28–9). It is a tradition that Hitchens also identifies in his essay on Paine:

> Paine belongs to that strain of oratory, pamphleteering and prose that runs through Milton, Bunyan, Burns and Blake and which nourished what the common folk like to call the Liberty Tree. This stream as charted by E. P. Thompson and others often flows underground for long periods. In England it disappeared for a long time.
>
> (Hitchens, 1988: 16)

Conclusion

These competing and overlapping traditions, so intimately connected with a view of society, are the source of the controversy that English provokes. It is hardly surprising that the moment anyone sought to formalise a view of the subject, in the form of a national curriculum, these competing traditions began to jostle for centre stage. Cox presented a consensual liberal arts curriculum which, by acknowledging different perspectives, attempted to be inclusive and so united the profession behind it, albeit with provisos. Inevitably it came under fire from those who, like Eliot, believed they had missed the opportunity to establish a dominant hegemony that did not allow for other voices.

And the arguments are not over. If the Conservative years were dominated by a nostalgia for a mythical past, a Labour future seems likely to be characterised by ever greater demands for skills to service the needs of tomorrow. What these may be, however, is also a source of contention and as likely to be dominated by a view of society as they have always been. As we approached the millennium, books like *Towards 2000* (Marum, 1995) and articles like 'A Curriculum for the Future: A curriculum built for change' (Tweddle, 1995) and 'The Future of English' (Davies, 1991) proliferated. Indeed, the millennium and the end of Dearing's five-year moratorium on the curriculum yet again created space for those groups who wished to establish their vision of the subject. The *English and Media Magazine* dedicated the whole of issue 34 to the future of English (Simons, 1996a). The NUT's *Educational Review* asked Anne Barnes of NATE (Barnes, 1997) to offer her views on where English was going; NATE itself published Kress's book *Writing the Future* (Kress, 1995). The National Literacy Trust also brought out a volume, *Building a Literate Nation: The strategic agenda for literacy over the next five years* (McLelland, 1997).

Yet, as Nigel Hall (1997) suggested in his aptly titled essay (from the same volume) 'Going Forward into the Past', our vision of the future is rooted in an analysis of the present and an understanding of the past. In another of these future-gazing collections, *English for Tomorrow* (Tweddle and Adams, 1997), which looks to the impact of IT, Tony Adams points out in the introduction:

> The book is essentially not about technology: it is about the curriculum and curriculum change in response to changing circumstances, 'a changing world'. We have begun with the eternal issues that have been debated by English teachers ever since the subject first began . . . it is the context that has changed rather than the fundamentals of our task and craft.
>
> (Adams, 1997: xii)

But as we have seen, there are contesting versions of what these fundamentals constitute. There is currently a utilitarian twang to much of the literature that surrounds Labour's Literacy Strategy (DfEE, 1998). David Blunkett, in the foreword to the National Literacy Strategy, demands that children 'master the basic skills of literacy and numeracy', because 'our children deserve to leave school equipped to enter a fulfilling adult life'. Although there is a nod in the direction of personal growth in the ameliorative use of the word 'fulfilling', the lists and clocks and regulations of the Literacy Hour would not sit as ill with Mr Gradgrind as many of the suggestions to be found in the writing of Messrs Hall, Kress and Adams, nor those of Ms Barnes. It is within this climate of change that my attempt to capture these competing philosophies of the subject exists, and to which I now turn my attention.

3 Finding a voice

In his play *Arcadia* about the eighteenth-century mathematician Ada Lovelace, Tom Stoppard attempts to use the structure of the play to convey the mathematics she is trying to describe. Scenes and scenarios appear over and over again, each time subtly different, to reflect the way in which the change of one element creates, like the twist of a kaleidoscope, a different pattern.

Unfortunately accounts of research are not dramas, though perhaps we would be better served if they were. For one of the difficulties in writing about the process of research is that the final version conveys, almost of necessity, the impression of strict chronology. The sheer temptation of narrative pull, not to mention the very linearity of the writing and reading process itself, forces the writer to order their experiences in a way that belies the often messy business of research. Here ideas bump and jostle back and forth with events; moments of epiphany occur while walking to the tube or in the bath, which cause the researcher to go back and reappraise their work. The patterns of thought shift and move many times before they settle. Yet the final version appears bereft of the very blemishes and quirks that breathed life into the research in the first place.

This is as true of this account as any other. In reality the content of the Rough Guide to English Teachers, an A5 booklet that contained the descriptions of five different philosophies of English teaching, emerged from what can best be described as an iterative process. The year that I spent on developing the Rough Guide took me backwards and forwards between three main points – my own experiences as an English teacher (to which we shall turn in the first section of this chapter), the history of the subject, and a review of the literature of others who have attempted to theorise views of English teaching (which we have already, in the main, considered). Threaded through this more focused activity were conversations with colleagues and friends, as well as the daily events of work. All I can attempt to do is to give some flavour of that process, of the internal debates that occurred in finding a final form for my research. Indeed, the first of these unwelcome divisions is to separate the form of the Rough Guide from its content, even though, as we shall see in chapter 5, they are intimately connected. For now, however, we will concentrate on the content.

So far we have looked backwards in our attempt to discover the current position of English teachers, for the contested history of English is one key element to understanding the present. As we have seen, it has meant that not one tradition but several traditions of the subject have coexisted almost from the beginning, each version both competing with and influencing the others.

A second element, however, contributed to the formation of the content of the guide. In his essay 'English for the English since 1906' (Ball, 1985) as well as in 'Conflict, Panic and Inertia' (Ball, 1984) Stephen Ball traces the lineage of views on the subject of English teaching to key players and their schools of thought. He looks, for example, at the influence of Leavis through figures like David Holbrook, whom he taught at Cambridge. He considers also James Britton and Harold Rosen, who affected generations of English teachers who trained at the Institute of Education in London. But these paths that Ball maps out are equally suggestive of the importance of the personal biography; almost of the provenance of anyone's views of English teaching. Moreover he adds, in 'English for the English',

> It would appear that the most profound influences upon the English teacher, in terms of his or her conception of English as a school subject and its concomitant pedagogy, is equally as likely to be the teacher's own experience as a pupil as their university or college training.
>
> (Ball, 1985: 81)

And here I must plead guilty. As this is to be, in part, an insider's account of the philosophies of English teachers I need to confess my own provenance as an English teacher, for undoubtedly my own experiences have affected the way in which I think, and it is best to make those influences explicit. For the last twenty or so years in which I have been involved with the subject (as a student, teacher and lecturer) have been marked by controversy. Interwoven with my own experience, along with thousands of other English graduates and teachers, has been a very public debate about the nature of the discipline. This has almost certainly influenced my understanding of those areas that provoke particular controversy, so that any pretence at neutrality is ill advised. Indeed, part of my aim is to indicate how any researcher comes to a project with their own history, for none of us exists in an ideological vacuum. How they use it is often part of the unwritten chapter of the final account. What follows, therefore, is a potted autobiography interlaced with a somewhat idiosyncratic selection of issues, which are only touched upon (there not being the space or time to do each one justice) that have arisen during my time in education. Each has found its way, in one form or another, into the Rough Guide to English Teachers.

Phase 1: school and university

I emerged from a direct grant girls' grammar school, which time had passed by, and where my love of reading had barely been kept intact by an ex-English teaching mother, to study English and American Studies at Nottingham University. Although I was probably one of the earliest cohorts to whom critical theory was taught, this influence was less significant than the general effect of those three years, which was to politicise my view of the arts.

My politics at school inclined to the left of centre, but this had been fuelled by a history teacher, Leslie Allen, not the English department. That university was to be a very different place was made clear in my very first seminar in the American Studies department. My tutor, Dave Murray, presented the group with Wordsworth's 'The Solitary Reaper' and asked us to consider the role of the absentee landlord in the poem. Murray's point, lost on me at the time, was that Wordsworth's picture of a romantic idyll failed to address the actual plight of the women he had idealised. It was my first encounter with Marxist literary theory.

The other key figure, and enduring influence, was the poet and critic Tom Paulin. Not a Marxist, Paulin emphasised the political nature of texts, a view espoused in his *Faber Book of Political Verse* (1986) where he wrote: 'We have been taught, many of us, to believe that art and politics are separated by the thickest and most of enduring of partitions' (ibid.: 15). This is not only an attack on Leavis but also on certain forms of critical theory. 'There is an influential school of literary criticism . . . which argues that the political and historical content of literature must be viewed as "extrinsic irrelevance"' (ibid.: 15). Paulin's central desire then was to wrest criticism from ahistorical, decontextualised disinterestedness, an aim he continually espoused in my three years of tutorials with him and which has now found voice in his critical book on Hazlitt, *The Day Star of Liberty* (Paulin, 1998).

Here, Paulin's portrait of the tradition of radical dissent contends that we have lost Hazlitt's concept of engaged disinterestedness to Arnold's view of impartial criticism. 'This has the effect of removing culture from the world of passions, so that it "returns upon itself"' (ibid.: 69). He continues: 'This idea of free-floating impartiality would have been incomprehensible to . . . Hazlitt', and argues that we should return to the pre-Arnoldian view of disinterestedness, a view that, until recently, has so dominated British literary criticism.

> This would involve recognising that all critical writing is essentially polemical, but at the same time stripping away many of the negative qualities which are so often associated with the term 'polemic'. The disinterested imagination takes a position, but is not entrenched, obdurate or rigid; rather it is based on an active flexible way of knowing that it is essentially dialogic. It doesn't talk to itself.
>
> (ibid.: 69)

The significance of these positions will become evident in the later more detailed discussion of the differences between the philosophies in the Rough Guide. From Nottingham I moved to Cambridge to study for a Postgraduate Certificate in Education (PGCE). It was here that I first encountered the notion of mixed ability teaching. Drawing on my own, somewhat fraught experience of setting, and concrete examples of the benefits of the way in which a visiting Head of English organised his own classroom, I became convinced, having been deeply sceptical to begin with, that this was the most educationally beneficial method of pupil grouping. Subsequent experience and research (see for example Boaler, 1997; Harlen and Malcolm, 1997; Sukhnanden with Lee, 1998) has only served to reinforce this view, although I am more than aware that it is not a position which many English teachers hold and, again, this is reflected in the Rough Guide.

Other underlying principles of practice also took hold at Cambridge, despite a degree of initial scepticism on my part. Teaching practice taught me the benefit of drafting. The value of allowing pupils to reshape and discuss their work with others, including the grammatical and technical features of their writing, made more sense in the classroom context than isolated lessons on points of grammar to the whole class. Interestingly, such an approach closely echoes Paul Black and Dylan Wiliam's research on formative assessment (Black and Wiliam, 1998a and 1998b) where teachers are encouraged to negotiate more individualised ways of improving work with the pupils. Such an approach to drafting was underlined in the work of the National Writing Project. This served to underline many of the principles I encountered first at Cambridge (see for example National Writing Project, 1989a, 1989b and 1990). Indeed so orthodox has the notion of drafting become that it is recommended by the National Literacy Strategy (DfEE, 1998) even though it still recommends decontextualised grammar exercises.

Certain other issues, however, still remain a source of contention, not least the debates that surround Standard English and knowledge about language. One of the notions I encountered at Cambridge was the view that the vernacular voice of the pupils should be encouraged. John Dixon's *Growth through English* was a seminal text in this respect. In the foreword to the 1975 edition of the book, James Britton, then chair of NATE, along with John Squires, also of NATE, wrote:

> It is unlikely that any other book in the past decade has had more influence upon English work in classrooms on both sides of the Atlantic, and we share the hope that this new edition may give that influence renewed hope.
>
> (Britton and Squires, 1975: vii)

Setting aside the modesty that made Britton forbear from mentioning his own contribution to the movement – with books like *Language and Learning* (1974) and his collaboration with Barnes and Rosen on *Language, the Learner and the School* (Barnes, Britton and Rosen, 1972) – Britton and Squires go on to substantiate their claim:

> The existence of the 'growth model' presented in John Dixon's book stimulated teachers to experiment with new approaches to language learning and literary education at a time when dissatisfaction with traditional models was widespread.
>
> (Britton and Squires, 1975: xv)

I needed little persuasion of Dixon's central tenet that 'language is learned in operation not in dummy runs' (Dixon, 1975: 13). Nor did I disagree with the notion that language is integral to the process of learning – an issue which Dixon believed was often overlooked in previous models of English. Such a view was well rehearsed through James Britton's readings of the influential psychologist Vygotsky (Vygotsky, 1984 and 1986). As we saw in the previous chapter Dixon characterised these previous models of English as a 'skills' view of the subject as well as one that stressed 'cultural heritage' (ibid.: 1–2). Yet I was uncertain as to the balance being presented on the PGCE course. It seemed to me then, as it seems to me now, that failure to recognise or make plain the power of Standard English was to disadvantage further the very children whom such an approach sought to enfranchise. Although Dixon and my college tutors acknowledged the need for some form of 'linguistic orthodoxy' (ibid.: 13), the balance erred on the side of general rather than appropriate communication skills.

The notion that standard English should be taught explicitly but within the context that it was the language of power began to have currency in the late 1980s. This was largely achieved through the work of the Language in the National Curriculum (LINC) initiative, the result of the Kingman Report (DES and WO, 1988) and the chair of Language in the National Curric-ulum, the linguist Ronald Carter (see for example Carter, 1991 and 1992; Richmond, 1991). It also brought to a wider audience the issue of bilingualism (see for example Savva, 1991) and the need to recognise not only dialects of English but other languages spoken by pupils. This was not new as such. The English and Media Centre, for example, had long been producing materials which encouraged teachers to understand and build on the linguistically diverse classroom. But their work, and that of others in the field had tended to be read by those to whom such work was immediately relevant, particularly those who worked in multilingual urban classrooms.

My own position at the time of my PGCE, however, arose less from any linguistic understanding than from an appreciation of the dissenting power of the vernacular and its relationship to standard forms. Again the influence of Paulin is evident. In the introduction to *The Faber Book of Vernacular Verse* Paulin writes:

> Perhaps it's the official gravitas of public discourse, its chilling lack of kinship ties, that is the real target in 'Latin is a dead tongue/dead as dead can be'. Many vernacular poets might want to join in that kids' chant. Latin belongs to institutions, committees, public voices, print. Against that Parnassian official order, the springy irreverent, chanting, quartzy, often tender, intimate, vernacular voice speaks for an alternative community that is mostly powerless and invisible.
>
> (Paulin, 1990: x)

He goes on to admire the 'vernacular energies' of poets like Whitman and Burns which are essentially 'democratic' (ibid.: xii) and the 'charged demotic ripples' of Clare's lines which 'become a form of Nation Language that rejects the polished urbanity of Official Standard' (ibid.: xix). For Clare, 'grammar in learning is like Tyranny in government' (cited in ibid.: xix). Paulin concludes:

> Many of the voices that speak here are disaffected and powerless. They know that out in the public world a polished speech issues

orders and receives deference. It seeks to flatten out and obliterate all varieties of spoken English and so substitute one accent for all the others. It may be the ruin of us yet.

(ibid.: xxii)

While such a position may seem to echo those held by Dixon and my PGCE tutors, it is subtly different. It more overtly recognises the creation of art as a political act, and the choice of language of that art as an expression of the power relationship between the state and the community it represents. Seen in this light, Paulin's view is closer to that of LINC, although his concern is more literary than linguistic. This difference in emphasis between the literary and the linguistic was another debate which I explored in the writing of the Rough Guide and one to which I will return. The stress, however, of the LINC materials (which were never officially published, but found their way into most schools – Carter, 1992) on knowledge about language, may be seen as an attempt to redress the balance, or at least elaborate on the position found in books like Dixon's *Growth through English*. Such a view is now certainly held by my former PGCE tutor, Anthony Adams.

The ability to review and revise attitudes in the light of new evidence is also symptomatic of the kind of philosophy of the subject that Adams took and in a sense this was the most abiding influence of the course. Even when I was on the PGCE course he was urging fellow professionals not to remain static in their view of the subject. Writing the introduction to a collection of essays called *New Directions in English Teaching*, he commented: 'One looks in vain in the journals devoted to English teaching for any attempt to remodel teaching to prepare students for the final twenty years of the century and beyond' (Adams, 1982: 1).

The title is in itself indicative of the approach he was taking and one which was reflected on the course. The role of the media was emphasised, as was the potential of information technology, then still in its educational infancy. These were both aspects of my future job as an English teacher that I felt no difficulty in adopting and quickly saw them as integral to my perception of the subject within school. Perhaps my own academic path had already encouraged me to see such work as complementary to rather than conflicting with a view of English.

But the title of the book is also representative of a change in mood in English teaching in the 1980s. As the subject began to unravel in university departments so those in education departments began to reconsider their own position. As Protherough and Atkinson (1994: 11) point out there was an explosion of titles like Adams' throughout the 1980s and into the 1990s. Titles like *Changing English* (Meek and Miller, 1984);

Barnes, Barnes and Clarke's *Versions of English* (1984); Creber's *Thinking through English* (1990); *Re-writing English* (Batsleer, 1985); *Bringing English to Order*, edited by Goodson and Medway (1990); even *Exploding English* (Bergonzi, 1990), all created an environment in which the parameters and the politics of the subject were under constant scrutiny and up for constant debate.

Phase 2: teaching in schools

Such was the intellectual climate at the time that I first entered the classroom, having retreated into academe for another year after my PGCE to gain an MA in English from Queen Mary College, London University. I began my teaching career in a west London school that received what was known as a social priority allowance. As at my teaching practice school, the department appeared to hold very different views about what it was to be an English teacher. This feature of many an English department (see for example Protherough, Atkinson and Fawcett, 1989 and Ball and Lacey, 1980), including all those I have subsequently worked in, proved to be an invaluable experience in my ability to tease out the differences in English teachers' philosophies.

Perhaps the most significant experience, however, was the fact that in my second year of teaching the school moved to examining its most able pupils by 100 per cent coursework. The rest of the pupils followed suit the next year. We will go on to consider the assessment of English in more detail in chapter 6, but it is worth examining the rationale of the school briefly. The move was brought about by the head of department, whose enthusiasm for the subject was palpable. It lay behind his drive radically to alter the system of assessment in English. Three years before the introduction of GCSE (General Certificate in Secondary Education) in 1987, he insisted that O level English was assessed entirely by coursework to liberate pupils from what he saw as the lottery of the London Board English Language multiple choice exam. Early in my career, therefore, I was introduced to the workings of the Joint Matriculation Board syllabus D, the mechanisms of which I will discuss in chapter 6. One year later, he abandoned CSE and examined all pupils through the NEA 16+ 100 per cent coursework exam. The positive impact it had on both the results within the department and the motivation of the pupils was immediate and dramatic. As important to me was the fact that it introduced me to the world of Inner London Education Authority (ILEA) English. Twice a year all participating schools met within a consortium. My particular consortium met at Holland Park School, and through these meetings I began to network with other teachers who held views of the subject that I recognised as my own. It was here also that I first heard of the London Association for the Teaching of English and the ILEA's English and Media Centre publications.

I left my first teaching post after four years and worked briefly at one other school before becoming a second in the English department and then head of media studies at another social priority school in west London. This appointment coincided with the introduction of the Technical and Vocational Educational Initiative into the borough. The influence of TVEI was also brought into English, using as a springboard Pete Medway's experiences in Leeds (Medway, 1997). As Mike Simons points out in his introduction to *Where We've Been: Articles from the English and Media Magazine*, 'This article was one of the many in the magazine that were beginning to question some of the old assumptions about the taken for granted orthodoxies of the personal growth model of English teaching' (Simons, 1996b: 2).

Phase 3: advisory and higher education work

The National Curriculum for English was introduced in my last year as a teacher. But my next post as a visiting lecturer at King's College, combined a year later with that of advisory teacher, meant that I witnessed its early implementation in a large number of schools across London. As Cox himself suggests (Cox, 1992) and others confirm (see for example Protherough, 1995, and Goodwyn, 1992) the National Curriculum was broadly welcomed by schools. Indeed, NATE itself published a response which recognised much of the Cox Report as good practice (Bain, Bibby and Walton, 1989). Those departments with which I was working were no exception. Yet there were elements about which they either felt less confident or had neglected as part of their general practice. These areas broadly covered knowledge about language (a new strand introduced through the National Curriculum), teaching pre-twentieth-century literature to less able children, and the media. Much of my work entailed providing in-service training for departments and piloting schemes of work alongside teachers.

Learning to work with these independently minded people gave me valuable insight into their philosophies of the subject, but it was the rewriting of the National Curriculum and the alterations to the assessment regime that were perhaps even more enlightening. Part of my brief was to run the termly meetings of the heads of secondary school English departments. Here the issues of the day were thrashed out against an increasingly tense background. It was their anger at the changes that pro-pelled so many to campaign against both the tests and Pascall's revisions to the English curriculum (DES and WO, 1993). Their views were echoed in the schools I visited in my role as a PGCE tutor. Many of these teachers were far from militant in their points of view, but, as Protherough (1995) points out, the whole process had the effect of politicising them. The debates that were set in motion by these changes at the beginning of the decade reverberated throughout the 1990s.

One other piece of work, which combined my work as an advisory teacher and lecturer, proved influential when writing the Rough Guide. This research was funded by SCAA (the Schools Curriculum and Assess-ment Authority) to look at the notion of progression in English. I was interested to discover whether or not one of the reasons for the perceived discontinuity between the primary and secondary phases was a difference in the models of English held by teachers in the different sectors. The findings eventually found their way into *Promoting Continuity between Key Stage 2 and Key Stage 3* (SCAA 1996), where a year of research was reduced to a single piece of advice. Under the subheading 'Joint work involving planning and assessing pupils' work', the document suggests that 'Joint work may focus on: similar units of work to be taught and assessed simultaneously in years 6 and 7 (for example, in English pupils' responses to literature)' (SCAA, 1996: 15).

This cursory description hides some of the central research findings (Marshall and Brindley, 1998), most notably that – even before the intro-duction of the Literacy Hour – primary teachers had, in the main, a much more skills-based view of the subject than their secondary counterparts, who appeared to place a premium on teaching literature. The importance of the research from the point of view of developing the Rough Guide, however, lay far more in the fact that it began to make me formalise my impressions of the ways English teachers approached their subject. And perhaps most significantly it demonstrated the limitations of question-naires for that particular audience, but this is a theme to which we shall return in chapter 5.

Developing the Guide

This then was the 'baggage' I carried when I began to write the Rough Guide to English Teachers. My first aim was to establish some sense of what the philosophies of English teachers might be, and to this end I needed to look beyond the scope of my own experience. As we have seen, one crucial element was the history of the subject itself. (For a summary of that history see Figure 1, p. 19.)

Investigating the models

Yet, significant as the history is for understanding English teachers' current philosophies, it is insufficient. Two of the main attempts to classify English teachers since the Cox report (Griffiths 1992 and Davies 1996) had only identified two broad categories – liberal humanists and cultural theorists. While not disagreeing with this general description these categories seemed too broad to make the kind of distinctions I wanted. In addition, both these accounts use evidence gained before the introduction of the National Curriculum, even though they were used to analyse the impact of the National Curriculum itself. My experience indicated that it was quite possible that the National Curriculum might have made a difference to English teachers' views. Possibly for this reason Goodwyn (1992) turns to the views of English to be found in the Cox Report as the basis of his account. It is worth reminding ourselves of them:

> It is possible to identify within the English teaching profession a number of different views of the subject. We list them here though we stress that they are not the only possible views, they are not sharply distinguishable and they are not mutually exclusive.
>
> (DES and WO, 1989: para. 2.20)

These included 'personal growth, cross curricular, adult needs, cultural heritage and cultural analysis'. As we have seen, Cox's attempts to codify English teachers have been thoroughly critiqued (Jones, 1991 and 1992; Snow, 1991) but part of the problem with the Cox views can be found in Goodwyn's own findings. His results indicate that English teachers themselves only really identify with the first and last in the list and this leaves one with another expression of liberal humanism and cultural theory. This is not to say that the other views do not have their supporters, but that strong attachment to these views tends to lie outside teachers of English (see Marshall, 1998).

I needed to find a vehicle that would problematise both these accounts and, more importantly, my own experience. All that I have described so far arises out of my experience as an insider. I was and am a part of the community I was attempting to explore in a more systematic way. It was important, therefore, to gain an outsider's perspective. To this end I turned to the work of Stephen Ball. During the 1980s he wrote widely on the subject subculture of English teachers, exploring both their practices and origins of the subject.

In 'English Teaching, the State and Forms of Literacy' (Ball, 1987) Stephen Ball examines some of the tensions in English teaching throughout the 1980s. Although it was written two years before the Cox curriculum,

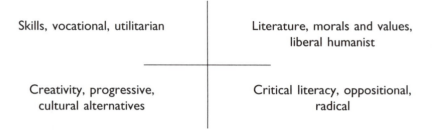

Figure 2 Ball's four main orientations of English teachers (Ball, 1987: 31)

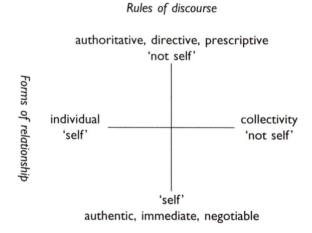

Figure 3 Ball's frameworks for English teaching (Ball, 1987: 31)

he considers the background against which it was produced, in particular the state of moral panic that surrounded the putative drop in standards of literacy and the fear caused by what he describes as the rise of the radical or London school of English (see also Ball, 1984). Using his categorisation, I began by exploring how his observations might be used to give another reading to the five models found in Cox.

In his article Ball identifies four main orientations of English teachers in the 1980s – Skills, vocational, utilitarian; Literature, morals and values, liberal humanist; Creativity, progressive, cultural alternatives; Critical literacy, oppositional, radical (see Figure 2). These he places within a framework, with the idea of authoritative, directive, prescriptive 'not self' at one end of a spectrum, and authentic, immediate, negotiable, at the other (see Figure 3). Broadly he locates the former with the Cambridge school of English, as characterised by F. R. Leavis, and the latter with what he describes as the London school of English, most influenced by the work of James Britton and, through him, by Vygotsky. In addition he argues that part of the nature of the oppositional stance of the London school comes from their legitimising the students' own voices against the received wisdoms of the canon, and places them along the axes shown in Figure 2. These he places within the framework shown in Figure 3.

At this point in the research process I had not eliminated the possibility that I would be looking at both the primary and secondary sector. I began, therefore, by reconfiguring these two figures using the different models of English in these two phases, based on my earlier research findings using questionnaires (Marshall and Brindley, 1998).

In Figure 2, it was possible to place the primary sector on the left-hand side of the grid and the secondary on the right. Both secondary teachers and the exam system place an emphasis on the teaching of literature. The two models on the right side of the page would then appear united by a sense of subject content but divided by the view taken of that content. Those on the left-hand side of the page give predominance to a more skills based, literacy approach.

Yet my reading of Ball's model is further complicated if we take into account the five types of English teacher identified by Cox and his working party. These views of English teaching cut across Ball's model in interesting ways. The 'cross curricular' and 'adult needs' views both fall into the skills sector but often manifest themselves differently in the primary and secondary sector. The primary sector is more likely to emphasise the cross-curricular nature of English. In many primary schools the post holder used to be called the language co-ordinator and is now often known as the literacy co-ordinator. Even though the Literacy Hour has now been given a specific timetabled slot to the subject, something that often did not happen in the past, the suggestion is still very much that literacy will give access to the whole of the curriculum. To that extent English is seen to be going on wherever reading, writing, speaking and listening are taking place.

In the secondary sector, however, many English departments resist the notion of becoming what they would consider to be a service department (see Ball and Lacey, 1980) to the rest of the curriculum. And, as Andrew Goodwyn (1992) points out in his early study and in his later survey with Kate Findlay (Findlay and Goodwyn, 1999), while English teachers acknowledge the need to prepare children for the world of work, and emphasise the technical aspects of English to that end, it is not a priority but more of a by-product of what they do. As we have seen, the origins of the antipathy to an 'adult needs' view of the subject go back to Sampson's highly influential *English for the English*. In it he states 'that it is the purpose of education, not to prepare children *for* their occupations . . . but *against* their occupations' (Sampson, 1952: 11). While such an unequivocal position has subsequently been modified, nevertheless the lack of sympathy for it as a position in Goodwyn's research shows that Sampson's view still has a hold, or rather it influences the way they read the phrase 'adult needs'. It has a ring of utilitarianism they wish to avoid, arguing that 'personal growth' prepares pupils for adulthood, which includes the workplace.

More significant, however, is the impact on Ball's remaining sectors of the other three views of English teaching found in Cox. When I looked at the 'personal growth' view I observed the way in which it cut across the literature and creativity sectors in Ball's model. Again Goodwyn's research suggests that 'personal growth' is still the dominant view of English teaching in the secondary sector. Using Ball's model, however, it seemed that different groups might interpret the notion of 'personal growth' differently. This view, for example has aspects of the London and the Cambridge schools. Its origins lie in Matthew Arnold's *Culture and Anarchy*, and it includes both the idea that literature improves, which Ball had identified with the Cambridge school, and that individuals should be given self-expression, which Ball sees as characteristic of the London school.

My initial reading of this split, however, was to see the way in which, on the whole, primary schools have emphasised the latter while secondary schools have pursued the former. Yet, as Ball points out and I had experienced, the right to self-expression is a key component of the oppositional stance in the secondary sector as well, particularly through the work of writers such as Dixon and, later, Britton. In addition, as Goodwyn suggests, most English teachers believed they prioritised 'personal growth', an idea not disconnected with self-expression. Nevertheless, my earlier research had suggested the dominance of literature teaching in the secondary sector. For this reason I went on to look at the way the idea of 'personal growth' and Matthew Arnold's legacy was interpreted in the teaching of texts.

I began by considering Cox's other two categories, 'cultural heritage' and 'cultural analysis'. The former is, apparently, Arnold transformed through Leavis, hence Ball's Cambridge school. Cox's 'cultural analysis' appears to fall neatly into the London school. But, as we have seen, Eliot is the dominant figure in Cox's 'cultural heritage' category and this makes a difference to the Arnoldian view of literature as a vehicle for 'personal growth'. For although in Leavis' great tradition only certain literature has value, for Eliot the real significance lies not in the quality of the literature but in its identification with Englishness. Instead of being a vehicle for promoting tolerance and empathy, literature becomes a heritage designed to exclude as well as to shore up the establishment.

Again, as we have seen, during the arguments surrounding the Pascall curriculum this 'cultural heritage' view of English further removed itself from Arnold's desire for personal growth. Arnold had used the notion of literature to oppose the utilitarian view of English teaching he found in the schools he inspected (see for example Matthieson, 1975). Yet the Pascall curriculum clearly articulates a skills-based approach combined with a sense of cultural heritage. This echoes the writing of John Marenbon (Marenbon, 1987; see also Marenbon, 1994). There was, however, considerable opposition to the views of Marenbon and the Pascall curriculum, which suggests that neither the five views found in Cox nor Stephen Ball's models sufficiently captured what English teachers thought.

At this point I began to explore the possibility that an Arnoldian view of personal growth was crucial to differentiating two types of English teacher. Although the lineage from Eliot to Arnold seems unbroken, Arnold saw growth occurring through the aesthetic properties of literature which allowed one to see the world differently. He believed in the importance of self-expression. Cox's autobiography reflected these ideas much more closely than any of the views he identified in his curriculum. As we have seen he attributes his own views of the subject directly to the influence of Matthew Arnold.

Yet it was clear, when I looked at those espousing what Ball describes as critical literacy and Cox calls 'cultural analysis', that, in part, they too owe their philosophy to Arnold. And their debt to Arnold is not limited to the idea of self-expression but in their whole approach to texts. As Snow (1991) points out, though he sees it as a danger rather than something to be endorsed, 'cultural analysis' seeks to encompass the idea of personal growth through a sense of empowerment. Indeed, in that it is possible to connect Dixon, who wrote *Growth through English*, so clearly with the London school, it is difficult to disconnect a view of growth from a more radical agenda.

As we have seen, Dixon's growth model was conceived in direct reaction to the two other models he identified, 'skills' and 'cultural heritage'. But his concept of empowerment can extend beyond the idea of self-expression and creativity to an ability to read the environment. This area of study extends beyond literature, therefore, to the more flexible category of text. Yet the role of literature in bringing about this more critical stance is central. Given that this category, in both Ball's and Cox's classifications, most closely reflected my own experience, I was aware that this group not only demands radical re-readings of canonical texts but carefully selects texts for their oppositional qualities. (See for example the English and Media Centre publications on *The English Curriculum: Gender* – English and Media Centre, nd; and on *The English Curriculum: Race* – Raleigh, Richmond and Simons, nd.) Books studied are likely to take a strong feminist or anti-racist stance. This strategy runs alongside the desire to develop the pupils' own tastes, and these two aims can, at times, come into conflict, but the sense that books can have a transformatory effect is never far from the surface.

Alistair West's comments in his essay 'The Centrality of Literature' perhaps best demonstrate this tension. Arguing against the limitations of a 'personal growth' model of English he comments:

> For the undeniable benefit of literature is just that process of locating oneself in history, putting together a selection of texts for which particularly resonant meanings have been made by individuals and groups. Opening up for discussion and analysis our students' experience of that process in their encounters with significant texts is an important part of 'critical literacy'. This entails taking our students' literary affiliations seriously.
>
> (West, 1995: 130)

It was important, therefore, to establish the ways in which this group's view of the transformatory view of literature differed from that of any other group's belief in its powers. For this I returned to the way in which 'personal growth' might be interpreted by differing groups. Again, based on my own experience, and the literature connected with this position, I sensed that what marked out the group interested in critical literacy from those who view their role simply in terms of personal growth is not their view of the individual, but their perception of the structures of society. Griffiths (1992) identifies this as a key difference between the liberal humanist and cultural theorist positions. In other words, those who see themselves as fostering personal growth in their pupils may be conservative or liberal but not radical if they avoid considering literature at any level beyond the impact it makes on the individual.

This may well encourage teachers into a seemingly radical stance, if they view the restrictions placed on the individual by the Pascall curriculum (or rather the opportunities to foster personal growth) as too great. Yet it would not necessarily cause them to challenge or question the structures of society which created them. In addition to this broad divide, however, I was aware, through my encounters with them, that there was another group with a foot in both camps. While some teachers might on the surface argue against the changes to the National Curriculum, in a language that reflected the views of the cultural theorists, they were often more ready to seek a path of compromise, within the context of school practice, than many who took a liberal humanist or Leavisite model.

Formalising the philosophies

It was at this point that it became clear that I needed to formalise my growing sense of the different kinds of English teachers that emerged during my study of both Ball's analysis and Cox's views. Using this critique and knowing how the battles over the English curriculum had been and still are being fought, I found that certain key points of debate emerged around which clusters of opinion could be formed. In their analysis of English as a subject subculture Ball and Lacey (1980) combined two elements to describe English teachers' views. These they called the 'subject paradigm' and the 'subject pedagogy' (ibid.: 157). Aspects of both are interwoven into the key elements of the debate I identified. These included personal growth, pedagogy, views on Standard English, literature, creativity, assessment, educational change and pupil grouping. It was at this point also that I decided to concentrate my attention on the views of secondary English teachers.

These key elements I placed in a grid against six types of teacher I had loosely identified, having written a thumbnail sketch of each of their positions. Broadly speaking I had mentally divided the liberal humanists and the cultural theorists into two groups. Within the former group I suspected that one group might place more emphasis on the liberal qualities of education, the other on mastery of the subject. But I subdivided these groups further, in each case believing that one inclined more to the literary view of the subject, the other towards emphasising the language. With the cultural theorists, however, I looked more to the way their view of society impacted upon the stance they took up within the school and in relation to the national debate. I was most interested in the extent to which their views led them to an oppositional stance.

As we have seen, these categories emerged from an interplay between the formal reading undertaken as part of my research and my experiences as an English teacher, education lecturer and local education authority (LEA) adviser. But these categories were also formed in informal discussions with colleagues and other English teachers.

From the outset I felt it was important to give these groups names almost as a way of giving myself a mental shorthand for their approaches. I began by calling these groups Old Grammarians A and B; Technicians A and B; Pragmatists; and Critical Literacy. The first four were broadly liberal humanist, the latter two, very loosely speaking, were cultural theorists.

The name Old Grammarians was intended both to denote an interest in language and to hint at the elitism of the grammar school as well as their own academic orientation. It also owed something to Brian Cox's auto-biography, in which he describes his indebtedness and commitment to this type of school. The Pragmatists suggested an attitude to educational change that was, I felt, a key marker of this group. Critical Literacy was intended to suggest left-wing orientation as well as an interest in theory. The term is commonly found in the literature of the English and Media Centre through their references to writers such as Freire and Bakhtin. It is also found in a publication called *The Redbridge Handbook* (NATE, nd), which was widely used in London English departments and distributed by NATE. The remaining group, the Technicians, were, I felt, dominated by an approach to accuracy and least interested in personal growth or the implications of English as an art.

I plotted what I believed would be each of these group's positions against the key points of debate that I had identified, but in many ways my approach at this stage was more like writing character sketches than any formal categorisation. I used individuals whom I knew well and, based on discussions with these people over the years, I held mental conversations with them to establish the nuances of difference between their positions. Inseparable from this process was my understanding of the literature which sought to characterise English teachers and clarify the history of the subject. But this reading was filtered through my knowledge of individuals who held strikingly different views, and it was these that I used to form the broad basis of the groups. I then sought to classify people whose position was less clear. This helped me clarify what some of the key dividers between positions might be, a process that I will discuss in more detail later as the groupings became increasingly defined.

This informal method of classification, using people I knew to create distinguishing features of views, became a significant factor in how, subsequently, I chose to validate my groupings. It became apparent at this stage that I needed to do this in a way that was as sympathetic as possible to their – admittedly unorthodox – conception. But I also wanted an approach that allowed English teachers to respond to the categories as character studies. Indeed, I did not finish filling in all the key points on the grid system, feeling constrained by the form that did not allow me sufficient room to explore and describe these people.

The next stage involved, therefore, expanding on these initial differences. This involved teasing out the various arguments between the positions, better to define their distinguishing marks. Although the manner in which I describe this process is, perhaps of necessity, chronological, at this stage the process of establishing an argument with one group had an

A Rough Guide to
English Teachers

Introduction

The booklet you are about to read is to form the basis of research into English teachers and in particular the way in which their understanding of the subject influences their view of assessment. In other words, what is it about English teaching that makes assessment such a contentious issue? Before looking at how English teachers assess, however, it is important to establish the different approaches they bring to their teaching, for not all English teachers are the same.

In order to do this I have loosely grouped English teachers around five broad views of the subject (not those used by Cox in the introduction to his report), each of which is described on the following pages. The contents of this booklet have already been modified as the result of an initial pilot involving two English departments, members of the MA group at King's and a number of willing PGCE students.

While everyone who has taken part so far has understandably resisted the notion of being classified, nevertheless all have found themselves broadly represented, to a greater or lesser extent, by one of the five groups found in the booklet. The aim is not to find a perfect match, for as with any classification there will be elements in any one of the groups with which we can sympathise, but rather to find the group in which we can most easily situate ourselves. However, at this stage the categories are still fluid and we would like your help in refining them.

Instructions

To find out what needs to be changed, added or dropped altogether, you are being asked to:

1   Find the group with which, broadly, you identify the most.
2   Highlight in one colour all those words and phrases in the description of that group that influenced your decision to choose it.

3   Highlight in another colour those aspects of the description that you think are mistaken.
4   Feel free to comment at any point. Marginal notes can be very helpful.

Thank you for your time and help in this research

Group A

This group are Arnoldian in their view of the subject. They believe in the improving and civilising qualities of literature. It is less, however, about books correcting behaviour than literature unlocking other worlds, other possibilities; a form of escape. And perhaps most importantly they are about developing an aesthetic sensibility.

This means that the literature they choose will have two purposes. The idea of the reading habit is fostered because, unlike television, it gives more scope for the imagination to roam. While there is an overtone of the Protestant work ethic – books are harder – there is also the sense that they allow more freedom than a television drama, where many decisions have already been made. In this sense there is a curious tension between moralistic aims – of hard work and improvement – and at the same time a kind of aesthetic hedonism – you read for pleasure. The former justifies the latter.

The tension is there in Matthew Arnold's writing, particularly on education. He posits many of his theories on poetry and reading against that which he views as Philistine utilitarianism and yet feels compelled to argue that there is a point to literature. He cannot argue art for art's sake, where his arguments tend. Books must have worth and value.

Leavis is the most obvious inheritor of this tradition, but his work focused the tradition more narrowly on the canonical value of texts. It is his legacy, however, that has made some uneasy that this tradition is in effect a rejection of working class culture. For literature is both an escape of the mind – the light in a dark place – and, through education, a route out of the slums. His emphasis on high and low culture reinforces this, but it is more tellingly worked out in the books of writers like Richard Hoggart, and evident in the biography of Brian Cox.

Literature, then, is intimately tied in with their view of what education is for – it is reformatory at the level of the individual; it is about personal growth, about personal fulfilment, both emotionally and in terms of life chances. This can lead to endorsing some form of selection as a means of enhancing the chances of those who will benefit from education the most. It is possible that many of this group will not 'set' in the early secondary years as they wish to provide every opportunity for latent qualities to emerge but they will probably introduce some form of setting, however broad, for exam classes. It is most likely to result in the creation of a top set with broad ability groups for the majority and then a bottom set. Some, however, will set that middle group more rigidly.

This is because at a certain significant point they do not believe that you can teach all children in the same way. And most importantly because you may hold back those who can escape or blossom. Their views lead them to concentrate their attention on the most able, with whom they have a rapport and a mission, and the least able, who have clearly identifiable needs. Even though they are concerned by literacy levels at the bottom end, they are unlikely to take a rigidly phonetic approach because they view reading as more than a mechanistic skill.

While such views are not clearly party political, and they take the class system as a given that can only be ameliorated at a personal level, their views on literature brought them into conflict with the Conservative government. This group seeks to foster empathy, the imagination and enlightenment in the students they teach. While they are not averse to the idea that some literature is better than others, they cannot have that choice imposed because teaching is about finding the book that will create the spark. It is about inspiration, which almost by definition cannot be produced by government diktat.

On the whole this group is also in favour of 100 per cent coursework because it avoids the reductive nature of timed tests. It is hard to produce inspiration to order. Similarly they are deeply suspicious of criterion-referencing because it is hard to predict originality. As this is one of the chief virtues they are trying to foster, criteria seem to miss the point, not least because they are perceived as bureaucratic. They view the current exams, and KS3 tests in particular, as reducing literature to the accumulation of facts rather than an opportunity to develop a personal response. In the pupils' own writing they will place a strong emphasis on flair and originality.

In addition, because they prefer impromptu ways of working to what they see as more formulaic methods, English departments run by this group often find themselves at variance with the senior management in their schools, who want 'checklist' assessment policies or rigid schemes of work. As teachers they are unashamedly teacher-centred because the teacher is the conduit of inspiration. Entitlement for the children lies less in the curriculum they follow, therefore, than in their access to good teaching. GCSE and the National Curriculum encouraged them to enter all sets for literature because the courses allowed for the possibility of finding appropriate texts and learning for all pupils.

The other way in which the National Curriculum influenced this group was in their views on Standard English. They are interested in the study of the grammar of English which relates to their position on Standard English. They would describe this in terms of command rather than ownership or empowerment. Yet their interest in grammar leads them away from any simple definitions of correctness towards the notion of a facility with language. Their emphasis on creativity resists the notion of the formulaic. The 'knowledge about language' strand in the National Curriculum gave them a diverse way of studying the language away from the old primers without necessarily involving them in discourse analysis or critical language awareness which takes a more oppositional stance to the language of power.

As with Leavis, *Hard Times* is a seminal text which defines their opposing views. They are with the circus people – the realm of the imagination. The Gradgrinds of this world are the enemy.

Group B

This group is significant because of the way in which they attempt to manage educational change, both within the school and at national level, and in particular the way in which they confront those changes which most impinge upon their beliefs and practice as English teachers. Many in this group, though by no means all, will have entered the teaching profession from the mid-eighties onwards so that their degrees may have been influenced by some form of literary theory and their training will have emphasised the rationale behind mixed-ability teaching as well as the benefits of coursework.

Many will never have taught O-level or CSE, a significant number will either not have taught long before the National Curriculum was introduced or never known a time when it was not there. The most recent entrants to the profession will not have had the opportunity to teach 100 per cent coursework. While some of these will have experienced its benefits as pupils, many will have just missed it both at school and then as a teacher. They will, to a person, say, however, that they oppose government reforms in terms of both the content and the assessment of the English curriculum.

Nevertheless they will place the emphasis on preparing pupils for what is in store for them. Some, though by no means all, will, for example, want to see the new grammar tests and perhaps pilot them because it is important to be ready for whatever is coming. Advanced knowledge may allow damage limitation. They are also keen to implement new initiatives and will set up working parties around issues such as boys and English, whole-school language and reading policies and the like.

Their departmental policy documents will reflect clear positions on equal opportunities including gender, race and often class. They have adopted a systematic approach to assessment policies, schemes of work and statements of aims partly from a desire to democratise the pupils' entitlement and partly from a belief that management systems will enhance the quality control and monitoring of the department.

For them, the English curriculum allows for the possibility of empowering pupils by giving them the ability to analyse critically the society in which they live. Again they are keen to equip and prepare pupils with the critical tools that they need to analyse any text. This view informs both their approach to literature and the study of language and has led them to consider the importance of the role of the media. Texts are chosen which highlight issues and critical possibilities. Teachers are likely to emphasise the social context in which they were produced. When considering the issue of Standard English they would be likely to look at the power relationships implied in the phrase and do work on dialect and regional variety. In pupils' writing they reward flair and originality as well as thoroughness and attention to detail.

Mixed-ability grouping is a problem area for this group. While it is an end devoutly to be wished, they argue, it is not always possible. They look to two sources of external pressure that have brought about their dilemma.

The first and most immediate pressure often comes from the senior management within the school. Many heads themselves claim to be sympathetic to the cause of mixed-ability teaching but place the blame on market forces. Parents, they claim, prefer setting and they have to give them what they want to maintain school rolls.

The second is connected. Government reforms, in particular the tiering of tests at KS3 and GCSE exams, have made mixed-ability teaching harder to organise. This has meant that the issue of setting has now affected lower school classes as well as GCSE groups.

This group accommodates these pressures into their view of pupil grouping. While they rarely allow, if in the position of head of department, more than a 'top-set and the rest' in year 9, and the possible inclusion of a bottom set at GCSE for those likely to be entered for the foundation tier, they will still argue that they are implementing mixed-ability grouping. They describe it, however, as a 'broad-banding' policy that maintains the spirit, if not the letter, of mixed-ability teaching.

Again they would share the belief that English is difficult to assess under the current arrangements, not least because acts of the imagination are hard to produce to order, and set books may dampen enthusiasm. But they believe it is possible to accommodate their ideas within the framework – that it is possible to make the best of a bad job. This group believes that the subject is being altered by external pressures and for the worse but continues to look for evidence of their view of English teaching, as a space to analyse and explore texts within the National Curriculum and its assessment arrangements.

Group C

This group is also very much in the Arnoldian tradition in that they have a strong belief in the benefits of English as a subject. They sense that it is perhaps the only space in the curriculum for unlocking doors and for exploring thoughts and emotions as well as promoting empathy, understanding and tolerance. Both the study of literature and creative writing are essential to this endeavour.

They are more likely to look to the literature of social realism to aid them in this process because they consider that, while style and aesthetic values are significant, they are less important than the content or message in the teaching of English as a school subject. They emphasise the notion that you start from the pupil's point of view and develop it by exploring issues, and are less driven by the idea of English as an Arts subject. That is not to say that they do not encourage the notion of reading for pleasure but the relationship with the book is more a beneficial friendship than a passion.

Their concern for social realism does not, however, lead to a radical, oppositional stance. They would, for example, be likely to be more comfortable with the notion of multi-culturalism than anti-racism because they would emphasise resolving issues at a personal level. In addition, they are likely to be concerned with themes in literature and may well organise schemes of work around extracts which illustrate an aspect of life, rather than a literary idea.

The written work they set is very much aimed at developing the personal voice and their approach to the teaching of Standard English is connected with this. While they will consider it important to teach children Standard English, in order to prevent them from being disadvantaged, they may well see the pupil's dialect or home language as being an essential part of their identity, which is to be valued. This view sits uneasily with the current model of 'correctness' which appears not to value authenticity but seems to encourage a somewhat mechanistic view of writing. They are also likely to value authenticity in the pupils' work over what they might consider 'flashy style' or writing that is 'too clever by half'.

They like to believe that the English teacher is the sympathetic face of the schooling system and this often leads them towards the pastoral system. Their emphasis on the personal leads them to mistrust management systems and bureaucracy for they are more likely to put their faith in human contact and dialogue than paperwork. But they now feel uneasy, if not beleaguered, because of what they perceive to be the changed ethos of schooling. They fear that schools are becoming more like building societies and are anxious that the pressures of the market place are making them more impersonal places. Initiatives such as appraisal and OFSTED inspections concern them because they do not believe you can summarise a person's worth at a glance or through generic 'tick-boxes'. They prefer words to numbers.

This attitude has also led them to oppose the changes to the National Curriculum and its system of assessment. They are keen to encourage pupils' reading habits by choosing texts that are relevant to them, in particular by teaching those authors who write specifically for teenagers. As such they are concerned by the emphasis on pre-twentieth century literature because they are afraid that it will 'switch-off' many pupils. Similarly they favour more coursework assessment because it allows more scope for expression and is less prescriptive than the demands of rigid syllabuses and timed tests.

Their strengths lie with teaching and developing the average child but they do not have defined views on mixed-ability versus setting and are likely to 'go with the flow' of the department. If they are the head of department they may well have experimented with varieties of pupil groupings. They will err towards mixed-ability for the younger classes as they are anxious for pupils to develop their potential, but again they would not necessarily turn this into a rigid policy.

Group D

The chief characteristic of this group is their desire to focus on the skills necessary to be good at English. They are likely to encourage pupils to study spelling, punctuation and grammar so that they can become confident users of the language. They are also keen to develop creative writing in order to encourage a more imaginative response to language because they believe that English is the only area in the curriculum where this can be done.

They may well, however, stress the importance of language in every day use, for example, writing letters or instructions, in order to ensure that pupils become competent in these forms. Teaching Standard English is important in this endeavour because it will increase pupils' command of the English language and their ability to communicate effectively and accurately.

In reading they are concerned to know how much pupils have understood of what they have read and to develop their reading skills. Comprehension is likely, therefore, to be an important teaching strategy, both as a means of assessing the pupils' understanding and as a means of increasing their reading skills. They believe that it is important that children read and are likely to commend it as an activity over computer games and watching television. Study of the media is not, therefore, a high priority in their classrooms, as they would prefer pupils to exercise their critical skills on more traditional texts.

They believe strongly that it is important for children to be taught appropriately according to their needs and that teachers should be able to focus on addressing the weaknesses of the pupils, particularly the technical and linguistic. They may well consider that not all pupils are capable of studying certain writers and that while it is important to stretch and challenge the most able, by presenting them with demanding literature, it is often preferable to give the 'less-able' books that are more relevant to them, or abridged versions so that they can appreciate the story. They are particularly aware that many less able children find poetry difficult.

This view of the appropriate needs of the pupils leads them to favour setting and they may well be sympathetic to the notion of selection. In a non-selective school, they are more likely to implement a system that is finely-tuned rather than broad-banding, because they believe it will allow them to concentrate more fully on each group's particular needs and set appropriate work.

They acknowledge the need for coursework because it offers more opportunity for creative writing but they are likely to argue for the discipline that exam work provides. For this reason they often opted for the 50 per cent exam/coursework divide when GCSE allowed such a choice, though they were more likely to take this option with literature, because it more obviously presented a body of knowledge to be tested. Given the importance of exams, they believe it is important to prepare children thoroughly for them. When assessing pupils' work they are likely to give priority to those pupils who are accurate and controlled users of English.

They are, however, not necessarily in favour of many of the education reforms because they believe that it has reduced their ability to control the curriculum and choose work that is appropriate for the pupils. They dislike the sense of something being externally imposed on them that will interfere with their ways of working, even if they are broadly sympathetic to some of the National Curriculum's aims. They are keenly aware of the workload implications. Initiatives such as OFSTED inspections or teacher appraisal may also be seen as an unnecessary imposition that detracts from the business of teaching. As a head of department, they are likely to value efficiency and like to see things well-run and organised with clear, definable aims.

Group E

This group have been described as 'cultural theorists' or interested in critical literacy, but in many ways they form a broader spectrum than this because not everyone who may be classified under this heading is as interested in critical or, more especially, linguistic, theory as this description suggests. They form a spectrum of opinion that is coloured by the degree of emphasis placed on literature. At one end can be found those influenced by linguistic theories which emphasise the notion of critical literacy arising out of theorists like Gramsci. At the other end are those influenced by a literary model of cultural dissent, which emphasises the political context and connotations of all literature and the need to challenge received norms.

Many teachers gravitate towards the middle of the spectrum, or modify their opinion depending on the area being discussed, so they do not form two distinct groups. As a group these teachers are marked chiefly by the rigour of their perception of culture and the way this impacts on their view of the subject, pedagogy and classroom organisation. As a group they are, of necessity, clearly to the left of centre.

This group sees personal growth in terms of empowerment. This has manifested itself in various ways over the last twenty years and may still change, depending on the position in the spectrum, but the aim is always similar. In the late sixties and early seventies much of the emphasis lay in discovering a personal voice. Spearheaded by teachers like Chris Searle in Hackney, and later through publications such as *Our Lives*, published by the English and Media Centre, this movement sought to empower pupils by allowing them freedom of expression. It was a way of breaking free of the dead weight of the Leavisite canon.

But this emphasis appears to have been amalgamated, in the late seventies and early eighties, with literary theory which allowed students to deconstruct texts, knowingly to debunk the canon and find

alternative texts that had been omitted. It also led to the rise of media studies and the examination of popular culture. Some have, however, been dissatisfied with the cultural relativism which this position implies and so have sought to explore more the idea of radical readings of canonical texts as well as suggesting alternatives to that canon.

The notion of discovering a personal voice has been maintained but refined. While the significance of non-standard variants is passionately defended, a new orthodoxy has emerged, namely that pupils are disenfranchised if they are not given access to standard forms of English, provided that these are discussed within the context of notions of the language of power and that notions of appropriateness are debated within the idea of critical language awareness. In some quarters, in fact, there is a hint of a movement away from the pre-eminence of literature within the English curriculum, and towards reconsidering language as an area of study. The emergence of knowledge about language in the Cox curriculum facilitated this development.

This flux in the ways of discussing empowerment is symptomatic of the mind-set of this group. Their position must constantly be reappraised and so its manifestations will continue to alter and this means, to an extent, that their classroom practice may alter also. They are likely to be influenced by ideas on learning theory as there is no rigid divide between theory and practice. Many will have been influenced by theorists such as Vygotsky, but they are likely to experiment with new ideas and theories within the classroom. While they pay lip service to the idea of teacher as facilitator, they are in fact highly directional in the way in which they teach.

Nevertheless, they are totally committed to mixed-ability teaching. This is mainly to do with their notion of democratic entitlement, not only in the desire not to treat one group differently by labelling them, but also to do with the idea that all children should have access to the same texts and ideas. Both these connect under the more general heading of equal opportunities. It is not, as has been suggested, saying all children are the same, but is insisting on the idea that all should have the same opportunities.

This insistence on mixed-ability teaching does, however, influence pedagogy, for while the teacher is highly directional they use the pupils to facilitate the learning. This is where the role of oracy and Britton's interpretation of Vygotsky is so significant. Group work and discussion are essential to the way in which the subject is delivered because it allows all pupils access to challenging texts. So, too, is coursework because it allows pupils to explore the same text in a far greater variety of ways than the terminal exam and allows for more scope in the way in which the pupils' work is approached. This emphasis may well lead them to value originality when assessing pupils' work.

All this has brought this group into direct conflict with government reform and it was this group that spearheaded the opposition to testing and the new curriculum. They have come round to the notion of a more prescribed curriculum and schemes of work through the notion of an entitlement curriculum as a form of equal opportunities, but are opposed to the way in which this currently manifests itself in legislation.

almost ripple effect upon the other positions. In other words, as I began to see more clearly the parameters of one group, it clarified my understanding of the philosophy I wished to capture in another. And it is this interplay between the ideas that I will attempt to reflect in this account.

Writing the descriptions

Critical Dissenters (Group E)

I began by writing about the group that I had initially described as Critical Literacy. I felt that if I started here, it might help to establish more clearly the boundaries and areas of overlap between this position and with other groups, given that this was the group with which I was most familiar. As with all the groups I was aware that the views I was about to explore covered a spectrum of opinions, but my knowledge of the debates within this group made me wonder at first whether or not this group, too, should be split in half. This was because I was aware of the tension between those who might broadly be characterised as taking a literary approach and those who emphasised language. This latter approach might loosely be categorised as one taken by Kress and Medway (see for example Kress, 1995 and 1997, or Medway, 1996), while the former can be seen in Traves' view of a literacy entitlement (see for example, Traves, 1996).

To compound the problem I was also aware that this group's position was in a state of constant flux. Tony Burgess, in an article for *Changing English* (1996), examines the way his approach to the subject has developed over the years. Mike Simons' introduction to the English and Media Centre retrospective *Where We've Been: Articles from the English and Media Magazine*, also published in 1996, charts a similar picture of internal debate and lack of stasis. While grappling for a solution to this dilemma I was asked to write an article on the English National Curriculum for *Critical Quarterly* (Marshall, 1996a). I had, at the time, been reading Tom Paulin's contribution to *Cultural Babbage: Technology, time and invention* (Paulin, 1996b). In it he reminds us of the half-forgotten legacy of rational dissent found in the work of the eighteenth-century scientist Joseph Priestley and the journalist and critic William Hazlitt. Part of the argument I intended to present, therefore, was the notion that opposition to the current form of the National Curriculum was not anti-traditional; rather, it was a call to another tradition, that of rational dissent.

It was this that gave me a way of unifying the two positions that I had feared I might have to separate. I believed that both the literary and linguistic approaches could be reconciled, using the notion of dissent. This would reflect the desire constantly to challenge both their own position and those of everybody else. Kress, for example, in *Writing the Future*, separates himself from what he describes as the 'liberal humanist position', precisely because of his desire to argue from a position that relates to the 'social, economic, political changes' with a view to 'intervention' (Kress, 1995: 15). To this end I changed the title of the group to Critical Dissenters. In this way I reflected its dissenting nature while keeping an echo of the notion of critical literacy.

Old Grammarians (Group A)

I was aware that those who were the most 'literary' (see Ball and Lacey, 1980) in this group might also share certain approaches with those that I chose to call, at this stage, Old Grammarians A, so it was to this group that I turned next. I was aware that the area of overlap was most likely to revolve around the notion of English as an arts subject, a view with which I had sympathy myself. It is this view of the subject to which Peter Abbs has most contributed, through books like *English within the Arts* (1982) and more recently with works like *A Is for Aesthetic* (1989a) and *The Symbolic Order* (1989b). Abbs wants to see 'English not as a literary-critical discipline, but as a literary-expressive discipline within the wider epistemic community of the arts' (Abbs, 1982: 33). Abbs himself, as we have seen, sees this as different from what he describes as both the 'Socio-linguistic school' (ibid.: 32) arising from the London Institute, and the Cambridge school of Leavis, characterised in educational terms by the work of individuals like David Holbrook. His third strand he calls the progressive school.

Abbs suggests an alternative to these three dominant forms, that of English as an art. While sharing his perception that aspects of the London school underplay the value of the aesthetic, what is perhaps significant about Abbs' analysis is that he cannot see room for the notion of English as an art either within the progressive or the London school. Indeed, this distinction is in itself interesting in that the London school owes much to progressive views of education. To this extent, Abbs' view of art becomes deracinated from any radical tradition. As Paulin (1986) suggests, art becomes apolitical. Abbs is at pains to separate his view from the discriminatory and critical purposes of Leavis, a tradition he traces back to Arnold, choosing instead to emphasise the creative and expressive act of art making. Yet without a specifically political or societal dimension to his view of art, he is still trapped within their same paradigm of 'culture' as examined by Raymond Williams (1961). This enables Abbs to include a piece by right-wing thinkers such as Roger Scruton in his collection of essays debating aesthetics (Abbs, 1989b). It is a difference that echoes

Griffiths' (1992) analysis of the difference between liberal humanist and cultural theorist views of the subject.

This then was to be the key difference between these two groups. While many Critical Dissenters may well share Abbs' sense that English is a 'literary-expressive discipline' and perceive it as placed within the arts, their view of the arts operates within a political context, within a dissenting tradition. The Old Grammarians, however, do not. For them art operates at the level of the individual. For this reason, rather as I had combined the literary/arts and linguistic approaches under the umbrella of Dissent, I now combined the Arnoldian tradition, which also values the aesthetic experience, with Abbs' sense of English as an art, under the heading of Old Grammarians. I kept the title the Old Grammarians because the presence of elements of the Cambridge school, as Abbs (1982) points out, were likely to give this group a predisposition to the academic. I am still not entirely happy with this name as it does not entirely capture the nature of the group. For what dominates their position is the enabling power of art, both of its appreciation and its creation.

Liberals (Group C)

Two other groups flowed from this position. Both are in a sense defined by the absence of this central position. The first was the group that I had originally called Old Grammarians B but now chose to call the Liberals. This was in part to indicate their debt to the liberal humanist position that I had outlined in the Old Grammarians, but it was also to suggest the more colloquial use of the term which, to an extent, connotes the promotion of tolerance and understanding. This latter position does not necessitate a view of English as an art, though I believed it might well show traces of the idea that books are beneficial. This view, however, is more connected to the notion that literature offers the possibility of empathy and so can be used to promote tolerance. The choice of literature is more concerned, therefore, with notions of relevance, with the children's writing with personal expression rather than with flair or artistic ability. In a sense this is not dissimilar to Ball and Lacey's (1980) category of the sociological approach to English teaching, which emphasises 'personal relationships, children's own culture, and free expression, opinions' (ibid.: 174). For this group the key words are 'pupils as individuals' (ibid.).

As with the Old Grammarians, however, such a view may have a dissenting dimension also. Indeed, Dixon's growth model of English also appears to promote this view. So does the work of Chris Searle, who edited and published pupils' poetry (see for example Searle, 1972) and many of the early publications of the English and Media Centre, such as

Our Lives (Ashton and Simons, with Denaro and Raleigh, 1979). Yet again the important difference between these groups lies in the view they take of the individual's voice. With the Critical Dissenters, the use of the vernacular, as Paulin suggests, is done almost in defiance of received norms, as a transgressive act. With the Liberals, it is done to allow the individual expression. It was this distinction also, again found in Davies (1992), that led me to differentiate between (for example) the Liberals' promotion of multiculturalism as opposed to the Dissenters' belief in anti-racism.

Technicians (Group D)

Whereas both the Old Grammarians and the Liberals had areas of overlap with the Critical Dissenters, the groups that I had initially seen as the Technicians A and B did not. My initial reason for separating the Technicians into two groups was to reflect the way in which they might be seen as almost mirror images of the Old Grammarians and the Liberals, or rather distorted images of these positions. Abbs' (1982) analysis of the shortcomings of the Cambridge school, with its emphasis on the critical and discriminatory, was suggestive of the way some teachers approached the subject. Interpreting English as an arts subject lends the Old Grammarians a more active view of the pupils' role. The notion of a 'literary-expressive discipline' involves some sense of the pupils' active participation. By contrast, an overemphasis on the 'great tradition' can lead to the passive absorption of received wisdom. The literary canon thus becomes knowledge to be acquired rather than literature with which to engage. The distinction is fine, but the difference is important to understanding why I believed it important to separate the Old Grammarians from the Technicians.

My experience in working with the heads of English had indicated that those who appeared to be coming from an arts perspective were likely to be far more vigorous in their opposition to the changes to assessment and their criticism of the testing regime at fourteen, than those who, I judged, were coming from a Technicians' point of view. To this extent, the Old Grammarians were closer to the progressive position, outlined by Dewey, and the Technicians to his description of traditionalists. It is this same difference that allows Cox to see himself as a 'moderate progressive' (Cox, 1992: 146) throughout his career. As we have seen, this may go some way to explaining how he could both contribute to the Black papers and staunchly oppose the changes to the National Curriculum.

To remind ourselves once more, as it is a useful definition, Dewey characterised traditional education in the following terms:

Since the subject matter as well as standards of proper conduct are handed down from the past, the attitude of the pupils must, upon the whole, be one of docility, receptivity, and obedience.

(Dewey, 1966: 18)

It was, in part, this view of education that enabled me to unite the Technicians A and B. For originally the Technicians, group B, were to be those who took a less literary view of the subject. I suspected, however, that their approach to language work, which I believed to be skills based, reflected the same attitude. They see language as a set of rules to be acquired, rather than as an opportunity for experiment and expression. Ball and Lacey (1980) identify a similar group, actually calling them the grammarians. This group emphasises 'functional use of language, communication and syntax' (ibid.: 174). Their key words for this group are 'basic skills' (ibid.: 74). To this extent also, the Technicians are the least child centred of all the groups I identified. Ball and Lacey connect this group, in part, to non-specialists, an impression that I shared. But like them it was a view I had encountered among specialists also.

This is, ironically, the view most often articulated by critics of what is seen as the mainstream of English teachers. Famously, Melanie Phillips, in an article on the Dearing review entitled 'Education's Guerrillas Prepare for War', described English teachers as 'cultural guerrillas' (Phillips, 1994). During the arguments over the revisions to the National Curriculum Dewey's traditional view of education, as it might be applied to English, was frequently given expression by writers and commentators in the broadsheets. Brian Appleyard's 'Loose Canons of Academe' (Appleyard, 1994) typifies this kind of writing, but perhaps its chief exponent is Melanie Phillips. Articles such as 'The Closing of a Teacher's Mind' (Phillips, 1992a) or 'English as She Is Tort' (Phillips, 1992b) exemplify the genre.

I suspect, though I do not know, that while I disagree with Phillips' position because we do not share a philosophy of the subject, the group I describe as the Technicians may well disagree with her on the grounds that she is criticising them for not doing something that they spend every day of their lives doing. Their resentment at her articles may well, therefore, arise out of the unfairness of her attacks. It is possible also that their experience of the classroom may well lead them to believe that the kind of standards she is proposing, particularly the teaching of canonical texts, is beyond the reach of many of the children they teach. Such an assumption may well lead them to the defensive position: 'What does she know?' Yet while Phillips may represent the extreme end of this position, and one which would, for the reasons I have explained, be unlikely to be held by teachers themselves, it was my perception that the Technicians occupied space on the same continuum.

Pragmatists (Group B)

This then left the Pragmatists to be defined. In many respects their position was closest to the Critical Dissenters. What separated them was their view of educational change. This is redolent of the process described in Woods, Jeffrey, Troman and Boyle (1997). They describe the tendency of teachers towards 'self-surveillance' (ibid.: 9). Woods and his co-authors analyse this tendency in relation to the changing culture of schools, particularly the new management culture, a phenomenon explored in detail by Gewirtz, Ball and Bowe (1995). As Woods, Jeffrey, Troman and Boyle (1997: 11) point out, 'This produces a variety of adaptations in the teacher workforce ranging from compliance with the new policy through mediation and accommodation to resistance and rejection.' My sense of this group was that they were more likely to manifest the first three approaches than the last two. Cooper and Davies (1993), in their study of English teachers and key stage 3 assessment during the SATs boycott, also noted that certain teachers took a more 'pragmatic' approach by seeking to 'prepare' their pupils for the SATs even though they did not agree with the tests.

Finding the form or characterising a philosophy

I now had brief descriptions of five philosophies of the subject. My problem was how to validate them. It was at this point that the idea of keeping them in this more descriptive form took a more concrete hold. I have alluded briefly to the difficulties encountered with questionnaires in my first attempt to glean models of English teaching. And it is an issue to which I will return in chapter 5, where I analyse further some of the possible reasons for English teachers' dislike of this form of research instrument. My aim in part, therefore, was to find a form that better reflected, or was more sympathetic to, this general view of English teachers. Undoubtedly this was in itself prompted by my own insider anxieties about the type of questions and answers found in questionnaires given their formal similarities to multiple choice questions. More significant at this stage, however, was my desire for the final form to echo the way the philosophies had been conceived.

As we have seen, there was a sense in which the emergence of these subject philosophies made them not unlike character studies, even though they were, in another way, archetypes. When writing them I had kept recognisable people in my head. As I tried to disentangle points of view, I had asked myself how so-and-so might react or what such-and-such might say. To this extent they were also like arguments for a position. The drafts I had produced thus far, then, were like texts to be discussed. I had in effect literally characterised a philosophy. To this end I decided to produce a final draft that allowed my text to be analysed by English teachers in a similar way that they would approach any text to be critiqued.

In order to produce some systematic sense of what I had got right and wrong I used a technique commonly used among English teachers to encourage close reading of a text. They might, for example, suggest highlighting different themes in different colours, or picking out two sides of an argument with different pens. Marginal notes are often included in such an activity to add as an additional gloss. In a similar vein, I decided I would ask teachers to select the description with which they most identified and highlight those words and phrases which had helped them make the choice. In a different colour they would indicate those elements of the description which they thought were mistaken. To an extent the success of the enterprise depended on the teachers' analytical ability, their own ear for the nuances of the language and the nuanced connotations which certain words carried.

For now I had to translate my perceptions of teachers into descriptions that they themselves would recognise and with which they would identify. At the same time these descriptions had to be sufficiently different to distinguish the variety of views I wanted to capture. To do this I constructed the text around key words and phrases (for a detailed account of how these were written, see Marshall, 1999). To begin with I used the cluster of issues that I had originally identified, such as attitudes to Standard English, pupil grouping, literature and so on, as a way of differentiating the content. At first I had intended to discuss each of these issues in the same order, but the logic with which each group approached these issues differed. Given that I wished to present each of the philosophies as the holders of the views might argue them, it was important to follow the logic of their argument in my description of their position, and so I abandoned this attempt, concentrating my efforts more on how these teachers might characterise their position.

But more significantly I used the language in which the descriptions were written to help me tease out some of the subtle distinctions between the philosophies. I infused, for example, the text of the Pragmatists with language of school management, while I talked of skills with the Technicians and opposition and dissent with the Critical Dissenters. I suspected that just as these would attract some teachers so they would repel others.

If we compare a section of the Pragmatists' text with that of the Critical Dissenters it may serve to illustrate the point. One of the paragraphs in the text describing the Pragmatists reads:

> Their departmental policy documents will reflect clear positions on equal opportunities including gender, race and often class. They have adopted a systematic approach to assessment policies, schemes of work and statements of aims partly from a desire to democratise the pupils' entitlement and partly from a belief that management systems will enhance the quality control and monitoring of the department.

If we look at a similar section in the text for the Critical Dissenters the difference becomes more apparent:

> The notion of discovering a personal voice has been maintained but refined. While the significance of non-standard variants is passionately defended, a new orthodoxy has emerged, namely that pupils are disenfranchised if they are not given access to standard forms of English, provided that these are discussed within the context of notions of the language of power and that notions of appropriateness are debated within the idea of critical language awareness . . . This flux in the ways of discussing empowerment is symptomatic of the mind-set of this group. Their position must be constantly reappraised and so its manifestations will continue to alter and this means, to an extent, that their classroom practice may alter also. They are likely to be influenced by ideas on learning theory as there is no rigid divide between theory and practice.

And so they both continue. Both are, to an extent, looking at the notion of equal opportunities in the broadest sense of the word. The crucial difference between the two is that one looks to organisational systems to ensure entitlement, the other to notions of teaching and learning, and this is also reflected in the langauge. Not only does the Pragmatist section specifically refer to management systems but it also uses some of its more hard-edged jargon such as '*monitoring*' and '*quality control*'. By contrast, the nature of the language in the Critical Dissenters' text is intended to reflect the notion of an ongoing debate. Now this is not to say that Critical Dissenters do not have departmental policy documents nor that Pragmatists are not keen to promote critical language awareness. The whole exercise allowed for overlap and common territory. What was important in trying to tap into teachers' philosophies was to find out which way they would jump when asked. The nature of the choices I had given them made them prioritise a point of view.

A comparison between the Old Grammarians and the Technicians also illustrates the way I tried to nuance the differences between the positions by the way they were phrased. Again, what differentiates the two passages is less the content – although in this particular section there is no mention of the Old Grammarians' approach to language teaching – it is the tone in which they are written. Part of the Old Grammarian text reads:

> This group seeks to foster empathy, the imagination and enlightenment in the students they teach. While they are not averse to the idea that some literature is better than others, they cannot have that choice imposed, because teaching is about finding the book that will create the spark. It is about inspiration, which almost by definition cannot be imposed by government diktat.

The Technicians' text, on the other hand, reads:

> The chief characteristic of this group is their desire to focus on the skills necessary to be good at English. They are likely to encourage pupils to study spelling, punctuation and grammar in order that they can become confident users of language. They are also keen to develop creative writing in order to encourage a more imaginative response to language.

In this latter description, creative writing and the imagination are both literally and metaphorically bolted on to the rest of the paragraph rather than, as with the Old Grammarians, being central to their motivation. In that they suggest a priority, the sequencing of the sentences in the Technicians' description is also suggestive of the order in which these are taught – the basics first and then the imagination. The description of the Old Grammarians indicates no such neat division.

So each of the descriptions was written in this way, with heed being paid to subtle variations in tone and vocabulary that would attract some readers and alienate others. The whole exercise, as I have said before, was dependent on an audience attuned to the niceties of language, to the way in which words resonate and connote meaning. Yet the idea of building key concepts and key phrases into the text was not only vital to the means by which I differentiated the positions, it was crucial to the data analysis. For it allowed me to count the positive and negative responses to my characterisation of teachers' philosophies, and it was this above all that allowed for the development of a large-scale research instrument.

Because the teachers were all responding to the same elements of the text, I was able to derive some systematic sense of what had drawn them to the particular description they had chosen.

Piloting the guide

At this stage, however, I was uncertain as to whether the groups I had defined would resonate with the reader. Moreover, it was important to pilot the work I had done so far, not least because no comparable research instrument had ever been tried. I had discussed and shown the descriptions informally to both my MA group and to some of my PGCE students, who had responded positively; but to establish a clearer, more formal picture I needed to pilot the work so far, so I selected two large departments which I knew contained a spread of views.

For my pilot to have any credibility at all these teachers needed to respond as I suspected they would. Because I was aware that there were tensions within one of the departments in particular, and that several of the teachers might be sensitive to being singled out as different, I wanted to ensure the anonymity of the respondents. I was afraid that they would respond in a way that they believed the head of department would want them to respond.

In the event, however, having distributed the survey, I established, through the heads of department, that all were willing to allow their identity to be known through the head of department to me. The descriptions were presented on A4 sheets of paper stapled together, and the names of the groups were omitted, in order that they might not prejudice response.

In all I received fifteen responses, and all the respondents had placed themselves in the groups I had anticipated. Only two respondents, however, made use of the opportunity to write marginal notes, and few highlighted much of the text. These responses allowed me little opportunity to modify the text and so only one phrase was altered as a result of the pilot. What these responses did allow me to deduce was that, in the broadest possible terms, the groupings appeared to work. Nevertheless the format was still not sufficiently different to encourage the kind of detailed response I wanted. Before sending it out on a large scale I began to explore ways of improving this element of the research instrument.

Refining the form

The final form of an A5 booklet came about after further discussion with colleagues, in particular Dylan Wiliam and Diane Reay. This would reflect even more closely the kind of material which English teachers were used to handling. To this end, during the conversation in which the suggestion arose, we considered the best size for the booklet. A5 was chosen because it was the closest to paperback fiction; the size of the font – 10 point – for the same reason; even the paragraph indentation was looked at. It was decided to produce it on a desktop package, again to help it look like a booklet.

In order to keep the booklet self-contained, I decided to include the instructions within it. Its layout on the second page made it seem almost like a contents page. In addition I felt it was appropriate to communicate the aims of the survey to those participating not only to make them feel part of the process but also further to encourage dialogue. This I also included in the booklet by way of an introduction. The page numbers for the introduction on the first page and the instructions on the second page were written in roman numerals. The page facing the introduction was blank to reinforce the impression of a front cover.

All that remained was a title. This was important because it was the first thing teachers would see and it would be the feature that would most create the impression of the contents of the survey. I toyed with a number of possibilities, all of which played with well-known titles, including 'The Anatomy of an English Teacher', which I decided was too heavy, and 'The English Patent', which I rejected on the grounds that it was too tricksy. In the end, I came up with the name 'A Rough Guide to English Teachers'. This had a number of advantages. Its echo of the tour guide series allowed it to connote both leisure reading and the suggestion that what was being presented was an alternative, informal view. The idea that the guide was only 'rough' also allowed teachers not to feel pigeon-holed, the descriptions not intended as definitive but open to negotiation. This was a theme I picked up in the introduction.

The sample

During this final stage I had begun negotiating with a number of schools. My involvement in NATE, my work as an LEA advisor and college lec-turer meant that I had fairly extensive contacts across the country, and I drew on this to obtain my sample. Often I only knew one or two members of the department. On three occasions my contact with the school was the head or the deputy. This personal contact, however, may well have aided the willingness of the schools to participate.

I selected twenty schools, in which the type and location of the school was as varied as possible. These included one independent school and two single-sex grammar schools in the south-east; two oversubscribed home

Table 1 School profiles

School	Type	Selectivity	Ages	Location
A	mixed	comprehensive	11–18	west midlands suburb
B	mixed	comprehensive	11–18	home counties
C	mixed	comprehensive	11–16	London suburb
D	mixed	comprehensive	11–18	shires
E	girls	comprehensive	11–18	west London
F	mixed	comprehensive	11–18	home counties
G	mixed	comprehensive	11–18	east London
H	mixed	comprehensive	11–18	north-east urban
I	girls	comprehensive	11–16	east London
J	mixed	comprehensive	11–18	east London
K	girls	selective	11–18	home counties
L	mixed	comprehensive	11–18	shires
M	boys	selective	11–18	London suburb
N	girls	independent	11–18	London suburb

counties comprehensives; four shire schools; seven London schools including one oversubscribed church school, five inner city schools – two of which were single-sex girls' schools, and one suburban school; two from the north-east; one from south Yorkshire and one from the suburban west midlands.

I sent copies of the Rough Guide with an accompanying letter to the heads of department. Included also was a prepaid reply envelope. These went out at the beginning of June and I allowed a month for completion. I chose this time of year, partly because the guides were now complete and partly because, traditionally, it is the quietest time of the school year. Most teachers have lost at least one exam class and have completed the standardisation of folders. In addition year 10 classes often go out on work experience during the latter half of the summer term, making the teaching load potentially even lighter. I allowed at least two weeks before the term ended, however, to give me a chance to follow up those schools who had not returned the Rough Guides. In the event fifteen of the twenty schools contacted replied (see Table 1 for the school profiles), though one, an 11–18 mixed comprehensive school in the north-west, replied too late for their results to be considered.

One last consideration has to be described before we go onto a more detailed look at the findings – how the texts were analysed. I have already described the process to an extent in the account of the development of the guide, as it was intimately connected with the way in which the groups were written and conceived. But it is sufficiently important to be worth recapping. As we have seen, embedded within the texts were certain key words and phrases. Respondents had been asked to select the group with which they had most sympathy and to highlight those words and phrases within the text that had led them to this choice. They were able to indicate in another colour those sections of the text with which they disagreed, and to annotate the text at any point.

I used the frequency with which the respondents highlighted or commented on key concepts and phrases as a way of measuring the success of the description. In addition I had invited the respondents to comment upon and annotate the text of the Rough Guide (see the appendix for an example). This was because part of the aim of the research instrument was to use textual criticism as a way of collecting and analysing data about the subject philosophies of English teachers. The respondents' comments are, therefore, woven into my text as I, too, use textual criticism to aid me in my analysis of their views. As we will see, their remarks add greatly to an understanding of their views in ways I had not fully anticipated. For ease of reference while analysing the text, I have italicised all quotations from the Rough Guide. I have, as far as possible, attempted to reproduce teachers' emphasis, punctuation and spelling.

One last dilemma in reporting the findings confronted me. Because I had chosen to make the responses completely anonymous, in the majority of cases I do not know the gender of the respondent. This left me with the problem of how to refer to them. When I began my analysis I coded each person with a letter which referred to his or her school and then a number to differentiate them from other members of the department. Respondents from school A would be called A1, A2, A3 and so on. After much internal debate I have chosen to keep this rather impersonal method of reporting despite its slightly clinical feel. I toyed with the idea of finding gender-neutral names like Kit, Pat or Hilary, but there were not enough, and giving an individual a gendered identity may well have coloured people's reading of their responses. Even where I do know the gender of the respondent I decided not to give them a name, partly for consistency but also because any name can create a mental image, and I wanted the responses to speak for themselves. If I do know the gender of the respondent I refer to them as he or she, otherwise all respondents are referred to in the third person plural. And so to the findings.

4 Analysing the characters

Two central aims motivated the construction of the Rough Guide. The first was to differentiate English teachers' philosophies of the subject. The second was to find a form in which this could be done. Any account of the success of the guide has to consider both these elements. For the sake of clarity I have chosen to look at them separately, yet, as we have seen, these two components were intimately entwined, and that makes any discussion of the findings which seeks to separate them slightly artificial and prey to inevitable overlap. For the moment, however, our purpose will be to examine the way in which teachers responded to the content of the Rough Guide and to consider the form in the next chapter.

Part of the difficulty in writing the Rough Guide was that I was attempting to find some means of categorising a group of people who have a tendency to resist the very notion that categorisation is possible. This is not to say that there is not open acknowledgement among English teachers that their views of the subject differ. Indeed, beginner teachers will often be introduced to the lack of consensus about English teaching early on in a course. Chris Davies and Peter Benton begin their Postgraduate Certificate in Education at Oxford by airing these differences:

> We approach the wealth of possibilities and complexities bound up in English teaching by emphasising the idea of diversity rather than consensus within the subject – the idea of different versions of the subject co-existing, often uneasily, in the thinking and practice of secondary English teachers. Our starting point with our interns is to get them thinking about the fact that there are no natural or correct answers to the questions, 'What is secondary English for?'.
>
> (Davies and Benton, 1991: 75)

Yet it is this very openness of approach that is a challenge to the notion that views of the subject can be easily identified within an individual.

Davies and Benton's aversion to correct answers echoes sentiments that have been characteristic of English teaching since its inception. Protherough cites the 1910 report, the first on the subject, which was written in response to the idea of an 'agreed or imposed syllabus' (Protherough and Atkinson, 1991: 15). 'English is the last subject in which teachers should be bound by hard and fast rules. No subject gives more scope for individuality of treatment or for varied experiment' (cited in ibid.: 15). The notion of individuality serves a double function in this context. It is a mark of both the teacher and the quality which the subject is trying to encourage, a point reinforced by the report's concluding remark, 'In none is the personal quality of the teacher more important' (ibid.: 15).

The way in which the teachers' personal qualities merge with their views of the subject, and the fact that teaching English becomes almost an expression of the individual, motivate Davies and Benton to encourage beginner teachers to find a voice, in much the same way as teachers encourage pupils to find theirs. That views of the subject can cause 'unease' is perhaps indicative of the way in which English teachers' perceptions of themselves are intimately bound up with their teaching. Such close identification is found in the comments written by one of the respondents on the Rough Guide. In the margin of their chosen group they write 'I think this is me.' To tap into English teachers' philosophies of their subject can, therefore, be seen almost as a personal intrusion and goes some way to understanding their resistance to categorisation. The researcher is not only capturing the views of a teacher but in danger of compartmentalising the person.

The Rough Guide to English Teachers was a response to this research dilemma. As we have seen, the idea was to produce a text which was sufficiently robust to be capable of differentiating responses, in a way that was compatible with this broad sense of the subject; that is, one that eschewed right and wrong answers, appeared open to negotiation and invited comment and analysis. One clear indication of the success or otherwise of the approach taken in the Rough Guide was the extent to which English teachers felt they could identify with the description without being pigeon-holed.

Perhaps the most significant validation of these teacher typologies, therefore, was the fact that all but three of the 62 respondents analysed were able to locate themselves within one of the descriptions. (For a breakdown of the responses by school see p. 72). Of these three only one was hostile to the exercise. Included in Table 2 are two additional replies from schools that took part in the survey but which I received too late to include in the analysis of the group texts. The school from the north-west

Table 2 Classification of teachers in the sample

School	Old Grammarians	Pragmatists	Liberals	Technicians	Critical Dissenters	Undecided
A	1	3				
B	4		1			1
C		1	1		5	
D	1	1		3	1	1
E			1	2*	2	
G				9		
F		2			4	
H	*	1			1	
I					3	
J					1	
K	3					
L		2	2	2		
M			1			1
N				1		
Total	9*	10	6	17*	17	3

* one replied too late to be analysed

sent in their booklets well beyond the July deadline and so I discounted them from my final analysis. They did, however, show a spread of groupings including one Old Grammarian, five Pragmatists, two Liberals, one Technician and two Critical Dissenters. Although none of these teachers annotated their descriptions, not one of them appeared to find completing the exercise difficult. If they, along with the two late replies, are added to the total of replies received, the number of respondents who were able to identify with a group rises to 72.

Before we go on to look in more detail at the actual replies, one more general observation is worth making. Any analysis of the respondents' replies is based on those aspects upon which they chose to comment. The nature of the task they were set meant that in some cases much of the text was left untouched. They neither agreed nor disagreed with my descriptions. Nevertheless, beneath this ability to identify with the types a more complex picture emerged. Each one of the descriptions was intended to reflect both a spectrum of opinion within the group as well as certain key markers that differentiated one group from another.

Inevitably certain aspects of the description would appeal or apply only to some members of that group; for example the completion of grammar tests in the Pragmatists, or the teaching of poetry and the media within the Technicians. Identification was intended, therefore, to reflect best fit rather than total adherence to the description. Given the spectrum of

Table 3 Breakdown of the type of response

Extent of agreement	OG	P	L	T	CD	U	Total
Clear match (up to two 'disagreements')	3	5	2	5	10		25
More than one 'disagreement' but no selection of features from another group	4	4	2	11	6		27
Identification with one primary group but with selection of at least one feature from another group	2	1	2	1	1		7
Identification with more than one group						3	3
Total	9	10	6	17	17	3	62

opinion within any one group some respondents would inevitably sit more centrally within a typology than others. As we can see from Table 3, this is reflected in the way those taking part responded.

But it is the nature of these responses – the way in which the respondents commented upon and highlighted the text – that is the most revealing. For it is the very detail of their replies, the fine grain of the text, that adds the real texture to this account and it is to this that we now turn our attention.

Please note that each section of analysis is preceded by the relevant part of the Rough Guide, which is printed in full in a separate section.

THE GROUPS

Old Grammarians

This group are Arnoldian in their view of the subject. They believe in the improving and civilising qualities of literature. It is less, however, about books correcting behaviour than literature unlocking other worlds, other possibilities; a form of escape. And perhaps most importantly they are about developing an aesthetic sensibility.

This means that the literature they choose will have two purposes. The idea of the reading habit is fostered because, unlike television, it gives more scope for the imagination to roam. While there is an overtone of the Protestant work ethic – books are harder – there is also the sense that they allow more freedom than a television drama, where many decisions have already been made. In this sense there is a curious tension between moralistic aims – of hard work and improvement – and at the same time a kind of aesthetic hedonism – you read for pleasure. The former justifies the latter.

The tension is there in Matthew Arnold's writing, particularly on education. He posits many of his theories on poetry and reading against that which he views as Philistine utilitarianism and yet feels compelled to argue that there is a point to literature. He cannot argue art for art's sake, where his arguments tend. Books must have worth and value.

Leavis is the most obvious inheritor of this tradition, but his work focused the tradition more narrowly on the canonical value of texts. It is his legacy, however, that has made some uneasy that this tradition is in effect a rejection of working class culture. For literature is both an escape of the mind – the light in a dark place – and, through education, a route out of the slums. His emphasis on high and low culture reinforces this, but it is more tellingly worked out in the books of writers like Richard Hoggart, and evident in the biography of Brian Cox.

Literature, then, is intimately tied in with their view of what education is for – it is reformatory at the level of the individual; it is about personal growth, about personal fulfilment, both emotionally and in terms of life chances. This can lead to endorsing some form of selection as a means of enhancing the chances of those who will benefit from education the most. It is possible that many of this group will not 'set' in the early secondary years as they wish to provide every opportunity for latent qualities to emerge but they will probably introduce some form of setting, however broad, for exam classes. It is most likely to result in the creation of a top set with broad ability groups for the majority and then a bottom set. Some, however, will set that middle group more rigidly.

This is because at a certain significant point they do not believe that you can teach all children in the same way. And most importantly because you may hold back those who can escape or blossom. Their views lead them to concentrate their attention on the most able, with whom they have a rapport and a mission, and the least able, who have clearly identifiable needs. Even though they are concerned by literacy levels at the bottom end, they are unlikely to take a rigidly phonetic approach because they view reading as more than a mechanistic skill.

While such views are not clearly party political, and they take the class system as a given that can only be ameliorated at a personal level, their views on literature brought them into conflict with the Conservative government. This group seeks to foster empathy, the imagination and enlightenment in the students they teach. While they are not averse to the idea that some literature is better than others, they cannot have that choice imposed because teaching is about finding the book that will create the spark. It is about inspiration, which almost by definition cannot be produced by government diktat.

On the whole this group is also in favour of 100 per cent coursework because it avoids the reductive nature of timed tests. It is hard to produce inspiration to order. Similarly they are deeply suspicious of criterion-referencing because it is hard to predict originality. As this is one of the chief virtues they are trying to foster, criteria seem to miss the point, not least because they are perceived as bureaucratic. They view the current exams, and KS3 tests in particular, as reducing literature to the accumulation of facts rather than an opportunity to develop a personal response. In the pupils' own writing they will place a strong emphasis on flair and originality.

In addition, because they prefer impromptu ways of working to what they see as more formulaic methods, English departments run by this group often find themselves at variance with the senior management in their schools, who want 'checklist' assessment policies or rigid schemes of work. As teachers they are unashamedly teacher-centred because the teacher is the conduit of inspiration. Entitlement for the children lies less in the curriculum they follow, therefore, than in their access to good teaching. GCSE and the National Curriculum encouraged them to enter all sets for literature because the courses allowed for the possibility of finding appropriate texts and learning for all pupils.

The other way in which the National Curriculum influenced this group was in their views on Standard English. They are interested in the study of the grammar of English which relates to their position on Standard English. They would describe this in terms of command rather than ownership or empowerment. Yet their interest in grammar leads them away from any simple definitions of correctness towards the notion of a facility with language. Their emphasis on creativity resists the notion of the formulaic. The 'knowledge about language' strand in the National Curriculum gave them a diverse way of studying the language away from the old primers without necessarily involving them in discourse analysis or critical language awareness which takes a more oppositional stance to the language of power.

As with Leavis, *Hard Times* is a seminal text which defines their opposing views. They are with the circus people – the realm of the imagination. The Gradgrinds of this world are the enemy.

The working title of this group, Old Grammarians, was intended, in part, to echo the idea of the grammar school, in their preference for the academic, aesthetic nature of English as a subject, as well as to suggest an interest in the way language was used. In addition I suspected that they would value originality, which made this group bookish with a hint of non-conformity. While making the aesthetic strand explicit, the academic tendency was embedded in the way the text was actually written, apart from one reference to a preference for teaching more able children. My sense was that in order to engage this group, the piece itself had to have the right 'academic' or 'analytical' ring; the text had to be seen to do with ideas rather than emotions. This latter preference emerged strongly in a number of the respondents' own comments.

Ability and pupil grouping

What is perhaps the most striking fact about this group is the type of school in which the respondents were found. While nine teachers, from four different schools, actually identified with this group, seven were found in institutions with an academic bias. There were three in a girls' grammar school (school K) and four in a Hertfordshire school (school B) which prides itself on a grammar school ethos and where nearly 90 per cent of pupils get between an A* and C grade in English and English literature. While only one person, respondent B3, actually highlighted the statement, 'their views lead them to concentrate their attention on the most able', and five actually disagreed with the statement, or claimed to be unsure, their choice of school seems overwhelmingly to support the observation. It is possible that the reluctance of the group as a whole to highlight this particular phrase is indicative of a certain internal conflict about the choice of pupils they teach.

Their views of pupil grouping reflect this tension also. All in this group agreed with the notion of some form of setting. Four did not highlight this section; three were from the grammar school, school K, and presumably saw selection as a given; the other was respondent B3, from the home counties school, who felt that 'their views led them to concentrate their attention on the most able, with whom they have a rapport and a mission, and the least able, who have clearly identifiable needs'. Of the remaining five who endorsed setting, all but one, respondent A1, underlined the phrase, 'this *group will not "set" in the early secondary years as they wish to provide every opportunity for latent qualities to emerge'.*

Interestingly the only debate around setting centred on the top and bottom sets, possibly reflecting again the concentration of this group on the most and the least able, along with the desire to be seen to give everyone an equal chance. Respondent D5 endorsed the notion of a top set but disagreed with the notion of a bottom set, adding 'not necessarily'. Respondent A1, however, disagreed with the *'creation of a top set'* adding, 'top sets not essential – but needs to be the largest, if it is to exist at all', but agreed with a bottom set, adding, 'bottom set should be the smallest'.

Aesthetics and the imagination

Other consistent patterns emerged from this group. Though only two actually highlighted the phrase that the *'group are Arnoldian in their view of the subject'*, and one that *'Leavis is the most obvious inheritor of this tradition'*, this was a dominant view that emerged. Two thirds believed in *'the improving and civilising qualities of literature'* and seven of the nine felt that literature was *'reformatory at the level of the individual'*. The word *'civilising'* is important in this context in that it implies an alteration of behaviour through the acquisition of culture and rational thought. Two thirds also agreed that English teaching is about *'developing an aesthetic sensibility'*.

Yet this is not necessarily an acceptance of received traditions or heritage. Eight of the nine respondents believed that literature is about *'personal growth, about personal fulfilment'*, and, perhaps more importantly, about *'literature unlocking other worlds'*. Eight out of nine agreed with this statement, seven with the notion that it was *'a form of escape'*. Both these hint at dissatisfaction with conformity. This view is reinforced by the qualities that they look for in written work. Seven out of the nine agreed that *'In pupils' own writing they will place a strong emphasis on flair and originality'*; an eighth, respondent A1, added 'but also value accuracy because it's a respect for language', suggesting that they did consider flair and originality to be significant.

Similarly seven out of the nine agreed with the statement: *'This group seeks to foster empathy, the imagination and enlightenment in the students they teach.'* While the notion of empathy echoes the Liberals, the words imagination and enlightenment again have different resonances, suggesting both artistic activity and ideas; a possibility of the spiritual alongside the sense of rational thought. Eight out of nine highlighted the phrase *'the reading habit'*; two thirds went on to endorse the notion that reading gives *'scope for the imagination to roam'*, while just over half felt it did this better than television. And though this latter observation emphasises again an anxiety about high as opposed to low culture, all these phrases touch on a desire for freedom against any form of confinement.

Nonconformity

What is significant about this group is the way in which this translates itself into practice and in particular against some of the outcomes of government reform. The streak of nonconformity meant that although two thirds were 'not averse to the idea that some literature is better than others', seven out of nine agreed that 'they cannot have that choice imposed, because teaching is about finding the book that will create the spark'.

Two thirds also applied the notion of inspiration to the activity of teaching itself, believing that teaching is 'about inspiration, which almost by definition cannot be produced by government diktat'. To ensure entitlement, over half placed their faith in 'access to good teaching' rather than the curriculum.

Assessment

The picture on the testing regime was similar, but provoked slightly more debate, for the way that debate is framed also reflects certain key characteristics of the group. Two thirds disliked 'the reductive nature of timed tests' and the same number were 'suspicious of criterion-referencing', with over half going on to add, 'because it is hard to predict originality'. Respondent A1, however, did not highlight the section on criterion-referencing, adding: 'on the other hand, criterion referencing is much fairer than norm referencing. You should reward everyone who can shoot through the goal post – if you then think it becomes too easy, you warn everyone that you're narrowing the goal mouth, then invite all to have further goes, raise the sights.'

His comments are less a disagreement with the premise than a continuation of the debate on ways of making assessment fairer and more flexible. Given that he is also 'in favour of 100 per cent coursework' his comments may be seen as a defence of what he considers to be an essential component of that form of assessment. When he disagrees with the phrase that criterion-referencing is 'perceived as bureaucratic' and adds 'less so than norm referencing', he is, in a sense, indicating that he wishes to endorse a system which he considers to be unbureaucratic. His comments are, therefore, an argument for 100 per cent coursework which is fair, capable of high standards and unbureaucratic, all of which are consistent with his position as an Old Grammarian.

Over half agreed with 100 per cent coursework, and all those who supported coursework also emphasised '*flair and originality*', as did respondent K2, who did not highlight the section on coursework but did highlight its corollary, the phrase '*reductive nature of timed tests*'. All these respondents clearly felt some kind of clash between the current testing regime and the kind of qualities they were trying both to foster and assess.

Respondent B4, who had highlighted the section on the current testing regime, added in the margin: 'yes but cannot be so easily dismissed', and went on to explore this conflict further at the end of the text. 'This [the description] seems to embrace many of the *ideals* involved in English teaching and should be the thrust of a good Dept. However exams at KS3 and KS4 are now a fact of life and it is essential that students are well prepared in order to get the grades so they too can access the very best opportunities and choices.' There is a clear sense of conflict between the respondent's 'ideals' and what they are currently being asked to do. The use of the word 'ideals' is interesting as it signifies both aspiration and the unattainable. There are echoes of the expression 'in an ideal world' – particularly in view of the respondent's comment that these exams are 'a fact of life'. Ideals are opposed to the harsh realities.

Three, however, disagreed with 100 per cent coursework. Two of these, respondents K1 and K3, were from the girl's grammar school, which may in itself be significant. K1 and D5 did, however, '*place a strong emphasis on flair and originality*', suggesting that they, unlike the other respondents, did not perceive the conflict in the same way. Interestingly D5, who teaches in a comprehensive, also added: 'I found it difficult to find one category which fully defined how I feel, parts of D [Technicians] were also important.' One of the key markers for the Technicians was their sympathy for timed examinations. It is possible that this was, therefore, one of the areas in which D5 identified more with that group.

Standard English and the language debate

Like respondent D5, B5 teases out two of the key markers that differentiate this group from the Technicians. In a lengthy response they query some of the assumptions behind the whole exercise but they do so in keeping with the tone of the description of this group and reinforce key markers. They start: 'My difficulty is that I ideologically comfortably aligned with group A [Old Grammarians] – and have therefore chosen this group. However, I have no difficulty with *some* systems of codifying and therefore think spelling punctuation and grammar must be rigorously taught – I have therefore also marked group D [Technicians], those parts with which I am happy.'

While I was aware that some would value technical accuracy, I felt that this group did so less because it was a set of rules to be obeyed than because they believed that it allowed for greater command or facility with the language that would either aid appreciation for the beauty of certain writing or allow pupils to create that kind of writing themselves. I anticipated a spectrum of responses, which was reflected in the gradation of statements on Standard English, which went from '*They are interested in the study of the grammar of English which relates to their position on Standard English*', through '*They would describe this in terms of command rather than ownership or empowerment*', to '*Yet their interest in grammar leads them away from any simple definitions of correctness towards the notion of a facility with language.*' One of the key markers that divided the Old Grammarians from the Technicians was the value they placed on the aesthetic and imaginative over the technically accurate. Given a choice they would place themselves with the former group rather than the latter, because they are interested in more than an adherence to a set of rules.

Thus respondent B5 is 'ideologically comfortably aligned with Group A [Old Grammarian]' but is at the end of the spectrum nearer to the Technicians on accuracy. Possibly for this reason this person only marked the statements on language up to the section on command and did not highlight the more radical statement on definitions of correctness. Four out of the nine respondents did go on to mark that section, including respondent A1, who added to the section on flair and originality: 'but also value accuracy because of its respect for the language'. Respect is an interesting choice of word in that it affords status both to the language itself and to those who use it well; yet with it comes the connotation of something that must be earned rather than given as of right.

Individual and society

Respondent B5 went on to consider their sympathy with the Critical Dissenters:

> There are also sections in group E [Critical Dissenters] which further expand my position. My basic problem with these groupings is that they rest, ultimately, on an alleged ideological divide which is [mirrored?] in left/right positions in government. Thus it is assumed that certain views on English lead or do not to a 'radical oppositional stance' to, it is implied, Conservative Party government. This is a fundamental misreading of the current political scene in advanced 'western' nations/states – as for example 'new right', libertarianism

and 'gay rights'. I have no problem with the literature as empowerment nor with radical readings of the canon, yet I would certainly
class myself as a 'cultural theorist'. This does not place me as 'left of
centre' in *British* political terms at the moment. Which brings me
back to my fundamental point – the divisions of the groups rest on an
ideological divide which is out of kilter with the 1990's. This little
booklet is like a sketch, an abstract of a political economy of English
in Education – I hope 'it', whatever 'it' is – succeeds.

This critique of the booklet as a whole is as interesting as the position it
portrays. The tone of the piece again is keen to establish analytical rigour
and a robustness in debate, talking of 'alleged ideological divide' and 'a
fundamental misreading'. This respondent does not only read between the
lines but between the texts also. They critique ideas, and phrases like
'radical oppositional stance', both by analysing the assumptions in the
text and by proffering alternatives of their own understanding of the
'current political scene'. They are keen to establish their 'own position',
their credentials, both in the way in which they respond and in their
endorsement of radical readings of the canon and cultural theory. But, in
line with the non-conformity of this group, they do not want to be bound
into any particular way of interpreting this position politically.

This desire to avoid categorisation and yet present a consistent position
also means that while respondent B5 does draw inferences that are
implicit, on occasion they make connections which are not intended
but are nevertheless consistent with their desire to avoid categorisation.
The divide between the Old Grammarians and Critical Dissenters along
political lines was intentional but it was not intended to be as party
political as respondent B5 suggests. The Old Grammarians were likely
to oppose specific Tory reforms, particularly in assessment, but, as I point
out, '*such views are not clearly party political*', nor does it make them systematically left of centre.

This respondent's reluctance to identify with a left of centre position
does again indicate that the key markers between the groups have been
reinforced, which is why they feel 'comfortable' with the Old Grammarians and not with the Critical Dissenters. Even the comments on the new
right, gay rights and the change of government since writing the booklet,
while valid, do not invalidate the difference between Old Grammarians,
who may or may not be left of centre, but want the freedom to choose, as
opposed to the Critical Dissenters, who will be left of centre. The emphasis on the individual will celebrate the idiosyncratic and fight shy of what
might be perceived as the coercion of the politically correct.

Conclusion

In conclusion, certain strong patterns emerge from this group. Consistently the strongest support came for those phrases that indicated that English was about fostering individuality, imagination and inspiration through literature. English, for this group, was not only about '*the improving and civilising qualities of literature*', it was about '*literature unlocking other worlds, other possibilities; a form of escape*'. Books give '*scope for the imagination to roam*'. The latter half of paragraph 7, which received the most positive response, sums up their position most coherently.

> This group seeks to foster empathy, the imagination and enlightenment in the students they teach. While they are not averse to the idea that some literature is better than others, they cannot have that choice imposed because teaching is about finding the book that will create the spark. It is about inspiration, which almost by definition cannot be produced by government diktat.

'*In the pupils' own writing they place a strong emphasis on flair and originality*' and see timed tests as '*reductive*'. Their understanding of '*personal growth, personal fulfilment*' has to be seen in this context.

The Pragmatists

This group is significant because of the way in which they attempt to manage educational change, both within the school and at national level, and in particular the way in which they confront those changes which most impinge upon their beliefs and practice as English teachers. Many in this group, though by no means all, will have entered the teaching profession from the mid-eighties onwards so that their degrees may have been influenced by some form of literary theory and their training will have emphasised the rationale behind mixed-ability teaching as well as the benefits of coursework.

Many will never have taught O-level or CSE, a significant number will either not have taught long before the National Curriculum was introduced or never known a time when it was not there. The most recent entrants to the profession will not have had the opportunity to teach 100 per cent coursework. While some of these will have experienced its benefits as pupils, many will have just missed it both at school and then as a teacher. They will, to a person, say, however, that they oppose government reforms in terms of both the content and the assessment of the English curriculum.

Nevertheless they will place the emphasis on preparing pupils for what is in store for them. Some, though by no means all, will, for example, want to see the new grammar tests and perhaps pilot them because it is important to be ready for whatever is coming. Advanced knowledge may allow damage limitation. They are also keen to implement new initiatives and will set up working parties around issues such as boys and English, whole-school language and reading policies and the like.

Their departmental policy documents will reflect clear positions on equal opportunities including gender, race and often class. They have adopted a systematic approach to assessment policies, schemes of work and statements of aims partly from a desire to democratise the pupils' entitlement and partly from a belief that management systems will enhance the quality control and monitoring of the department.

For them, the English curriculum allows for the possibility of empowering pupils by giving them the ability to analyse critically the society in which they live. Again they are keen to equip and prepare pupils with the critical tools that they need to analyse any text. This view informs both their approach to literature and the study of language and has led them to consider the importance of the role of the media. Texts are chosen which highlight issues and critical possibilities. Teachers are likely to emphasise the social context in which they were produced. When considering the issue of Standard English they would be likely to look at the power relationships implied in the phrase and do work on dialect and regional variety. In pupils' writing they reward flair and originality as well as thoroughness and attention to detail.

Mixed-ability grouping is a problem area for this group. While it is an end devoutly to be wished, they argue, it is not always possible. They look to two sources of external pressure that have brought about their dilemma.

The first and most immediate pressure often comes from the senior management within the school. Many heads themselves claim to be sympathetic to the cause of mixed-ability teaching but place the blame on market forces. Parents, they claim, prefer setting and they have to give them what they want to maintain school rolls.

The second is connected. Government reforms, in particular the tiering of tests at KS3 and GCSE exams, have made mixed-ability teaching harder to organise. This has meant that the issue of setting has now affected lower school classes as well as GCSE groups.

This group accommodates these pressures into their view of pupil grouping. While they rarely allow, if in the position of head of department, more than a 'top-set and the rest' in year 9, and the possible inclusion of a bottom set at GCSE for those likely to be entered for the foundation tier, they will still argue that they are implementing mixed-ability grouping. They describe it, however, as a 'broad-banding' policy that maintains the spirit, if not the letter, of mixed-ability teaching.

Again they would share the belief that English is difficult to assess under the current arrangements, not least because acts of the imagination are hard to produce to order, and set books may dampen enthusiasm. But they believe it is possible to accommodate their ideas within the framework – that it is possible to make the best of a bad job. This group believes that the subject is being altered by external pressures and for the worse but continues to look for evidence of their view of English teaching, as a space to analyse and explore texts within the National Curriculum and its assessment arrangements.

The ten respondents who identified with this group were found in a range of different types of schools (six altogether): inner city, suburban and shire schools. None was found in selective schools.

Cultural analysis

A quick glance at all the replies seemed to indicate that paragraph 5, which referred to their commitment to cultural analysis, received the greatest endorsement. Four of the respondents highlighted virtually the whole of the paragraph. Two more highlighted more of this paragraph than any other, and the remaining teachers, while highlighting less, picked the key markers contained within the paragraph. All but one of the respondents highlighted the words '*possibility of empowering pupils*' and '*to analyse critically the society in which they live*'. Respondent A4, having underlined only these two phrases, added in the margin a double tick by these statements and wrote, 'definitely'. Eight out of the ten also highlighted the phrase '*has led them to consider the importance of the role of the media*'. Again, respondent A4 reinforced the link between these two markers by ticking the word '*media*', adding an arrow to the phrase '*analyse critically the society in which they live*', and writing, 'media and IT part of this'.

Pragmatic language

There was also much support for the key words which were intended to differentiate the tone of this group from that of the Critical Dissenters.

Seven out of the ten highlighted the words '*equip*' and '*prepare*'. Respondent G5 went so far as to select these words, along with the other key markers in this paragraph, for particular attention. While for most of the paragraph they put a line down the side of the text to show general endorsement (they scribbled out those parts of the text with which they disagreed), they also underlined the phrases '*empowering pupils*', '*analyse critically the society in which they live*' as well as '*equip*' and '*prepare pupils*'.

While not highlighting this phrase, respondent H3 did highlight a corresponding phrase in paragraph 3, which says that they would place the '*emphasis on preparing pupils for what is in store for them*'. And, along with over half the others, they highlighted the phrase '*critical tools that they need to analyse any text*', another phrase used to lend a slightly more mechanistic tone to the text.

Again, over half agreed that '*this view informs both their approach to literature and to the study of language*' and went on to say that they would '*look at the power relationships implied in the phrase* [Standard English] *and do work on dialect and regional variety*'. It is possible that the four who did not highlight this phrase were simply less interested in language work. None disagreed with the statement and all supported either the study of the media or the notion of empowering pupils.

Respondent A4 commented on the phrase '*Texts are chosen which highlight issues and critical possibilities*': 'yes – although literature is an escape it (English) is also a survival tool for the C21st.' The notion of literature as an escape is subordinated to the more important aim of English as 'a survival tool'. The contrast is significant. Not only does it echo my choice of word, '*tool*', but it also reinforces the pragmatic approach taken by the group. English becomes less an aesthetic experience than a survival pack. Behind the word 'although' lies the feeling that escape is an indulgence in the face of the more immediate practical need to survive, for which you need tools. Flights of fancy are contrasted with real equipment. While in some ways this links them to the Technicians, the emphasis on the twenty-first century is also important. Again there is that sense of the new, which is important for this group. A4 looks forward for confirmation rather than back to past traditions and rules. It is almost as if literature as an escape takes one back into the past, or certainly it is seen as a flight away from the fast approaching future.

Accommodation and the management of change

This pragmatic endorsement of the new was also found in the paragraph (paragraph 3) which is the first to characterise this group's approach to the management of change and included key markers which differentiated them from the Critical Dissenters. Eight out of the ten highlighted the sentence: '*They are also keen to implement new initiatives and will set up working parties around issues such as boys and English, whole-school language and reading policies and the like.*' The initiatives are '*new*'. The word '*initiative*' itself was chosen for its management connotations. The emphasis lies less in the ideas, however, than in what is to be done with them. They are '*keen to implement*' and '*will set up working parties*'. Respondent A4, who only highlighted the phrase '*working parties*', added 'very valuable, cross curricular working parties', which again suggests that it is the fact of working parties, rather than their content, that is significant.

It is the last paragraph, however, which acknowledges both their dislike of the current arrangements and their means of coping with it; for, to an extent, they avoid opposition by looking to ways of accommodating change. Again, there was more support for the pragmatic manner in which this group dealt with the situation than for those who expressed opposition. Seven saw '*English teaching as a space to analyse and explore texts within the National Curriculum and its assessment arrangements*'. Six felt that even though '*English is difficult to assess under the current arrangements*' and that '*set books may dampen enthusiasm*', it was '*possible to accommodate their ideas within the framework – that it is possible to make the best of a bad job*'.

L6 is typical of the general tone of this group's reaction. She disagreed with the clause: '*they will, to a person, say, however, that they oppose government reforms in terms of both the content and the assessment of the English curriculum*' and added 'not opposed to it all'. She did, however, highlight the whole of last paragraph, including '*this group believes that the subject is being altered by external pressures and for the worse*'. It is possible that she objected to the slightly bald tone of the first statement, for implied in her phrase is the idea that she does oppose some of the reforms. It is also possible that what she felt more keenly is the sense of the pressure for change coupled with a desire to see a way through. She highlighted all those phrases in the last paragraph which suggest this to be her approach. Nevertheless there is an ambiguity within the Pragmatists between what they say they believe and what they often end up doing, and this is reflected in the tension between these two sets of responses, along with respondent L6's admission that they had done the grammar tests, adding 'I did!' to the margin where they were mentioned. It should, however, be noted that the reference to the grammar tests received more disagreement than any other section of the text. Several remarked on their clear opposition to them, most notably C7, who added 'Absolutely not. These tests do not fulfil my criteria for effective useful, assessment. Rather than damage limitation I would be looking for boycotts.'

Like L6, A4's response reveals a tension. This person believed that '*set books may dampen enthusiasm*' but failed to highlight any other more negative statements. In addition A4 fully endorsed the notion of accommodation by adding 'yes' in the margin next to the highlighted phrase '*it is possible to accommodate their ideas within the framework – that it is possible to make the best of a bad job*'; and under the highlighted words '*English teaching . . . space to analyse and explore texts*' wrote, 'This is in itself an exciting challenge.' The notion of an 'exciting challenge' is in itself descriptive of the mind-set of this group.

Management language and culture

The group's endorsement of the key markers in paragraph 4 is equally strong. Four highlighted the whole paragraph. Only H3 failed to highlight anything, explaining that they were not a head of department. Again the key feature of this paragraph, which was to differentiate the Pragmatists from the Critical Dissenters, who were likely to be sympathetic with the content, was the tone. The content separated them from the Technicians, who were likely to see it as too politically correct. The key phrases that established the tone were '*management systems*', '*quality control*' and '*monitoring of the department*'. Not only are all these are buzz words but they also convey a sense that the Pragmatists, instead of looking towards the curriculum and teaching and learning strategies to ensure entitlement, look towards systems. The words have a bureaucratic resonance with which the Critical Dissenters, Old Grammarians and Liberals are uneasy.

Eight of the ten respondents highlighted the phrases '*management systems*' and '*monitoring the department*' and seven the phrase '*enhance quality control*'. Respondent G5, who had put a line down the side of this latter section of the paragraph, selected the word '*monitoring*' and underlined it twice, thus emphasising the approach and not flinching from the hierarchical and bureaucratic connotations of the word. Interestingly respondent A4, while again specifically highlighting the phrase '*monitoring the department*', softened the tone by their interpretation of the phrase, 'vital, i.e. positive comments to each other'. Yet they added another buzz phrase, 'professional development', as if the first comment had not seemed rigorous enough, had appeared like idle chat without the benefit of a framework.

Six highlighted the phrases '*clear positions on equal opportunities*' and '*adopted a systematic approach to assessment policies, schemes of work and statements of aims*' as well as the phrase '*from a desire to democratise the pupils' entitlement*'. Only half highlighted the phrase '*gender, race and often class'* as if the content of the policies was less important. This first sentence, was, however, for respondent G6 the only significant section of this paragraph 3. Given that they scribbled out the whole section on grammar tests and mixed ability teaching, in paragraphs 6 to 8, it is possible that this respondent is nearer to the Critical Dissenters than others in this group. While they did not disagree with the latter half of paragraph 3 they may well have felt out of sympathy with its managerial tone. The need for a clear policy would therefore have more to do with the importance of the issues than the method by which that importance was conveyed.

Mixed ability

This group's attitude to mixed ability teaching was another key marker that differentiated them from the Critical Dissenters and was one of the clearest indicators of the difference between theory and practice in this group. Only respondent D4 highlighted the clause '*mixed-ability grouping* [was] *a problem area for this group*' and, significantly, went on to agree with the whole description other than the section which suggested that the head teacher and parental pressure was to blame. Six, however, asserted that while it was to be '*wished*' it '*was not always possible*'. These respondents may have read into the word '*problem*' the implication that lay behind it, namely that external pressures were not the only cause of their agreeing to some form of pupil grouping. As we shall see, there is a sense in which this group's views on mixed ability teaching reflect the departments in which they work. Yet there are hints, in some of the respondents' remarks, that it is indeed '*a problem area*'. H3, who did not highlight any of the section on pupil grouping, for example added in the margin: 'I must confess to feeling very ambivalent about mixed ability teaching at the moment'. Respondent A2 also added: 'Unsure about this point. Does/ can mixed ability teaching ever allow every pupil to maximise potential?' Interestingly, three of the four who highlighted the reasons for being pressured into some form of setting also highlighted the section on testing: '*tests at KS3 and GCSE have made mixed-ability teaching harder to organise*'.

Three respondents, however, remained firmly committed to mixed ability teaching. But again it is possible that their approach simply reflects the kind of school in which they find themselves. All three of the respondents who disagreed with the section on pupil grouping teach in schools in which the rest of the department are Critical Dissenters and where mixed ability teaching occurs in all years in the English department. This contrasts with those respondents who described problems with mixed ability teaching. Respondents G5 and G6, who teach in the same inner city school, scribbled out all four paragraphs on ability grouping and the pressures that lead to setting.

Respondent C7, who also disagreed with this section, highlighted the sentences '*Mixed ability grouping is a problem area for this group. While it is an end devoutly to be wished, they argue, it is not always possible*', and commented 'I am fully committed to mixed ability teaching and therefore mixed ability grouping is not a problem. Although there are external pressures, mixed ability teaching can still be maintained successfully.' She put a line beside the text which discussed the external pressures that often cause the abandonment of mixed ability teaching, and commented in the margin: 'These are real pressures but if a department is strong they do not have to bow to these pressures', and she highlighted the whole of the fourth paragraph, adding 'not my view on pupil grouping'.

Significantly all three of these respondents highlighted the section in the first paragraph which said '*their training will have emphasised the rationale behind mixed-ability teaching as well as the benefits of coursework*'. Respondent L6 was the only other person to highlight this section, adding 'definitely' to the margin. She disagreed with the notion that '*mixed ability [was] a problem area for this group*' and both agreed and disagreed with the suggestion that '*it is not always possible*', thus reflecting both her own perception and the school's practice. Interestingly she went on to highlight, where her head of department had not, the section: '*parents, they claim, prefer setting and they have to give them what they want to maintain school rolls*'. Respondent L6 added 'happens in this school', which suggests that she locates the pressure to set outside the teaching of English itself. In fact respondent L6 disagreed with the whole of the section, which suggested that the assessment arrangements led to setting, which others had highlighted.

However, she also commented at the end of the text, 'I believe special needs need specialist skills which I do not possess. But I strongly feel mixed ability teaching helps to empower the weakest and does not disadvantage the brightest.' While there is more of an ambivalence about its efficacy for all children than with the other respondents who defended mixed ability teaching, there is, nevertheless, a clearer articulation of the principles of mixed ability teaching than is found among the six other respondents who did not disagree with my description. The fact that L6 felt it was an area in which she needed to explain her more positive position in more detail is another indication of her conviction. It is possible, therefore, that the training these respondents received was as influential as the department in which they found themselves, but it is also possible that circumstances have reinforced that conviction. The more ambivalent answer of respondent L6 would tend to confirm this perception, though not conclusively.

Conclusion

Certain strong patterns, then, emerge from this group as a whole which validate my perceptions of them. Their convictions are to an extent tailored by their circumstances, and while they describe a preference for cultural analysis as a guiding principle in their approach to texts and how they should be taught, the implementation of these ideas suggests a greater debt to management theory and a desire to prepare pupils for the future, than it does to critical or learning theory. They respond positively, therefore, to the bureaucratic tone of much of the text and go on to echo this tone in their own writing. All these tendencies are typified by the additional comments of respondent A4. In her key for the way in which she has highlighted the text, she provides a label for a section called 'Other thoughts', which is found at the end of the text under the heading, '*VALUE OF TEAM SKILLS*' and highlighted subheading, 'Added?', implying that these 'thoughts' might be added to my text.

> Combination of some thoughts in E [Critical Dissenters] – ie management – encourage a range of working situations for students ie never leave them with the same person twice – aim – mixed pairs. Develop 'team work'. Few jobs expect their employees to work alone and early experience of working with a wide range of people will enable young people to foster effective working relationships quickly. – Keen to ask students to evaluate their team – to be self critical and offer constructive advice.

She begins by indicating an affinity with the Critical Dissenters, but her interpretation of learning theory causes her to use a phrase from management theory, 'group dynamics'. Her emphasis, then, lies less with how this will aid pupils learning from or about a text, and more with classroom organisation: 'never leave them with the same person twice'. That her aim is 'mixed pairs', rather than some learning outcome related to the content of the study, is again telling. Her own belief in certain working practices becomes her prime concern, rather than any notion of critical literacy. She wants to 'encourage a range of working situations'; 'develop team work' and thus prepare children for future work. Again the language is that of business, 'jobs', 'employees', 'effective working relationships', 'working situations', rather than education. The pupils are disconnected from the school context and become that more generic group, 'young people'. Even when they are described as 'students', a word that has a broader connotation than 'pupil', it is to ask them 'to evaluate their team'. The verbs are all positive and look to the future: 'will enable', 'foster', 'constructive'. As with this respondent, the Pragmatists are above all 'keen'.

The Liberals

This group is also very much in the Arnoldian tradition in that they have a strong belief in the benefits of English as a subject. They sense that it is perhaps the only space in the curriculum for unlocking doors and for exploring thoughts and emotions as well as promoting empathy, understanding and tolerance. Both the study of literature and creative writing are essential to this endeavour.

They are more likely to look to the literature of social realism to aid them in this process because they consider that, while style and aesthetic values are significant, they are less important than the content or message in the teaching of English as a school subject. They emphasise the notion that you start from the pupil's point of view and develop it by exploring issues, and are less driven by the idea of English as an Arts subject. That is not to say that they do not encourage the notion of reading for pleasure but the relationship with the book is more a beneficial friendship than a passion.

Their concern for social realism does not, however, lead to a radical, oppositional stance. They would, for example, be likely to be more comfortable with the notion of multi-culturalism than anti-racism because they would emphasise resolving issues at a personal level. In addition, they are likely to be concerned with themes in literature and may well organise schemes of work around extracts which illustrate an aspect of life, rather than a literary idea.

The written work they set is very much aimed at developing the personal voice and their approach to the teaching of Standard English is connected with this. While they will consider it important to teach children Standard English, in order to prevent them from being disadvantaged, they may well see the pupil's dialect or home language as being an essential part of their identity, which is to be valued. This view sits uneasily with the current model of 'correctness' which appears not to value authenticity but seems to encourage a somewhat mechanistic view of writing. They are also likely to value authenticity in the pupils' work over what they might consider 'flashy style' or writing that is 'too clever by half'.

They like to believe that the English teacher is the sympathetic face of the schooling system and this often leads them towards the pastoral system. Their emphasis on the personal leads them to mistrust management systems and bureaucracy for they are more likely to put their faith in human contact and dialogue than paperwork. But they now feel uneasy, if not beleaguered, because of what they perceive to be the changed ethos of schooling. They fear that schools are becoming more like building societies and are anxious that the pressures of the market place are making them more impersonal places. Initiatives such as appraisal and OFSTED inspections concern them because they do not believe you can summarise a person's worth at a glance or through generic 'tick-boxes'. They prefer words to numbers.

This attitude has also led them to oppose the changes to the National Curriculum and its system of assessment. They are keen to encourage pupils' reading habits by choosing texts that are relevant to them, in particular by teaching those authors who write specifically for teenagers. As such they are concerned by the emphasis on pre-twentieth century literature because they are afraid that it will 'switch-off' many pupils. Similarly they favour more coursework assessment because it allows more scope for expression and is less prescriptive than the demands of rigid syllabuses and timed tests.

Their strengths lie with teaching and developing the average child but they do not have defined views on mixed-ability versus setting and are likely to 'go with the flow' of the department. If they are the head of department they may well have experimented with varieties of pupil groupings. They will err towards mixed-ability for the younger classes as they are anxious for pupils to develop their potential, but again they would not necessarily turn this into a rigid policy.

The Liberals attracted the smallest number of respondents in the actual survey, six in all, although in one of the departments in the pilot survey three teachers, in a department of seven, had identified with this group. Interestingly also, in more recent research that I have carried out to discover how teachers' views change over time, it emerged that many beginner teachers hold this view (Marshall, Turvey and Brindley, 2000).

When writing this particular category I had used words and phrases as markers that were intended to emphasise two predominant strands that differentiated this group from the others. The first was their emphasis on personal growth almost as an end in itself. The second, a related strand, was a desire to avoid prescription and to err towards a position of compromise. The title which I had given this group – Liberals – was intended to reflect this characteristic.

Personal growth

When analysing the results of the survey for this group, I found it particularly striking that they had all highlighted the phrases that I had identified as being the essence of the group – the emphasis on the personal. Although only four of them highlighted the word '*benefit*' and five the fact that English provided '*space*' in the curriculum '*for unlocking doors*', all six highlighted the phrase, '*exploring thoughts and emotions as well as promoting empathy, understanding and tolerance*'.

Again, all agreed that writing was '*aimed at developing the personal voice*' and that '*they are keen to encourage pupils' reading habits by choosing texts that are relevant to them*'. Coursework again received strong support, none of the respondents actively disagreeing with it. Five of the respondents identified the notion that it allows '*more scope for expression*', while four also agreed with the alternative '*rigid syllabuses and timed tests*'.

Similarly, in the section on Standard English, all highlighted the section that read '*the pupil's dialect or home language as being an essential part of their identity, which is to be valued*', but that it was important to teach them Standard English '*in order to prevent them from being disadvantaged*'.

In terms of school organisation there was again a universal dislike of '*generic "tick-boxes"*', and near-universal acclaim for the phrase '*prefer words to numbers*', along with the belief that you cannot '*summarise a person's worth at a glance*' and that they are '*more likely to put their faith in human contact and dialogue than paperwork*'.

There was substantial agreement on some of the more detailed working out of teaching methodology that the group might employ to foster personal growth. Four emphasised '*the notion that you start from the pupils' point of view and develop it by exploring issues*', and again that '*they are likely to be concerned with themes in literature and may well organise their schemes of work around extracts which illustrate an aspect of life*'. Half agreed that they would organise work this way rather than around '*a literary idea*'.

Management of change

Response to the detail of change and school management (found in paragraph 5) again varied, apart from the broad principles outlined at the beginning of this analysis. Half of the respondents claimed to '*feel uneasy*' with the changes in the schooling system, and half also felt they were likely '*to mistrust management systems*'. Half again highlighted their sympathy with '*the pastoral system*' but overall only respondents L3 and L4 highlighted the majority of paragraph 5, which described their attitude to the management of change. Interestingly both of these came from the

same school in a small shire town, which is seen locally as less academi-
cally successful than its main local rivals, and it may be that they feel the
external pressures more keenly.

Within paragraph 5 certain interesting anomalies emerged. Both respondents M1 and L3 agreed with most of the first half of the paragraph.
Respondent L3 highlighted the whole section down to '*anxious*'. Respondent M1 endorsed the phrase that the English teacher was the '*sympathetic
face of the schooling system and this often leads them towards the pastoral
system*' and went on to underline twice – something that this respondent
did not do anywhere else – '*leads them to mistrust management systems and
bureaucracy for they are more likely to put their faith in human contact and
dialogue than paperwork*'. That this teacher felt the need to underline the
phrase twice suggests that it is a subject about which they feel keenly.
Both respondents M1 and L3 also highlighted the notion of preferring
words to numbers.

Neither of these respondents, however, agreed with the sentence on
OFSTED and appraisal, even though respondent L3 agreed with the second half of this sentence: '*because they do not believe you can summarise
a person's worth at a glance or through generic "tick-boxes"*'. Respondent L3
also disagreed with the phrase in the next paragraph, '*this attitude has
also led them to oppose the changes to the National Curriculum and its system
of assessment*', but then went on to agree with the idea that there was
a detrimental over-emphasis on pre-twentieth-century literature. It is
possible that this respondent agreed with the sentiments of opposition
but did not want these spelt out in a way that implied confrontation with
authority.

Respondent M1, however, disagreed with the whole of the latter section of paragraph 5, from '*they fear that schools*' to ' "*tick-boxes*" '. This was
the only respondent to disagree with a dislike of tick-boxes, while curi-
ously agreeing with the phrase '*prefer words to numbers*'. It is possible that,
being a grammar school teacher, this particular respondent simply did not
recognise these pressures in the same way as the others – the direct effects
of market competition being less acute, except in terms of results.

Respondent B1 also disagreed with much of this section. They agreed
that the '*teacher is the sympathetic face of the schooling system*' and were
'*more likely to put their faith in human contact and dialogue than paperwork*'.
And they did '*not believe you can summarise a person's worth at a glance or
through generic "tick-boxes"*', preferring '*words to numbers*'. Yet they did not
feel drawn to the pastoral system, did not distrust management systems, or
feel anxious about the changed ethos of schooling or OFSTED. It may
again be that B1 teaches in a highly successful school, but their disagreement with the text occurred at the point where they felt that it appeared

to offer opposing positions that they felt were false dichotomies, for they added 'accountability, efficiency and good management are important, as are passion, spirit etc – being a good English teacher surely doesn't stop you from being organised'.

What is interesting here is the choice of words. Throughout, B1 has affirmed concepts that appear positive and rejected others that have negative connotations, so here they have transformed the notion of management systems, OFSTED and appraisal into 'accountability, efficiency . . . good management . . . being organised'. This may have something to do with the fact that this person is a newly qualified teacher who is determined to keep an open mind in the face of a cynical profession.

The only phrases that respondent E5 disagreed with were '*this often leads them towards the pastoral system*', '*to distrust management systems*' and '*this attitude has also led them to oppose the changes to the National Curriculum*'. Significantly, however, she added at the end of the text: 'However I fit very well into group B [Pragmatists] too', where the significant marker is the attitude to management systems and change. In addition she disliked the current form of assessment.

Mixed ability

Finally, there was greater endorsement of mixed ability teaching than I had anticipated. Here all but the teacher in the selective school agreed with the following sentence: '*They will err towards mixed-ability for the younger classes as they are anxious for pupils to develop their potential.*' Also, while respondents E5 and L4 '*did not have defined views on mixed-ability versus setting*' and highlighted the corresponding phrase, '*would not necessarily turn this into a rigid policy*', respondents B1, L3 and C6 disagreed with the former statement. Respondent L3 added in the margin 'Yes I do', and commented that they would 'definitely not' '*go with the flow of the department*', while respondent C6 highlighted the whole of this paragraph, adding 'I agree with group E [Critical Dissenters] here', and went on to add: 'I have marked the relevant section.' The whole of the paragraph on the rationale for mixed ability teaching in the Critical Dissenters is highlighted, as is the section on Vygotsky and coursework. What is potentially significant about C6's response is that, like those respondents we saw in the Pragmatists, she works in a department committed to mixed ability teaching throughout, and in which five out of the seven in the department were Critical Dissenters.

Conclusion

Certain patterns emerge from this group as a whole. As individuals they highlighted little that they disagreed with, and they disagreed with different things. Yet they were all more likely to disagree with statements that sounded negative than those that sounded positive, even if the negative statement was criticising values that prevented their beliefs being realised. It is also possible that had I slightly altered the tone I might have had a more universal response on more than simply the key markers. Several, for example, disagreed with a negative statement but agreed with identical statements when expressed positively.

It is significant, however, that although they only endorsed certain key phrases, all those phrases were key markers defining the group. All are affirming in nature and, in the main are about avoiding conflict – empathy, understanding and tolerance. In a sense, therefore, while they apparently disagree with the more critical sections of the text, they are, in their disagreement, endorsing a liberal position of tolerance and the dislike of being pushed into a defined position.

The Technicians

The chief characteristic of this group is their desire to focus on the skills necessary to be good at English. They are likely to encourage pupils to study spelling, punctuation and grammar so that they can become confident users of the language. They are also keen to develop creative writing in order to encourage a more imaginative response to language because they believe that English is the only area in the curriculum where this can be done.

They may well, however, stress the importance of language in every day use, for example, writing letters or instructions, in order to ensure that pupils become competent in these forms. Teaching Standard English is important in this endeavour because it will increase pupils' command of the English language and their ability to communicate effectively and accurately.

In reading they are concerned to know how much pupils have understood of what they have read and to develop their reading skills. Comprehension is likely, therefore, to be an important teaching strategy, both as a means of assessing the pupils' understanding and as a means of increasing their reading skills. They believe that it is important that children read and are likely to commend it as an activity over computer games and watching television. Study of the media is not, therefore, a high priority in their classrooms, as they would prefer pupils to exercise their critical skills on more traditional texts.

7

They believe strongly that it is important for children to be taught appropriately according to their needs and that teachers should be able to focus on addressing the weaknesses of the pupils, particularly the technical and linguistic. They may well consider that not all pupils are capable of studying certain writers and that while it is important to stretch and challenge the most able, by presenting them with demanding literature, it is often preferable to give the 'less-able' books that are more relevant to them, or abridged versions so that they can appreciate the story. They are particularly aware that many less able children find poetry difficult.

This view of the appropriate needs of the pupils leads them to favour setting and they may well be sympathetic to the notion of selection. In a non-selective school, they are more likely to implement a system that is finely-tuned rather than broad-banding, because they believe it will allow them to concentrate more fully on each group's particular needs and set appropriate work.

They acknowledge the need for coursework because it offers more opportunity for creative writing but they are likely to argue for the discipline that exam work provides. For this reason they often opted for the 50 per cent exam/coursework divide when GCSE allowed such a choice, though they were more likely to take this option with literature, because it more obviously presented a body of knowledge to be tested. Given the importance of exams, they believe it is important to prepare children thoroughly for them. When assessing pupils' work they are likely to give priority to those pupils who are accurate and controlled users of English.

They are, however, not necessarily in favour of many of the education reforms because they believe that it has reduced their ability to control the curriculum and choose work that is appropriate for the pupils. They dislike the sense of something being externally imposed on them that will interfere with their ways of working, even if they are broadly sympathetic to some of the National Curriculum's aims. They are keenly aware of the workload implications. Initiatives such as OFSTED inspections or teacher appraisal may also be seen as an unnecessary imposition that detracts from the business of teaching. As a head of department, they are likely to value efficiency and like to see things well-run and organised with clear, definable aims.

This group, along with the Critical Dissenters, was the largest single group in the survey. Seventeen respondents identified with this group and they were found in all types of school – urban, shire and selective. Six different schools had Technician members of department, but almost half the group, eight respondents, came from one home counties school. This interested me, not least because this was the group with which I felt the least affinity. In a sense the fact that so many identified with this group might be seen as a tribute to my ability to empathise with their position, but, as we shall see, unlike the other four groups no single section struck a clear chord with the readers. The key markers in the text were its overall tone, the constant emphasis on skills and the need to teach to the perceived ability of the pupil. But it was the absence of certain concepts, of any form of personal growth or individuality, that was also intended as a key marker. Their ability to identify with this group was intended to indicate that this concept was less important to them than any of the others, and this again was to be a rationale for their name, the Technicians. It was important, therefore, that the overall tone of the text was devoid of jargon. And because I suspected that this emphasis on the concrete might make them suspicious of any form of theory – their beliefs arising out of "common sense" – I also avoided any sense of abstraction within the description. The language of the text was permeated with words that suggested a lack of fuzziness – '*skills*', '*confident*', '*command*', '*effectively*', '*accurately*', '*discipline*', along with concrete examples that to them might reflect this approach – comprehensions, letters, exams. There was only one reference to the imagination, two to the creative and no mention of personal growth.

Creativity and the imagination

The dominance of the technical over the imaginative becomes clear when we look at the number of respondents who failed to highlight any reference to the imaginative. The first paragraph contained the sentence: '*They are also keen to develop creative writing to encourage a more imaginative response to language.*' Only eight respondents highlighted the words '*imaginative*' and '*creative writing*'. Three more highlighted only '*creative writing*'. F1 actually disagreed with this statement, adding in the margin, 'I don't agree totally with this point.' The fact that for half the group the imagination is either unimportant or apparently unconnected to creative writing is in itself significant. It may indicate that, for them, the ability to write creatively is simply another skill to be acquired, rather than an attempt at the expression of self through art.

Language skills

This may also correspond with their prioritising of the practical uses of language found in the second paragraph. Thirteen respondents highlighted the phrase '*stress the importance of language in everyday use*', twelve spoke of the importance of '*writing letters or instructions*', and eleven endorsed the notion of competence. All these suggest a skills-based approach, and one that, on the surface, seems to stress a conformity to the external rather than a development of the internal.

The idea that there is a sequence in learning to write is hinted at in some of the respondents' additional comments. Respondent F7 comments at the end of the text: 'The basics of the language should be <u>thoroughly</u> grounded in the junior school and secondary years used to fix these and develop style.' The fact that they chose to conclude with a comment on skills is in itself significant, but it is the way in which they chose to describe their concern that is more revealing. They have a clear sense of the order of learning: 'basics' come before 'style'. The word 'basics' resonates with Tory party – and increasingly with Labour – rhetoric and is not used by any other group, either in my description or in their comments.

As a metaphor, it has more to do with the idea of building blocks than it does with the more holistic approach of the other groups. The notion of a thorough grounding echoes a sense of laying the foundations. The word 'thoroughly' is also telling, because it implies that attention to detail is important to this group. It is even underlined for emphasis, suggesting that this respondent is not confident that this thorough grounding occurs. The choice of phrase 'fix these' is again interesting, indicating both something broken that needs mending as well as the sense of something being cemented on or attached, that, once in place, will be difficult to remove. In this context 'style' is to be developed, and even here the language has a utilitarian ring: the 'secondary years' are to be 'used'.

Respondent L2 also sees the acquisition of skills as a precursor of success, and adds at the end of the text: 'You need to master technical accuracy to get on in careers, other subjects and, indeed, English.' The use of the word 'master' is interesting in that it suggests a desire to control. But it is the use of the imperative phrase 'you need' that is possibly the most revealing, for rather than being reflective, as many of the other groups are, frequently using the first person in their comments, this addresses the thought to an unspecified external audience. For the comment appears to be intended as a statement of incontrovertible fact rather than an engagement or even disagreement with the text or me as its author.

While neither of these respondents, F7 or L2, highlighted the key marker found in paragraph 4 that indicated this group's particular deficit model of learning, '*that teachers should be able to focus on addressing the weaknesses of pupils*', they did not disagree with it either. (Respondent L2 also highlighted the additional phrase, '*particularly the technical and linguistic*'.) Eleven respondents, however, did highlight this phrase and no one disagreed with it. This willingness to identify with the negative rather than the positive capabilities of the pupils they teach may be a function of their disposition to focus on those aspects of the curriculum that are more clearly right or wrong, or certainly those areas that are bounded by definable rules.

Notions of correctness

This sense that a desire for accuracy can lead to a predisposition to look for right and wrong, or a reliance on rules and procedures, can be found in the comment made by H2, who writes at the end of the text: 'I have underlined all that is accurate; there is nothing here which is actually wrong – merely some issues on which I am neutral, or not actively engaged in.' There is a faint air of condescension in this comment, a feeling that the text has been marked rather than engaged with as a set of ideas. It has been checked and they have found 'nothing here that is actually wrong'. The use of the word 'here' is interesting in that it implies that elsewhere, possibly in the rest of the booklet, much may be 'wrong'.

Yet they also seem to feel the need to justify to someone that they have done what they were told. They are seeking to confirm that they have done the 'right' thing. By writing 'I have underlined all that is accurate' they are telling me, the task setter, what they have done. Despite the throwaway 'merely' and the stated sense of neutrality on certain issues or lack of 'active engagement' on others, they clearly need to explain why they have not totally complied with the procedures. Read this way, H2's stance becomes defensive and highlights the tension within this group. Adherence to rules and procedures allows for confident judgements on the one hand but can cause anxiety and defensiveness on the other. Both types of response tend to close down debate.

Teaching literature and pupil ability

I translated my sense of this group's deficit model of language, and their sense that there was an order in which subject matter might be taught, into their teaching of literature. I did so by giving it more positive expression in the sentence '*It is important for children to be taught appropriately according to their needs.*' That the pupils had '*needs*' was intended to hint at the deficit model. Thirteen of the respondents highlighted this phrase. Ten went on to highlight its more explicit expression, that '*not all pupils*' were '*capable of studying certain writers*' and twelve agreed, including all those who had highlighted the first phrase, that the '*less-able*' should be given '*relevant*' or '*abridged*' texts.

There was, however, more disagreement over the statement that '*less able children find poetry difficult*'. Six disagreed. Yet what is interesting is the way they expressed that disagreement. Several of those who disagreed with this statement had agreed with the first sentiment that less able children should study different books from the more able. Had I suggested a similar approach with poetry more may have agreed, for their disagreement does not suggest that these children should study the same texts as their more able peers. E3 for example writes: 'No – it depends on poetry chosen.' And F2, having conceded that not all children can study the same texts and having agreed with the statement on poetry, adds 'but should still "do" some poetry selected by the teacher with knowledge of the group'. The use of inverted commas is interesting here, suggesting as it does that the study of poetry for this kind of child will not be the same as it would be for other groups. They will '"do"' poetry in the loosest sense of the word. This slightly patronising note is also found in the comment of F4. On one side this respondent writes 'This is possibly true, but I am often surprised by what students take to', and on the other side adds 'But they often enjoy it!' While this is partly a defence of these pupils and does imply that this respondent is prepared to experiment, to an extent, with the texts they choose, it does betray a certain persistence in this teacher's low expectations, given that F4 is 'often surprised'. The exclamation mark at the end of the comment 'But they often enjoy it!' also suggests that the pupils' enjoyment is unexpected.

F6, who wanted '*to focus on addressing the weaknesses of the pupils*' and believed that '*not all pupils were capable of studying certain writers*', also wanted to comment on their poetry lessons: 'I have often found poetry lessons very rewarding with "less able" classes. I concede, however, that they do find it difficult. But (a) so do some able students (b) the less able find everything quite difficult.'

It is possible that the slightly defensive note in these last four respondents (E3, F2, F4 and F6), and their desire to describe their poetry lessons, arises out of their sense of an implied criticism in my comment on their attitude towards teaching poetry to the less able. To an extent their concern is justified in that the comment was intended to reflect those departments and teachers I had encountered who had barely taught lower sets any poetry at all.

D1's comment is equally revealing for different reasons. Having highlighted the whole section on focusing on '*the weaknesses of pupils, particularly the technical and linguistic*' and agreeing that not all pupils '*are capable of studying the same writers*', D1 adds to the section on poetry:

> Yes and no – I have found – with experience that less able students may not be able to cope at *same level* – that does not mean that they cannot cope with the same text. In mixed ability grouping they *may*

be more aware of their limitations. Again they may find it difficult because it is 'culturally' believed to be. I do think any child can respond and benefit to any text.

There is an interesting ambiguity within this response beyond their own uncertain 'Yes and no'. On the one hand it is a clear expression of a deficit model. They emphasise the 'less able' pupils' ability to 'cope' by underlining '*same level*'. The comment on 'their limitations' is also interesting in that the evaluation is a given, the only question is, in which environment will the pupils themselves 'be more aware' of this given? There is an implied desire to protect them from the realisation of 'their limitations'. This, and the idea that all pupils may 'respond and benefit to any text' (despite the awkward construction of the phrase) may mean that this respondent is closer to the Old Grammarians than other Technicians. Indeed, D1 writes copiously around the text and, as we shall see, admits a sympathy with the Old Grammarian position.

Pupil grouping

What respondent D1 does not question is the need for some form of pupil grouping. And while D1 adds 'this *may* be "broad banding" – does not have to be strict', this person is in favour of meeting '*the appropriate needs of the pupils*' through some form of setting, as opposed to differentiating work within a class. This notion was also intended as a key marker within this group, and indeed there was less ambiguity about setting in this group than in any other. Seven of the Technicians agreed with selection. Only two in this group, F4 and L2, actively disagreed with it, F4 adding 'Selective schools? No way!'.

Nine of the respondents agreed with the statement that they were likely to implement a system that is '*finely-tuned rather than broad-banding*'. E3, L2 and D3 still wanted some form of setting, but like D1 preferred broad banding. Next to the section on the '*appropriate needs*' L2 comments 'yes – but can be done in broader bands'. Similarly, against the notion of '*fine tuning*' D3 added 'not in the lower school'.

Only D2, E4 and N1 appeared to disagree with the notion of some form of setting, but none of their responses suggests that they would rather teach mixed ability classes. D2, for example, supported the notion that not all pupils are capable of reading the same texts and N1 teaches in a highly selective independent girls school. E4's response is slightly more complex. Next to the section on setting, she wrote in the margin 'This isn't necessarily the result of a "skills" approach.'

What is interesting about this response is that she appears to have understood the implication behind the text, for I do not actually explicitly connect these two concepts. It is also possible that she has read into the text the suggestion of a deficit model of learning, for she circled the word '*weaknesses*'. Again, however, E4 works in a school where pupils are taught in mixed ability groups for the first three years, and thereafter in broadly banded groups. It is possible, therefore, that E4 is at pains to separate out a skills-based view of the subject, which she endorses at every other point in the text, from the deficit model implied in my rendition.

Accuracy

This interpretation is in part borne out by the way in which E4 queried my suggestion that this group gives '*priority to those who are accurate and controlled users of English*'. She ringed the word '*priority*' and added in the margin, 'what does this mean?' The note of caution sounded in the question may be connected with a hesitancy to sign up for a position with which she is not wholly comfortable. The exact nature of her caution is unclear but may be amplified by the comments of F2. This respondent also ringed the word '*priority*', adding 'does this mean higher marks for the better spellers and "punctuators". That's the dilemma – you can't grade an emotional response to a piece of literature without taking into account the accuracy of the technical aspects.' Interestingly the respondent classifies this as a 'comment' rather than a 'disagree'.

As with E4, part of the comment is a desire for clarification, and to this extent neither E4 nor F2 are actually disagreeing with the statement. But in a sense F2's question, 'does this mean higher marks for better spellers and "punctuators"' and F2's ensuing 'dilemma' is directed as much at themselves as it is at my statement. The absence of a question mark adds weight to the idea that this is an internal musing rather than a question that expects a response. And indeed they go on to answer it themselves, '– you can't grade an emotional response to a piece of literature without taking into account the accuracy of the technical aspects'. The use of the words 'emotional response' rather than, for example, the more commonly used 'personal' or 'imaginative' is also interesting. It has a faintly pejorative ring, not least because it is a term often used to contrast feminine irrationality with masculine rationality and control. Juxtaposed as this phrase is with an insistence on accuracy, there is a curious sense in which 'the technical aspects' act as a restraint on the 'emotional'; that rules prevent unseemly displays. This is, of course, to stretch the point slightly but there is a hint of it within the text.

Only F6 and F8, however, clearly disagree with the statement. F6 adds: 'I believe that "accurate users of English" should be rewarded for their accuracy; but not necessarily *more* than those students who are imaginative, inspired etc.' Significantly, perhaps, in their disagreement this respondent does contrast accuracy with the 'imaginative, inspired etc' rather than the 'emotional'. In addition, this response seems to allow scope for rewarding, on occasion, the imaginative over the technically accurate, which F2's does not. F8 simply highlights the statement as something with which they disagree. Only six respondents actually agreed with this statement, eight making no comment at all, but the fact that only two respondents clearly disagreed is indicative of the group's approach to technical accuracy as a whole.

Exams and coursework

I suspected that their predisposition to value those aspects of English which are more easily assessable would make them more likely to be sympathetic to examinations than any other group. When writing this paragraph, therefore, I linked the notion of technical accuracy with their approach to examinations through the use of key words and phrases such as '*discipline*' and '*prepare children thoroughly*'. In this context, thorough preparation was meant to carry the hint of cramming or drilling, in that I did not include any qualifiers to the process as I had done with the other groups, namely some comment on either the limitations or distorting effects of the current testing regime.

Indeed, almost three quarters of the respondents agreed with the idea that children should be '*prepared thoroughly*'; just over half supported a notion of the '*discipline of exams*' while just under half argued for '*50 per cent coursework*'. Not all respondents highlighted all these phrases, but if we consider that these statements are more supportive of examinations than any other group, we find that just under three quarters supported some form of formal examination.

While ten did '*acknowledge the need for coursework because it offers more opportunity for creative writing*', only three elaborated upon my somewhat tokenistic nod in this direction. Again, one of these was F2, but, as with their comments on accuracy, their apparent gesture towards a less rigid approach is belied by the way in which they express it. They add to my statement 'and work geared & directed towards the group's or *individuals'* needs'. Instead of seeing coursework as an opportunity for differentiation by outcome, as opposed to the tiering arrangements of the current exams at key stage 3 and 4, this respondent appears to sanction the tiering of papers by seeing coursework as a better means of differentiating by input.

Such a view is clearly connected to their support for a system of setting that '*is finely tuned*'. Indeed, their language echoes my own description of the rationale for setting: '*it will allow them to concentrate more fully on each group's particular needs and set appropriate work*'.

Conversely, F4's clear criticism of the notion of selection – 'Selective schools? No way!' – and a lack of comment on setting, may not be disconnected to their stronger support for coursework. This respondent adds: 'Not the only reason, by far, that I think c/wk is a good idea. What someone can achieve over a range of time and activities is more important than what they can achieve in one two hour exam.' They go on to add next to the section on examining literature, 'Literature is much better appreciated through c/wk and discussion.'

D1's ambivalence about coursework and exams, however, illustrates the way in which a belief in terminal exams may be connected to an emphasis on technical accuracy as opposed to the imaginative. In addition D1's discussion of these two parts of the Technicians' description demonstrates why these are key markers of this group. Along with eight other respondents D1 agreed with the statement that '*they are likely to argue for the discipline that exam work provides*'. Unlike the other eight, however, D1 chooses to modify the statement '*acknowledge the need for coursework because it offers more opportunity for creative writing*', replacing '*acknowledge*' with 'welcome' and '*need*' with 'value'. This is interesting because they are substituting a negative argument for coursework, one which echoes the language and tone of the deficit model, with a positive one. They annotate the statement further by adding: 'and personal response'. More significantly still they add to the comment on the '*discipline of exams*': 'Certainly in the past I have argued this but after teaching 100 per cent coursework and losing it I'm not so sure!'

This respondent, while placing themselves among the Technicians, also identifies with much in the other groups, with the Old Grammarians, the Liberals and the Pragmatists. As we have seen before, such respondents on the cusp of a group reveal much about the way in which key markers in the text help to differentiate teacher's positions. D1 is no exception. Each time, as with their comments on coursework, in their desire for balance they expose a tension between their views of skills and the imaginative. At the beginning of the text they write that they want 'a *balance* between exploring literature for all its imaginative and explorating values'. At the end they comment 'I do not think language skills should be taught at the expense of the exploration of literature' and then go on to borrow from the text of the Old Grammarians and the Liberals '– unlocking of other worlds – and development of empathy'. Both their opening statement and their conclusion borrow from the Pragmatists. At the beginning of the text they write: 'Teaching language skills to "empower" pupils is essential.' While at the end, they note 'I would study language through literature – but do believe that "competence" in language should be encouraged and *yes* – is part of "empowering" pupils.

There is a defensive stance in the underlined '*yes*'. Not only does D1's underlining give the word emphasis, but the rhythmic awkwardness of the placing of 'and', which precedes it, makes the reader pause and so reinforces the stress on the word '*yes*'. It is almost as if D1 is saying 'I know you don't believe me but . . .'. Yet they betray their own lack of ease with the concept of empowerment by insisting that it is placed in inverted commas each time it is mentioned. The comment on the discipline of exams indicates that this is a respondent whose ideas are in a state of flux, that their position is on the move. What is interesting about the response is the issues on which this movement appear to be based. Clearly, in that they have picked the Technicians and frequently mention the importance of skills, they still identify most strongly with a technical view of English than any other. For D1, this used to suggest a belief in the discipline of exams. Now they are 'not so sure'. Similarly, they want accuracy but this is no longer sufficient either, and so they seek to borrow from the other groups a sense of imagination, empathy and empowerment that they no longer see in the Technicians.

D1's voluntary use of such language separates them from all the others in this group. For D1 is the only one who makes any reference in their comments to personal response, empathy or the imagination. And yet D1's belief in the importance of skills unites them with the rest of the Technicians. In this way D1's selection of the Technicians re-emphasises the key markers of the group which separate the Technicians from the rest. But D1's ambivalence about their choice is equally telling. What is so interesting about this teacher's response is that in identifying their sympathy with other groups D1 selects the key characteristics of those other groups which differentiate them not only from the Technicians but also from each other, namely the Old Grammarians' belief in the imagination, the Liberals' desire for empathy, and the Pragmatists' espousal of empowerment.

OFSTED *and the management of change*

A similar tension is also evident in D1's comments on the management of change. Here again they consider the tension between structure and freedom. D1 comments:

> I think definable aims are important but would wish to trust each
> member of the department to work to their strengths – responding

to pupils' strengths and weaknesses. Do not value over prescriptive approach – but a *basic, defined* policy of aims and objectives gives teachers the 'freedom' to develop those as appropriate to their class and situation.

Again the language oscillates between 'strengths and weaknesses', between 'definable aims' and 'trust'. They 'Do not value the over prescriptive' but want '*a basic, defined* policy of aims and objectives'. ' "Freedom" ' is not only circumscribed by the use of inverted commas, but also by the notion of the 'appropriate'. This last sentence is particularly telling, for those are the words which most echo the language of the Technicians. '*basic, defined*' are given all the weight of an underlining, while the concept of ' "freedom" ', as with ' "empowerment" ', has all the frailty of a word surrounded by inverted commas. It is as if this respondent needs to hang on to the certainties which skills offer while hankering after the ambivalence, or the freedom, of the emotive and aesthetic. For the rest of the group this last paragraph struck a chord. Only two respondents disagreed with any part of it. The section on OFSTED invited some comment but little actual disagreement.

Studying the media

The Technicians' broad sympathy with the National Curriculum may go some way to explaining the one key marker which I appear to have misjudged. It is possible that I had underestimated the impact that the requirement to teach the media would have on their practice, not least the fact that it is a component of GCSE. I had written '*study of the media is not a high priority in their classrooms, as they would prefer pupils to exercise their critical skills on more traditional texts*'. Ten respondents disagreed with the statement, several pointing out that they do indeed teach the media in their lessons. But a closer look at this section makes a simple reading of this failure to strike a chord more complex, for many of the respondents did support the notion that they privileged reading over watching television and playing computer games.

Read in this light only five respondents are unsympathetic to the general thrust of my understanding of this group's attitude to the media – D3 and F2, along with L2, F4 and E3. These last three respondents did not disagree with the key marker on reading, but all three not only disagreed with the statement on studying the media but commented as well. L2 writes 'not true at all!', while F4 comments 'I would say study of the media is important – it is about using language in conjunction often with other visual messages.' E3 adds 'No! "Reading" includes other texts/forms.'

Conclusion

This last section on the media is, in a way, illustrative of the key features of this group. In part it is indicative of my ability to get the broad thrust of their philosophy right, without managing to hit the nail, as it were, on the head. Unlike all the other groups no single clear key marker emerges. While there are a number of statements for which I can get general agreement, as with the statements on skills, the language of everyday use, examinations and setting, all of which are important in separating them out from the other groups, no more than thirteen respondents ever agree with any particular manifestation of these concepts. Only with a more complex reading, as with the one on the media, does a more supportive, or a less negative, picture emerge.

As I suggested at the beginning of this section, it may well be that my lack of empathy with this group meant that I was unable to get the nuances right, but it may also suggest that my failure to gain total agreement on any single key marker is simply symptomatic of a group which is hard to please. It is just possible that the Technicians' desire to find fault makes pleasing them with any element of the description difficult. F5 confesses as much:

> I was sorely tempted to highlight the whole piece in blue as I found myself sympathetic to almost everything in it. I couldn't keep the blue [pink] highlighter from it however! The only piece I find slightly out of place is the comment about the media which does feature quite highly in my teaching programme. Not much left – but as I implied I don't object to any of it.

Again this respondent highlights the section on the media as mistaken, but, as they point out themselves, they are simply correcting a factual error on my part. They do not actually 'object' to my analysis of their attitude to the media, they simply cannot 'keep the . . . highlighter from it'. This trait is in itself a key marker of the Technicians, and significantly their use of red ink also exceeds that of all other groups. Of the seventeen respondents ten used the red pen copiously.

As we have seen, they alone use the language of skills to analyse my text. But it may be their corrective tone, their instinct to look for mistakes, as much as my lack of sympathy for their position, that explains why so many identify with the Technicians without any particular statement attracting their whole-hearted support. There is, of course, sufficient evidence to validate my picture of a group which values technical skills, examinations and setting. Nor are they thrown by my lack of emphasis on either the imagination or personal growth. Nevertheless, the overriding impression is of a group which responds to a generally negative tone and so cannot entirely agree on what they actually support.

Again their comments bear out this observation. While in all other groups many of the comments are supportive, even declamatory in their agreement, the copious comments of the Technicians, which have made this section so long, are almost entirely negative in nature, even when they are ostensibly not actually disagreeing. It is as if they cannot be content with the approximate, but have to get it absolutely right and this prevents them from being positive.

Critical Dissenters

This group have been described as 'cultural theorists' or interested in critical literacy, but in many ways they form a broader spectrum than this because not everyone who may be classified under this heading is as interested in critical or, more especially, linguistic, theory as this description suggests. They form a spectrum of opinion that is coloured by the degree of emphasis placed on literature. At one end can be found those influenced by linguistic theories which emphasise the notion of critical literacy arising out of theorists like Gramsci. At the other end are those influenced by a literary model of cultural dissent, which emphasises the political context and connotations of all literature and the need to challenge received norms.

Many teachers gravitate towards the middle of the spectrum, or modify their opinion depending on the area being discussed, so they do not form two distinct groups. As a group these teachers are marked chiefly by the rigour of their perception of culture and the way this impacts on their view of the subject, pedagogy and classroom organisation. As a group they are, of necessity, clearly to the left of centre.

This group sees personal growth in terms of empowerment. This has manifested itself in various ways over the last twenty years and may still change, depending on the position in the spectrum, but the aim is always similar. In the late sixties and early seventies much of the emphasis lay in discovering a personal voice. Spearheaded by teachers like Chris Searle in Hackney, and later through publications such as *Our Lives*, published by the English and Media Centre, this movement sought to empower pupils by allowing them freedom of expression. It was a way of breaking free of the dead weight of the Leavisite canon.

But this emphasis appears to have been amalgamated, in the late seventies and early eighties, with literary theory which allowed students to deconstruct texts, knowingly to debunk the canon and find

alternative texts that had been omitted. It also led to the rise of media studies and the examination of popular culture. Some have, however, been dissatisfied with the cultural relativism which this position implies and so have sought to explore more the idea of radical readings of canonical texts as well as suggesting alternatives to that canon.

The notion of discovering a personal voice has been maintained but refined. While the significance of non-standard variants is passionately defended, a new orthodoxy has emerged, namely that pupils are disenfranchised if they are not given access to standard forms of English, provided that these are discussed within the context of notions of the language of power and that notions of appropriateness are debated within the idea of critical language awareness. In some quarters, in fact, there is a hint of a movement away from the pre-eminence of literature within the English curriculum, and towards reconsidering language as an area of study. The emergence of knowledge about language in the Cox curriculum facilitated this development.

This flux in the ways of discussing empowerment is symptomatic of the mind-set of this group. Their position must constantly be re-appraised and so its manifestations will continue to alter and this means, to an extent, that their classroom practice may alter also. They are likely to be influenced by ideas on learning theory as there is no rigid divide between theory and practice. Many will have been influenced by theorists such as Vygotsky, but they are likely to experiment with new ideas and theories within the classroom. While they pay lip service to the idea of teacher as facilitator, they are in fact highly directional in the way in which they teach.

Nevertheless, they are totally committed to mixed-ability teaching. This is mainly to do with their notion of democratic entitlement, not only in the desire not to treat one group differently by labelling them, but also to do with the idea that all children should have access to the same texts and ideas. Both these connect under the more general heading of equal opportunities. It is not, as has been suggested, saying all children are the same, but is insisting on the idea that all should have the same opportunities.

This insistence on mixed-ability teaching does, however, influence pedagogy, for while the teacher is highly directional they use the pupils to facilitate the learning. This is where the role of oracy and Britton's interpretation of Vygotsky is so significant. Group work and discussion are essential to the way in which the subject is delivered because it allows all pupils access to challenging texts. So, too, is coursework because it allows pupils to explore the same text in a far greater variety of ways than the terminal exam and allows for more scope in the way in which the pupils' work is approached. This emphasis may well lead them to value originality when assessing pupils' work.

All this has brought this group into direct conflict with government reform and it was this group that spearheaded the opposition to testing and the new curriculum. They have come round to the notion of a more prescribed curriculum and schemes of work through the notion of an entitlement curriculum as a form of equal opportunities, but are opposed to the way in which this currently manifests itself in legislation.

As I have already explained, this is the group in which I would place myself, and to that extent, therefore, it makes the group on the one hand more difficult and on the other easier to analyse. The danger always lies in the tendency to see their position as more beneficially coherent because I agree with it. Similarly, in writing this I tried to ensure that my description did not assume that this position was 'correct' or lend itself to pejorative readings of the other groups. I was, however, aware of this group's tendency constantly to reappraise their position and also to be very precise about the way in which these views were articulated. Within the text, therefore, many of the paragraphs include similar ideas expressed in slightly different ways. Whereas in the other groups these statements were often graded in terms of the strength of support for a particular idea, here the statements carried equal weight but allowed the respondents to reply with that sense of precision.

Certain very strong patterns do, however, emerge from this group. They, along with the Technicians, formed the largest grouping. Seventeen placed themselves in this category and were found in six different schools of all types except selective. (One respondent, while placing himself in this category, explained that he had not filled in the booklet due to 'end of term stress!' I have, therefore, omitted his reply from the calculation throughout.) They clustered predominantly, however, in urban schools and in particular inner city schools. This in itself may well be a significant feature of this group. While it is hard to know whether they choose this kind of school because of the kind of teacher they are, or whether they become this kind of teacher because of the school they are in is difficult to tell from these replies. Nevertheless a key feature of this group is their radical oppositional stance and the way in which this is systematically worked out in their views of the subject, approach to pupil grouping and pedagogic theory; hence their name, Critical Dissenters.

Mixed ability

Undoubtedly, however, as I had suspected, the most important key markers are their commitment to mixed ability teaching and coursework, which I will consider later. All but one of the respondents highlighted their commitment to mixed ability teaching. The only one who disagreed with it was D6, a head teacher in a shire school. This contrasts with the rather more hesitant commitment of other groups to mixed ability teaching. The response of this group is unequivocal, although their rationale varies slightly.

All but one of the respondents linked the idea of mixed ability teaching to some notion of *'democratic entitlement'*, including the idea that all children *'should have the same opportunities'*. These general principles were given educational expression in the phrases *'the desire not to treat one group differently by labelling them'*, along with *'the idea that all children should have access to the same texts and ideas'*. All but two gave at least two reasons for their belief in mixed ability teaching, and two thirds of these linked the notion of democratic entitlement or equal opportunities to educationally specific outcomes.

Pedagogy and learning theory

Their pedagogy is so intimately tied up with the notion of entitlement and equal opportunities that for some they are inseparable. One respondent (E1), while *'insisting on the idea that all should have the same opportunities'*, disagreed with *'the notion of democratic entitlement'* as a rationale and wrote in the margin: 'No I believe it is the best way to learn.' This focus on 'the best way to learn', or the attempt to integrate *'learning theory'* into best practice, is also a key marker in this group. Again, certain clear patterns emerge when paragraph 6, which discusses this aim, is subdivided into five key phrases. Two are related to the practical outcome of this tendency – *'their position must constantly be re-appraised'* and *'they are likely to experiment with new ideas'*. The others are concerned with learning theory – *'they are likely to be influenced by ideas on learning theory'*; they see *'no rigid divide between theory and practice'* and, more specifically, they may *'have been influenced by theorists such as Vygotsky'*.

Thirteen of the respondents highlighted at least one of these five phrases. Eleven of the respondents highlighted at least one of the phrases concerned specifically with learning theory. Of these, seven highlighted the section on the influence of *'learning theory'*; five went on to highlight the phrase that they saw *'no rigid divide between theory and practice'*, along with one other, who had not highlighted the phrase on *'learning theory'*. Nine noted the influence of Vygotsky. Eleven also highlighted one or other of the phrases on reappraising practice or experimenting with ideas, all but two highlighting one or the other. Of those that highlighted this paragraph only two respondents did not add that they either experimented or reappraised their practice; both those who failed to highlight specific phrases on learning theory did, however, '*re-appraise*' their position.

Interestingly, respondent G2 went on to add to the section on '*new ideas and theories in the classroom*' 'True – eg. interest in practising textual theory à la Scholes – to see if it works in a mixed ability setting.' They also commented 'True – there is always a theory in place – it seems only right to make it explicit.' This sense that there is 'always a theory in place' again highlights the mind-set of this group, which does not separate theory from practice, believing that the one will influence the other. The desire to 'make it explicit' is indicative of the tendency to lay everything open to challenge, to criticism. The idea that this is the 'right' thing to do suggests that other practices, which are by implication more covert, are wrong. For this respondent, therefore, to ignore the place of theory is almost to be dishonest.

The idea that integrating theory with practice is nothing more than good practice is again echoed by respondent E1. Next to the section describing the way in which this group's classroom practice may alter in the light of '*re-appraising their position*', she writes: 'this is an odd way of expressing what should surely be good practice?'. This idea that reappraising your position is connected to good practice is reinforced by her comment on the passage describing the role of the teacher – '*While they pay lip service to the idea of teacher as facilitator, they are in fact highly directional in the way in which they teach*' – 'I don't understand this either – I do not see a conflict between the different roles a teacher needs to take on. Classroom culture demands a multiplicity of positions of all participants.'

What is perhaps most interesting is the language in which she chooses to express her views, for again it reflects the integration of a kind of discourse theory with pedagogy. Rather than talking of classroom management, as the Pragmatists might have done, this respondent chooses to call it 'classroom culture'. The notion of 'multiplicity of positions' again echoes the idea of different readings of a text and almost of code switching.

It is, however, the belief in 'all' participating that is intended to act as the chief rebuttal to the notion of a '*highly directional*' teacher. The choice of the word 'participant' reinforces a notion of equality, implying as it does engagement in a common goal. But the apparent incomprehension at my comment, in her 'I don't understand this either', betrays an unquestioning confidence in the rightness of her view which echoes the implicit sentiment behind my phrase '*highly directional*'. This confidence is felt also in the triumphal 'of course!' added next to my comment '*for while the* teacher is highly directional they use the pupils to facilitate the learning'. It is as if she feels I have conceded on a debating point, which should have been obvious in the first place.

Curriculum, group work and coursework

This latter comment comes in paragraph 8 which discusses the pedagogical implications of this group's stand on mixed ability teaching. Again we see the linking of theory and practice throughout; the way in which they connect the what and the how of their teaching. Thus the key phrases in this paragraph all relate the methodology of teaching to the content.

Indeed, all respondents (apart from D6) connected some notion of discussion or group work – be it a specific mention of Vygotsky or Britton, the notion of oracy or the idea that '*they use the pupils to facilitate the learning*' – to an aspect of the curriculum, in particular, coursework. This may in itself be significant, for although D6 highlighted an earlier reference to Vygotsky in paragraph 6, they alone in this group disagreed with mixed ability teaching. Fourteen of the respondents agreed with coursework, none disagreeing, and ten of these went on to agree that it allowed '*pupils to explore the text in a far greater variety of ways*', as well as allowing '*for more scope in the way in which the pupils' work is approached*'.

Radical readings and the media

I3, along with eight other respondents, did agree with the idea that group work '*allows all pupils access to challenging texts*'. While on the one hand this relates to their belief in mixed ability teaching, it is also connected to their approach to literature. Thirteen of the respondents said that they sought to explore '*more radical readings of canonical texts*', found in paragraph 4, as well as suggesting '*alternatives to the canon*'. All but two highlighted both these phrases.

In fact, seven of the respondents highlighted only the section on literary texts, ignoring the reference to media studies and popular culture. It might be argued that '*alternatives to the canon*' includes a notion of popular culture. Yet it may also refer to the under-representation within the traditional canon of certain groups, such as women and those from ethnic minorities, rather than popular culture per se. This view is given some credence by the fact that I10, who highlighted only the phrase '*alternatives to the canon*', also underlined the phrase '*challenging texts*'. In other words, alternatives have to be challenging. Interestingly, respondents C2 and G3, who highlighted only the section on media studies and popular culture, also gave '*access to challenging texts*' as one of the reasons for mixed ability teaching. In the case of G3 it was the only reason.

Indeed, if we combine the endorsement of '*radical readings of canonical texts*' in paragraph 4, with the notion of pupils encountering challenging texts in paragraph 8, only G4 and E1 fail to highlight either of these phrases. And even E1, along with seven others, supports the notion that '*literary theory*' '*allowed students to deconstruct texts*'. All this suggests that many of this group have a much stronger affinity with the Old Grammarians than would seem likely at first glance. So despite only a quarter of this group agreeing that they were '*dissatisfied with the cultural relativism*' implied in the rise of popular culture, their response shows more of a dissatisfaction than would at first seem apparent. It would appear that the key marker which differentiates this group from the Old Grammarians is not necessarily the kind of texts studied, because some in this group may also be interested in literary theory. The key marker, as I anticipated, lies more in the way in which the Critical Dissenters systematically apply their understanding of '*cultural dissent*' – the key words here being '*radical*' and '*alternative*' – to mixed ability teaching. In other words, if the reading of a certain text or choice of text considers social exclusion, racism, class or gender theory, then pupils cannot be placed in ability sets because such a move may well reflect those negative values which the Critical Dissenters are attempting to expose in the teaching of these texts.

Elitism

That they share some of the implicit elitism of the Old Grammarians is found in the comments of G2. Like several of the Old Grammarians they name-drop in the margins. Significantly, however, they cite literary theorists rather than writers. In the first paragraph this respondent declares themselves by writing: 'Not sure where I stand on linguistics actually. More interested in literary/textual theory', and we have already noted their reference to Scholes. To paragraph 4 they add 'Rise of media and cultural studies is v. important', '"Cultural" Materialism is important too Dollimore/Sinfield', but perhaps most significant is G2's concluding comment. Discussing the notion of '*an entitlement as a form of equal opportunities*', they add 'True – I am for entitlement but clearly this should be left in the hands of people who "know"'. While this comment is an endorsement of an oppositional stance to Conservative legislation, it does nevertheless betray an unequivocal sense of rightness in their own position. The addition of the word 'clearly' to the qualifying 'but' rules out the possibility of argument. This, combined with the notion of 'people who "know"' and the way in which the rhythm of the sentence demands that the word 'clearly' is stressed, adds almost a note of disdain to the idea that anyone could disagree, despite the fact that '"know"' is placed in inverted commas to suggest irony.

This dominance of literature was, nevertheless, greater than I had anticipated, for while I had recognised that there would be an affinity to the Old Grammarians at one end of the spectrum, I had not realised how strong this would be.

Empowerment and Standard English

What became apparent was a sense that this group took a structural rather than an individualistic approach to empowerment. This is evident in the apparent dominance of the *'literary model of cultural dissent'*, in that texts are placed within an overall context where all aspects of canonical traditions are questioned. But it is even clearer in the way in which they dealt with the issue of Standard English, where a clear position on the teaching of language emerged. This did to an extent confirm my sense of a new orthodoxy. Only respondents D6, G3 and C4 failed to highlight some aspect of paragraph 5, which looked at the teaching of Standard English. Again the text was divided into key phrases, but in this instance I was aware of the possibility of a fluctuating approach. The defence of *'non-standard variants'*, while still prevalent, was being superseded by the notion of *'the language of power'* and the belief that pupils were *'disenfranchised'*, both of which were framed by a notion of *'critical language awareness'*. I was also aware, as a member of this group, that there was an ongoing debate about the role of *'language as an area of study'* and that this debate was partly a reflection of the group's tendency to reappraise its practice.

In many respects the way in which this paragraph was highlighted reflects this flux of opinion and the more structural view of the issues involved. Ten respondents felt it important that pupils should be given access to *'the language of power'*, and eleven highlighted either this phrase or the corresponding phrase *'that pupils are disenfranchised if they are not given access to standard forms of English'*. Nine went on to highlight the notion of *'appropriateness'* *'debated within the idea of critical language awareness'*.

Although there was support for the idea that *'the notion of discovering a personal voice has been maintained and refined'* there was slightly less support for the development of a personal voice per se. I had suggested that this group, in the late 1970s, used *'personal voice'* to *'break free from the dead weight of the Leavisite canon'*. And while the notion of *'empowerment'*, at the beginning of paragraph 3, was highlighted by thirteen of the respondents, only half translated this into a notion of '*freedom of expression*' and only half the respondents highlighted one or other of the references to '*personal voice*'. If these two concepts are combined, however, the number rises to ten. Yet only six highlighted the phrase about '*non-standard variants*', and of these only two did not go on to highlight either the section on '*the language of power*' or the notion that '*pupils are disenfranchised*'.

When these two are combined with the other eleven who highlighted one or other of these phrases, however, a stronger sense of the importance of language as a vehicle of empowerment does emerge within '*a new orthodoxy*'. While only I2, C2 and G1 highlighted this phrase, there does seem evidence of its existence; that although '*freedom of expression*' and '*personal voice*' are still important, the actual commitment to non-standard variants is less significant.

In some respects C1 represents the ambiguity within the shift. This respondent demonstrates a strong commitment to the 'old' orthodoxy, highlighting all those phrases in the third paragraph (as well as in the fourth) that indicate this, including '*personal voice*', '*Our Lives*', '*freedom of expression*' and '*breaking free of the dead weight of the Leavisite canon*'. In addition she disagrees with the idea that a new orthodoxy had emerged, as well as with the whole section on the language of power and critical language awareness. Yet she did agree with the notion that '*pupils are disenfranchised if they are not given access to standard forms of English*' and did not highlight the section on non-standard variants. Thus in many respects she confirms the new orthodoxy in general, if not in some particular expressions of it.

Home language

But significantly for this group, language is almost more important as an aid to learning than an object of study. A number of the respondents refer to the significance of home language in the teaching of English. G2, G1, I3 and I2 all make some comment. G2 writes next to the paragraph on mixed ability teaching 'yes, + multi-lingualism'. G1 adds to the same paragraph 'provides models for English as an additional language', while I2 writes, 'use of home language as a huge resource in the learning of English language and literature' at the top of the second page, possibly linking it to the section on the study of language.

I3's comment next to the paragraph on mixed ability teaching, while not specifically mentioning language, includes a similar sentiment and adds to the phrases '*use pupils to facilitate learning*' and '*pupils' background*'. They go on to write at the bottom: '– Focus on teaching skills to empower students. Learning should be student focused – mixed ability teaching works and has worked.' While this response came at the end and no arrow linked it to any other part of the text, it is in many respects a rebuttal to the idea that this group is *'highly directional in the way in which they teach'* – a comment with which they disagreed, highlighting the first part *'teacher as facilitator'* instead. While four agreed with the former statement, five did not.

Dissenting discourse

I have already discussed how E1 rejected the notion of highly directional teachers. C1 also disagreed without commenting, but C3 argued the point in a similar way to E1, writing 'SEE *BELOW'*. Next to the section on *'they use pupils to facilitate learning'* C3 writes: 'So surely they do facilitate learning, not direct it? INCONSISTENCY?' What is interesting is that, like E1, the tone is argumentative and combative. The riposte begins with the words 'So surely . . .', and again there is a triumphant note, despite the question mark, which appears with a rhetorical flourish, in the use of capitals and underlining of the word 'inconsistency'. This echoes E1's 'of course!' but it also betrays the desire not to be seen as inconsistent and the need to be on one side of the debate or the other. This wish not to be seen as inconsistent and, more importantly, to score the debating point, apparently overcame another impulse, which was to engage in the argument. Next to the section on the highly directional teacher on the other side of the page, they have scribbled out the comment 'How can teachers not be directional in some way?' Clearly, for C3, the charge of 'inconsistency' wins the day better than this more questioning tone.

And it is this willingness to take on a fight in a style which is confrontational that marks out this group, from the Pragmatists in particular, but also from the Liberals and, to an extent, the Old Grammarians. If we consider the last paragraph, which looks at their role in opposing Conservative reforms, three key phrases describe, in differing ways, this opposition: *'direct conflict with government reform'*, *'opposition to testing and the new curriculum'*, and opposition to the curriculum as it *'currently manifests itself in legislation'*. Twelve highlighted either all or some aspects of this paragraph. E1 is already suggesting opposition to the new Labour government, adding to the phrase *'brought this group into direct conflict with government reform'* 'Too right', and going on to comment at the end, 'especially parts of the new White Paper (DfEE July 97)'.

Entitlement

There was some debate around the notion of an entitlement curriculum. C1 and C4 simply disagreed. C5, while not disagreeing, added this rider:

dept. working together on schemes of work-sharing notions of practice, applications of theory in practice and ensuring all students given the same experience.

The prescribed curriculum has ensured that we continue to cover breadth in the curriculum and integration study of language, literature and different cultures, but has become too prescriptive and stifling of growth & development.

In these comments this respondent makes interesting distinctions between entitlement and prescription, between local practice and national imposition. The need to qualify my assertion, the values which they espouse, particularly in the first paragraph, and the language in which they choose to express those ideas are all characteristic of this group.

J1 circles the word entitlement and comments, 'questionable! "entitled" to get what someone else decides is good for you! not entitled to discover your own curriculum etc. . . .' This response is again, however, characteristic of this group. The word 'questionable' is interesting in this context in that it has a slightly pejorative tone; the placing of 'entitled' in inverted commas reinforces the notion that it is a 'questionable' concept. But what emerges most strongly is the dislike of being told what to do, a sentiment he describes in terms of ownership of ideas. What is at fault, perhaps, is that 'someone else decides'. It is quite possible, however, that in the hands of Critical Dissenters, G2's 'people who "know"', J1 would be less unhappy, as he agreed with the notion of a '*highly directional*' teacher.

The London connection

G2, as we have seen, queried the notion of entitlement, and while they do not highlight any section of this paragraph their stance is evidently oppositional. They highlight the whole section in the first paragraph on the '*literary model of cultural dissent*' and '*the need to challenge received norms*'. They also agree with the notion that this group is '*clearly to the left of centre*'. The response of G4, who also fails to highlight any of the last paragraph, is also interesting because they, along with I2, suggest the importance of a London network. I2 adds at the end of the text: 'The teachers in this group use each other as a resource and enjoy the idea of an English teacher's network.' The most significant factor in establishing the London link between these teachers is that all but two, D6 and H1, currently teach in London schools and both of these have spent much of their career in the capital.

G2's comment, at the bottom of the whole text, provides a possible explanation of this clustering of Critical Dissenters. This respondent writes:

Although I can see aspects of each section which I feel are appropriate to myself, overall this one is the closest to my beliefs around English teaching – I think lots of this influence has come from the PGCE tutors at the Institute and the views which they held. In turn within the context of the classroom which is strongly placed in mixed ability, this rationale works.

At the beginning of the text, against the first paragraph, they also write: 'The influence of the E and M Centre has often informed what I teach through their publications – support for NQTs [newly qualified teachers], English departments.' This sense of 'the context of the classroom' which supports 'the rationale' coming from the influence of key London institutions, is important in establishing this group and has implications for the way in which it is formed and maintained.

There is some evidence of this, albeit tentative, if we consider the influence of D6, who highlighted the section on Gramsci. He was respondent I2's English Inspector in an east London borough before moving to a shire county – first as an English inspector and then as the head of a school in the same authority. Here he is the sole Critical Dissenter. Respondent I2 refers to D6 when discussing the section on debunking the canon. Significantly I2 disagrees with the idea of debunking the canon and adds: 'notions of literary entitlement, [D6's] idea that any text can be usefully taught'.

It is possible, therefore, that you already have to be a Critical Dissenter before you are influenced by such theorists, or in a situation where the issues seem relevant. Moving away from London has not altered D6's position, except perhaps on mixed ability teaching, which may in itself be significant; but his ideas seem to strike less of a direct chord in his present context. For not one of the teachers in his current school shares his views, while all in the east London school do.

Conclusion

When writing this, although I knew that Critical Dissent was a position held by many London teachers, I had not anticipated that the influence of this group would be so localised. Nor is it entirely clear why this is so, though there is a sense in which the network maintains a view espoused in training, with which this group already has a sympathy. In addition, those who teach in London have an opportunity to see those ideas work in practice, in a situation where the need for them seems applicable. It may also be significant that this is the only group which refers to the notion of a teachers' network, thus reinforcing the idea that they belong

Table 4 Disagreement with the description of setting arrangements

Old Grammarians	Pragmatists	Liberals	Technicians	Critical Dissenters
1 out of 9	5 out of 10	1 out of 6	6 out of 17	1 out of 17

to a distinct community. The presence of institutions such as the English and Media Centre, the Institute of Education and organisations like LATE appears to facilitate and reinforce this strong sense of identity. Like me, however, these teachers would be unlikely to confine this sense of community to London, despite this tentative evidence to the contrary.

What emerges overwhelmingly from this group is that they are self-confessed radicals who apply this to a theory of culture and also learning, which necessitates mixed ability teaching. Perhaps because I locate myself within this group there was very little disagreement with my description, except in those areas which registered change or where I challenged their image of themselves. The only statements that prompted any real disagreement were those on the extent to which they were '*highly directional in the way in which they teach*', and a definition of entitlement. This is in itself indicative of how, despite their assertion that all is open to question, they are confident that they have got it right and are prepared to argue openly with any one who says otherwise.

Final observations

Before we finish looking at the content of the Rough Guide it is worth considering certain strands that emerge across the groups, one of the most interesting of which is the respondents' attitudes towards pupil grouping. For while most agreed with the way in which I had described their setting arrangements, a number did not (see Table 4).

What these raw figures do not reveal, however, is the strong influence of departmental setting arrangements within the school.

All but two of the respondents who disagree with my comments on pupil grouping reflect the department in which they find themselves (see Hargreaves' theory of 'balkanisation', Hargreaves, 1994). While A1 quibbles whether there should be a top or bottom set, L6, a Pragmatist, is still hesitantly sympathetic to mixed ability teaching, despite being in a school that sets rigidly. And this is the other significant feature of the comments on pupil grouping. All but one of the respondents (D6, a head teacher who is a Critical Dissenter) only question my general categorisation of their view on pupil grouping to broaden it – that is, from sets to broad bands or from broad bands to mixed ability. Moreover, it would appear that those who deviate in this fashion are influenced by their experience of a form of setting that is closer to broad banding or mixed ability than is characteristic of other members of the group.

The commentaries

One other feature is worth noting, namely how respondents chose to disagree with my descriptions. I have, to an extent, already addressed this in the analysis of each of the groups but it is a feature worth revisiting. If we consider those respondents who were able to identify solely with one group, but who found more than two statements with which to disagree, we find that there are patterns within those responses that are found only within that group. For the purposes of coding these responses I have characterised them as *academic, managerial, compromising, corrective* and *theoretical with elements of dissent*. These five categories broadly reflect the five groups I identified. There is an element of overlap between two of these – the academic and the theoretical with elements of dissent – but there are sufficient differences to make them worth coding differently.

Academic

If we begin by looking at the Old Grammarians we find that their responses are characterised by a desire for rigour, analysis and a tendency to quote literary figures to support their arguments, which is not found among the other groups. It should be noted that two of the respondents who wrote in this way came from the same girls' grammar school, school K, which might be seen to cultivate an academic ethos. But they were not alone in their response. K1 commented: 'Essentially it's teaching people to *think* about emotional areas and also training thought generally. I would stress the analytical and academic a bit more.' K2 concluded: 'You've over-emphasised this group's attachment to empathy in studying literature. I think it values analysis, argumentation, "rigour".' In a marginal note K2 also comments: 'it's about teaching people to think' and talk of 'the pleasure to be derived from intellectual challenge', along with, 'Personally I'm with John Donne and other metaphysical poets in their understanding of the almost sensual pleasure in intellectual activity – "the felt thought".' B2 also values 'the ability to analyse'.

B5, while not using any of these terms other than 'rigorously', exemplifies the kind of analytical, argumentative prose style to which these other respondents refer. While there is debate about whether the notion of academic writing or "literacy" can be applied generically (Street, 1996), B5's comments at the end of the text read more like an academic essay than the comments of respondents from other groups, not least in the use of the passive voice; he uses connectives to add cohesion, and illustrative quotation (like K2) to aid analysis and argument. He writes, for example:

> Thus it is assumed that certain views on English lead or do not lead to a 'radical, oppositional stance' to, it is implied, Conservative Party government. This is a fundamental misreading of the current political scene in advanced 'western' nations/states – as for example the 'new right', libertarianism and 'gay rights'.

When I wrote the Rough Guide I was concerned that suggesting that this was the only academic group might have a harmful knock-on effect on the other groups, in particular the Critical Dissenters, who I believe also put a premium on analysis. To this end I stressed the aesthetic aspect of the Old Grammarians to differentiate them from the rest. I was aware that this group set a high store on academic success, hence, in part, their name. I had tried to imply the academic in the general tone and the use of key figures, but this was evidently insufficient for some of the respondents. Given the evident desire for an academic tone by this group it is possible, therefore, that I should have stressed it more in my initial description. While the Critical Dissenters would not be looking for an emphasis on the academic, it is also possible that the description in their text implied an analytical framework better than the text of the Old Grammarians, in that the Critical Dissenters did not comment at all on the need for more thought or analysis within the description.

Managerial

If the Old Grammarians' comments are characterised by a desire for and use of academic discourse, the Pragmatists rely on what might loosely be described as generic school management and school improvement jargon (see for example Chubb and Moe, 1990, or Sammons, Hillman and Mortimore, 1995). This is not used by respondents outside this group except for D3, a Technician, who while using the term 'new initiative' does so in the context of critisising OFSTED. A4 is the chief exponent of this style. Under the subheading 'combination of some thoughts', A4 speaks of 'group dynamics', 'classroom management'. They wish to 'encourage a range of working situations' and 'develop team work', 'team skills' and the ability to 'evaluate their team'. They want 'professional development', talk of the National Curriculum as 'an exciting challenge', find 'cross-curricular working parties' 'very valuable' and want 'more time to spend analysing exam results etc.'.

While A4 provides the clearest example of this kind of discourse other respondents do hint at it. A2 talks of the need to set in order to 'maximise potential', a common school improvement phrase; while C7 criticises the grammar tests because they do not 'fulfil my criteria for effective, useful assessment'. Perhaps all these respondents are, however, simply reflecting back the language of the text I offered, their phrases echoing mine. Given, however, that such 'management speak' was a key marker of this group, and one that would alienate many in the other groups, it would appear that their absorption of this language has less to do with imitating the text and has more to do with their sympathy for this form of discourse.

Compromising

What is interesting about the Liberals is that their comments do actually challenge the text and do not reflect its language, but they do so in a way that is characteristic of the group. Their comments suggest a desire to compromise. L4, for example, on the section which discusses seeing dialect as an essential part of a pupil's identity, annotates the phrase '*This view sits uneasily with the current model of "correctness" which appears not to value authenticity*' with 'Not necessarily contradictory'.

B1 asks: 'why are these mutually exclusive?' when referring to the comment in the text that these teachers might find '*the content or the message*' as more important than '*style and aesthetic values*'. This respondent also highlights the comparative phrase '*they are less important than*'. Later when looking at the section on writing where I suggest '*They are also likely to value authenticity in the pupils' work over what they might consider "flashy style" or writing that is "too clever by half"*', again B1 highlights the comparative to show disagreement and adds in the margin: 'again these are not exclusive are they?' At other points in the text B1 highlights the words '*more*' and '*than*' in the phrase '*the relationship with the book is more a beneficial friendship than a passion*', and adds in the margin 'both'. And in the phrase '*organise schemes of work around extracts which illustrate an aspect of life, rather than a literary idea*', they agree with the first half of the statement, do not go on to agree with the second half but do disagree with the comparative '*rather*'. Even their comments on management suggest a desire not to rule anything out rather than to endorse bureaucracy: 'accountability, efficiency and good management are important, as are passion, spirit, etc. – being a good English teacher surely doesn't stop you from being organised'. Management systems are converted into a personal attribute with which they can agree.

All other groups modify or qualify my comments but none shows this penchant for compromise. Other groups use phrases like 'not always', 'not necessarily', 'to a degree', 'to a limited extent' or 'only in a minor way'. They add 'possibly but not necessarily', 'not the only reason' or 'yes but it can be done'. They comment also on the tone, 'rather judgmental' and 'too strongly put' but they do not resist the comparisons. Even the phrase 'yes and no', used by an Old Grammarian to comment on the idea that entitlement for pupils lies in access to good teaching not a curriculum, while equivocal, does not have the same ring as 'both'. The phrase 'yes and no' recognises some truth in the statement but wishes to register hesitancy. Only the Liberals seem anxious to avoid the comparisons, desiring compromise instead.

Corrective

While such qualifications do show a desire to resist some of the assumptions made by the text, they are not corrective in tone or content. This is the preserve of the Technicians. We have already considered H2, who 'underlined all that is accurate', adding 'there is nothing here that is actually wrong', but such language is characteristic of many of the respondents within the group. Redolent of Honey (1997) and Phillips (1997), the Technicians' comments, like those of H2, suggest an approach to the subject which emphasises accuracy. L2 describes the 'need to master technical accuracy'; F2 writes 'you can't grade an emotional response to a piece of literature without taking into account the accuracy of the technical aspects'. F6 believes that '"accurate users of English" should be rewarded for their accuracy'.

Linked with this emphasis on accuracy is the notion of acquiring the basics and skills. Again, their language reflects this. F6 talks of teaching 'language skills', though they do add the rider that these should not be 'taught at the expense of literature'. F7 demands that the 'basics of language should be thoroughly grounded' and E4 talks of the 'need to develop higher order skills'.

Theoretical with elements of dissent

Only two respondents outside the Technicians mention the word 'skills' and both refer to teachers rather than the taught. L6, a Pragmatist, writes 'special needs need specialist skills'. I3, a Critical Dissenter, comments 'focus of teaching skills to empower student learning, student focused'. Despite the use of the word 'skills' this response is characteristic of many of those within the Critical Dissenters, referring as it does to some notion of both teaching and learning. C3 talks of the need to 'facilitate learning' and E1 comments that mixed ability teaching is 'the best way of learning'. Several connect this to some form of theoretical model which sometimes connects language and learning. C5 talks of 'application of theory in practice'. G2 writes that there is 'always a theory in place', cites Dollimore/ Sinfield, and notes 'The rise of media and cultural studies . . .' and 'cultural materialism'. They mention Scholes and 'textual theory', and talk of the importance of 'multilingualism'. G1 believes that mixed ability teaching 'provides models for English as an additional language,' while I2 adds that the teacher can use the 'home language as a huge resource in the learning of English – language and literature'.

This use of named writers within the comments echoes the Old Grammarians, though the kind of writers in both cases, one a poet, the other literary theorists, reflects the orientation of the groups. Also similar is the discursive nature of some of their comments, but there are subtle differences. While the Old Grammarians have a slightly more formal feel to their arguments, the Critical Dissenters have a more conversational feel. Their tone of voice echoes more closely the pugnacious or dogmatic style for taking on and winning the argument which Tom Paulin identifies with dissenting prose in his book on Hazlitt, *The Day Star of Liberty* (Paulin, 1998). The rhetorical use of the question mark implies not only a tone of voice but a flourish that is designed to have the last word. Rhetorical questions are not intended to have a response. This is particularly evident in C3, who writes comments like 'so surely they do facilitate learning, not direct it? <u>INCONSISTENCY</u>?', and 'Isn't this giving Cox too much credit?'

It is also evident in E1, who writes on the need to reappraise practice in the light of experience, 'this is an odd way of expressing what should surely be good practice?' However, she also shows the dogmatic tendency in other ways. Commenting on mixed ability teaching she writes 'No – I believe it is the best way of learning'. The tone of J1 combines both these features when he writes of the belief in an entitlement curriculum: 'questionable! "entitled" to get what someone else thinks is good for you! (not entitled to discover your own curriculum etc.)'. While the syntax again suggests a rhetorical question, the use of the exclamation mark helps convey the emphatic tone in which the phrase is to be delivered. The content of the phrase implies the need of the individual to challenge and question received opinion, a sentiment characteristic of the group.

Idiosyncrasies

This desire to question and challenge manifested itself in another more idiosyncratic feature of the Critical Dissenters. (See Table 5 for group idiosyncrasies.) Of all the groups, this one paid the least attention to the detail of how the booklet was to be filled in. Nine out of the seventeen respondents provided no coding on how they had done this. This compares to one of the Old Grammarians, two of the Pragmatists, two of the Liberals and three of the Technicians. Without wishing to push the point too far it does suggest a lack of interest in conforming to the minor procedures.

This contrasts with the idiosyncratic feature of the Pragmatists, who more than any group used a ruler. Whereas not one of the Liberals did this, and there is only one example of ruler use in each of the other groups, four of the Pragmatists – almost half – used one. Again, while not wanting to read too much into this, it is interesting that the group that most prizes organisational features of school life should be the one to make most use of the ruler, suggesting that they are sufficiently organised to have a pencil case to hand.

If the neat pencil case is an outward symbol of organisational prowess and efficiency, the flourish of the red pen symbolises the over-critical teacher. Here again the respondents appear to conform to type. By far the highest percentage of red pen use is found among the Technicians, followed by the Old Grammarians. Whereas three of this latter group of teachers make minor use of the red pen to indicate disagreement, and only one of the Pragmatists and one of the Liberals, ten of the Technicians make copious use of the instrument. Four Critical Dissenters do also use the red pen, in each case to disagree – in no case with more than two points and once only with a word. The effect of the red pen on these pages is, therefore, considerably less dominant than on the pages of the Technicians.

Table 5 Group idiosyncrasies

	OG	P	L	T	CD
No adherence to the instructions for filling in the booklet	1	2	2	3	9
Use of the ruler	1	4	0	1	1
Use of the red pen	3	1	1	10	4
Total of respondents in the group	9	10	6	17	17

Conclusion

There were, of course, shortcomings in the content. I should have made more reference to ICT (information and communications technology) given that this may either be or become a significant feature of English teachers' work. Yet not one of the 62 respondents mentioned ICT in their comments either. Perhaps this omission suggests that they do not, as yet, see it as integral to their teaching, or it may simply mean that they view it as another tool, like a pen, rather than as something to consider in its own right. It may also indicate that attitudes to ICT are less dependent on general philosophies of English teaching and may well be more connected with teachers' own confidence or the school's resources. For that reason in particular I am not sure that I could have nuanced the responses to ICT in the same way as other aspects of English teaching. Clearly the teachers themselves did not believe it to be sufficiently important an oversight to mention it, which probably says as much about their view of ICT as it does mine, even though I used it and still use it extensively in teaching and in my work.

Moreover, as with all surveys, the information dates. At the time I wrote the booklet the grammar tests were the subject of much debate and their implementation seemed likely, hence their inclusion in the text. That possibility appears, for the moment at least, to have receded and to have been replaced by a series of publications on the teaching of grammar (QCA, 1998 and 1999b), along with strategies for improving pupils' writing (QCA, 1999c). The more discursive approach of these documents has been received, albeit tentatively, more favourably by teachers. They have done little, however, to appease the demands of those advocating a return to formal, prescriptive grammar teaching (see for example Phillips, 1998).

Similarly, the Rough Guide was written in the summer before the government's Literacy Strategy (DfEE, 1998) hit staffroom desks. Although this is aimed predominantly at the primary sector, it spawned a debate in the secondary sector about literacy which has reached fruition in the new guidelines for year 7 (DfEE, 2000), along with the literacy test to be taken at the end of that year. Many schools had already implemented literacy policies and appointed post holders before these new measures were introduced. Unlike the ICT element this would, possibly, have been easier to characterise according to the categories I had conceived in the Rough Guide, given that there is evidence that schools have approached the task very differently.

Yet despite these omissions, the content of the guide does appear to allow us to understand the variety of views English teachers hold. By analysing the nuances of their responses, as well as the manner in which they treated the text, different discourses of the subject emerge. In subtle but significant ways the language of description, either their own or their response to mine, enables us to differentiate their positions.

5   The medium and the message

We have come thus far without ever really engaging with what is arguably the most controversial feature of the research – its form. Without wanting to become overly embroiled in what can often be a fraught and on occasion sterile debate it is worth pausing for a moment to consider how research is carried out. For this provides an important context for understanding the genesis of the Rough Guide to English Teachers. Part of my desire to engage in this debate arose out of the community I wanted to survey. In other words, unusually in the field of research methodology, my eventual choice of form was driven by a consideration of the audience that was to receive it.

One of the central dilemmas facing anyone involved in what might loosely be described as attitudinal research is how to get at the information. Two paths have traditionally been open to the researcher – the questionnaire and the interview. Yet, as with so much in the field of education, choosing between these two apparently innocent methods of enquiry can place the researcher firmly in one of two camps – in this instance the quantitative or the qualitative. On the surface the dilemma is easily resolved. The former offers the opportunity for a large-scale survey, while the latter can provide a detailed illuminative study. Indeed, many researchers use both of these for different ends. But this neat solution ignores the politics of these choices. For while the questionnaire has the ring of objectivity, the interview appears to be more prone to the subjective interpretation of the interviewer.

Part of the reason for this perception must lie in the form of the questionnaire. Unlike the interview, the researcher is not present. The variables of human dialogue, such as gesture, intonation, even leading questions, are eradicated. Everyone is apparently asked the same thing in the same way. Such an approach is seen to correspond more closely to science, which has historically been seen to generate 'purer' forms of knowledge and has thus acquired a higher disciplinary status than that of the social sciences. As with science the relationship between the researcher and subject is an impersonal one and such 'scientific' methods protect the findings from the contamination of subjectivity (see Wittig, 1985).

Perhaps as important in understanding why questionnaires are considered more objective, however, is what you can do with the answers once you have been given them. It is possible to write a questionnaire that requires open responses from those filling in the form. These are then coded by the researcher. Yet, more commonly, questionnaire design uses closed responses, such as an agree/disagree metric of scale as developed by Rensis Likert (1931).

The great advantage of this design is that the responses can be number crunched to form what appears to be 'hard' statistical evidence. Despite the old adage 'lies, damned lies and statistics', numbers still seem more reliable, more 'scientific' and less subject to interpretation or misinterpretation than words. The 'hard' data generated through surveys is seen to stand free of either subjectivity or prejudice (O'Connell, Davidson and Layder, 1994). So large-scale surveys have traditionally been seen as generating both superior knowledge and a generalisability unobtainable through small-scale qualitative research. Part of this conflation undoubtedly stems from the seductions of measurement. For many years the academic orthodoxy in relation to empirical research has been 'When you cannot measure it, when you cannot express it in numbers, your knowledge is of a meagre and unsatisfactory kind' (Berelson and Steiner, 1964: 14).

This attitude has irked those in the qualitative research community, who argue that quantative research methods offer only positivist forms of enquiry which are concerned with a search for facts. Indeed, Sayer has been moved to comment that quantitative work constitutes a form of methodological imperialism within the social sciences in which scientism 'uses an absurdly restrictive view of science, usually centring around the search for regularities and hypothesis testing' (Sayer, 1993: 4).

What gets lost, even in this analysis of the limitations of quantitative methods, however, is that not only are mathematical techniques not always applicable, but that the so-called 'scientific' methods themselves may also be subjective. Even though the logic of such methods (and even their language) prescribes both prediction and control (Unger, 1983: 1), quantitative research methods such as questionnaire surveys can be just as messy and subjective as qualitative approaches. For the respondents themselves bring their own subjectivities and prejudices to bear when they fill in the questionnaires, an element often ignored by advocates of this method. Despite, therefore, the assumption that large-scale surveys provide the researcher with unproblematic 'facts', a number of studies have shown otherwise.

Robert Coe (1999) was attempting to discover teachers' attitudes to ALIS, the A level Information System (Fitz-Gibbon, 1996) by using a questionnaire. In particular he wanted to know whether the raw data provided by ALIS was of benefit to teachers or whether they needed additional feedback for it to find it useful. On the surface his analysis of the data appeared to suggest that those who had been given additional feedback were less positive about ALIS than those who were simply working with the raw data. But he also did follow-up interviews with some of the respondents. He goes on to qualify his findings:

> The interpretation of these apparent attitude changes was rendered somewhat problematic by some of the responses given during subsequent interviews. Several people commented on the difficulty of representing a complex attitude on a single numerical scale and also on the changeable nature of their feelings:

> 'It depends on . . . well take today for instance – I'm feeling quite good. I had two really good lessons this morning. Tomorrow, I'll probably have an extremely bad one and feel awfully depressed and give you a different answer. It's sort of patchy.'
>
> (Coe, 1999: 6)

He goes on to cite a number of research studies that demonstrate how the very phrasing of the question alters the way people respond. For example, when asked 'Should divorce in this country be easier to obtain, more difficult to obtain or stay as it is now?' 41 per cent said it should remain the same, 36 per cent felt it should become more difficult and 23 per cent said it should be easier. When the question was phrased 'Should divorce be easier to obtain, stay as it is now or be more difficult to obtain?' 29 per cent wanted to stay with the status quo, 46 per cent wanted it to be more difficult and 25 per cent felt it should be easier (Shuman and Presser, cited in Coe, 1999). Coe also looked at research by Belson (1981) which suggested that respondents routinely misinterpret the choices given to them by standard market research questionnaires.

Work by Diane Reay (Marshall, Reay and Wiliam, 1999) suggests that not only do some respondents simply misinterpret the question, they deliberately distort the data as well. Again, Reay followed up a questionnaire with interviews. During one of these a male Bangladeshi student revealed that he had entered both his parents as having degrees because he believed that any other response to the questionnaire 'would show them up as uneducated and I didn't want any stuck-up academic looking down on them'. Other respondents confessed to equally unpredicatable ways of responding to questionnaires:

> Just tell me what you want me to put down. I hate filling these things in. I just try and work out what they want me to say and put that down so if you tell me it'll save me the bother of having to figure it out.
>
> (Carol, access student, HE project)

> You know they're all lies. People like me just make it all up.
>
> (Patricia, access student, HE project)

In an attempt to overcome the difficulties of interpreting traditional questionnaire responses, Ian Stronach and Maggie MacLure write about devising a 'report and respond' questionnaire which provided respondents with the space for 'emotional colouring-in' (Stronach and MacLure, 1997: 108):

> As the name suggests, the report and respond (R&R) questionnaire was created to combine feedback based on preliminary interview and data analysis (a kind of potted case study) with an invitation to agree or disagree with feedback, as well as add to it.
>
> (ibid.: 104)

They go on to explain how

> The questionnaires were administered after semi-structured interviews had been carried out with a small sample of teachers and headteachers (n = 20). Questions were framed, not as questions *per se*, but as a series of summary statements about the programme.
>
> (ibid.: 104)

Stronach and MacLure also note how it was intended to encourage dialogue 'as a provocation to both summative and formative comment' (ibid.: 105) and that many of the respondents read it in this way. It was also designed to encourage a more 'informal register' (ibid.: 104) as well as a more 'open' response (ibid.: 105). Of the respondents 81 per cent did use the possibility of going beyond the simple agree/disagree part of the rubric.

Despite this, the report and response method does still contain elements of the questionnaire. Although the questions are presented as statements, they are still numbered and can, therefore, appear as isolated and decontextualised. These statements are fragmented around particular aspects of the programme to which respondents are being asked to reply. No holistic picture of the course is being presented. Similarly, although additional response is encouraged, the rubric does ask for a simple agree/disagree response to the whole statement. Although Stronach and MacLure describe the way in which teachers play around with the text within these statements, report-and-response can nevertheless be seen as an attempt simply to broaden the scope of a questionnaire. The format did provoke two teachers to add: 'Just putting in a [tick or cross] is too restrictive' (ibid.: 105).

The Rough Guide

This last observation and the type of attitude it denotes was particularly significant when I began considering how I was going to capture the philosophies of English teachers, and it is to that specific challenge that I now turn. English teachers are not a uniquely problematic group, but their well-documented hostility to certain forms of what they would describe as atomistic forms of assessment (see for example Wiliam, 1995a; Marshall, 1996b; Furlong, 1998) has, as we shall see, many parallels with their attitude towards questionnaires.

I had already used a questionnaire with secondary English teachers, and my urge to find a different form of research arose in part from this experience (Marshall and Brindley, 1998). As an advisory teacher I worked not only with secondary schools, but with the primary sector also. As I worked increasingly in the primary sector I became more and more concerned with issues related to curricular continuity. This concern arose in part, from my growing sense that primary school practice in English differed considerably from that of the secondary sector, and also because I wanted to develop some way of avoiding the secondary schools' perceived need to rely on reading tests as a way of assessing pupils' ability in English on transfer. English departments were being pressurised into administering these tests because their schools, and indeed they themselves, trusted neither the primary teacher assessments nor the key stage 2 test scores (the National Curriculum tests for eleven-year-olds).

Wanting to lend support to teacher assessment, but needing to find a vehicle to make it more reliable and valid, I organised a moderation meeting that was attended by both primary and secondary teachers. This created a dialogue between the two sectors that had not previously existed. I was able to extend and refine this research with funding from SCAA, who were looking for pilot case studies for a forthcoming publication on promoting continuity and progression.

One of the questions with which I had begun the research was whether primary and secondary teachers had different models of English. I wondered if it was this, rather than any essential difference in how these groups assessed, that caused the breakdown in communication between the two phases. Although the research was only tentative, it did confirm this suspicion. When they met to moderate, teachers were able to agree on grades, but the questionnaire that accompanied the research showed very different models of the subject. The secondary sector had an almost exclusively literature-based view of teaching, while the primary sector looked to an approach based either on skills or on creative writing.

What was more relevant, however, to the development of the Rough Guide was the English teachers' attitude to the questionnaire itself. The initial questionnaire was sent to 24 schools, 12 in each phase. While the primary teachers had no difficulty in filling in the questionnaire, the secondary teachers did. Only half responded, and of those six, all filled in the form incorrectly or subverted the questions. In order to ascertain their views of the subject I had asked them to prioritise certain elements of their teaching, first by asking them to rank order them on a scale of 1 to 4, where 1 was the highest, and then by asking them to place these elements, and any others that they might want to add, along a continuum from most to least important.

One respondent had that page missing. Two reversed the rank order. One answered only the rank order question and failed to respond to the continuum. Another changed the word 'rank' to 'rate' and then only ticked two of the options, literature and oracy. Yet another wrote 'meaningless' beside the rank ordering question and placed an exclamation mark in the middle of the continuum. When I extended the survey to a much wider sample a similar pattern emerged. From one LEA, only the primary sector replied. This experience proved formative and encouraged me to find a way, other than the traditional questionnaire, which enabled teachers both to respond more positively and to feel that they were being given an opportunity to express their views.

My own experience with questionnaires is far from unique. Indeed, it is not uncommon for those researching English teachers to begin by apologising for the inadequacies of the questionnaire as a research instrument before presenting their findings. At the start of their influential *Versions of English* Dorothy Barnes, Douglas Barnes and Stephen Clarke feel moved to comment: 'Direct questions are frequently an inappropriate tool for eliciting the deep seated beliefs and principles which govern our actions' (Barnes, Barnes and Clarke, 1984: 40).

Kate Findlay and Andrew Goodwyn express a similar caution. They had used a questionnaire to ascertain whether, based on the Cox models, the views of English teachers had substantially changed in the intervening years since the introduction of the National Curriculum. This research was a follow-up to Goodwyn's original work on the Cox models (Goodwyn, 1992). Introducing their research, they noted that 'The weakness of all surveys is the constraints they place on respondents and some teachers remarked on this difficulty' (Findlay and Goodwyn, 1999: 19). They add by way of passing: 'However we were very struck by the significant number of teachers who added lengthy and detailed comments and who clearly felt some relief in expressing their views and concerns to an interested audience' (ibid.: 19).

Part of the challenge of developing the Rough Guide, therefore, was to find a way of both capturing and representing English teachers' views where, without sounding too McLuhan-like, the medium was part of the message. To this extent one significant element of the research had to be the extent to which English teachers responded not only to the content of the descriptions but also to the form of the Rough Guide.

Debating the form

In the event, only one respondent commented negatively on the form, and even then it was only to suggest bullet points rather than continuous prose. Yet because I had not asked for any comments on the form of the Rough Guide itself, it seemed reasonable to suppose that this element of the research instrument might need further exploration.

One of the schools taking part in the survey had also participated in Kate Findlay and Andrew Goodwyn's research. Although the models of English teaching used by Findlay and Goodwyn were different from my own, both Findlay, Goodwyn and I were asking teachers to contribute to research on their views of the subject. While the differences between the Cox models and those of the Rough Guide should not be underestimated, the main difference between Findlay and Goodwyn's approach and my own was the method by which we chose to collect the data.

It seemed worth asking those who had participated in both surveys what they felt to be the major advantages and disadvantages of the two approaches to data collection, how they responded to the two research instruments as activities, how they engaged with the form. The school was approached by a colleague, as I felt it would be inappropriate to carry out the research myself, believing that it would be harder for the teachers to speak freely about the research instruments if I were conducting the interviews. The department of school L, a shire comprehensive, contained Pragmatists, Liberals and Technicians. The interviewer, who was familiar with my research, chose to use a focus group (Morgan, 1988 and 1995) consisting of three teachers from the English department, including Lawrence, the head of department, and two others. Laura was a young female teacher who was also head of year 7; Lucy had been teaching for six years. (All names are of course pseudonyms.)

There were immediate contrasts in the way in which these teachers responded to the questionnaire and the Rough Guide, which go some way to supporting the form I had chosen. While both are texts of a sort, my aim in creating the Rough Guide was to create a text which had the qualities of a book or booklet, which would allow teachers to respond to it in this form. In other words I wanted them to be able to analyse it and empathise with both its form and content in a way that more closely reflected their subject discipline of reading books. At a superficial level, therefore, it was important that teachers viewed it as a text with which to be engaged. Laura and Lucy responded to the Rough Guide in this way. Lucy comments:

> Once you got started it got . . . It had its own momentum. It drew you in like any good book. It got you going. Then it was interesting because it related so directly to who and what we were. So it was a really interesting read.

Laura adds: 'Having read through it . . . I agree with you . . . it draws you in.' Both Laura's and Lucy's comments on the Rough Guide 'pulling the reader in' are also suggestive of the way in which these teachers view the Rough Guide as a leisure activity, rather like a good book, as opposed to a repetitive administrative chore. That they should view it in this way was also important, as encouraging the pleasure principle in reading is central to English teachers' view of their role (see for example DES and WO, 1989; Barnes, 1998; Wilkes, 1998). Again, Laura found the Rough Guide 'quite entertaining to do' precisely because it was not like work. She adds: 'Because when you sit down at the end of the day and you've got an hour and a half marking to face at least, even at that time of year, to actually have something a bit different to do is pleasurable.'

Lawrence, who twice describes filling in the Rough Guide as 'fun', and also describes the way in which it 'draws you in', contrasts this with the process of filling in a questionnaire.

> You get fatigue with a questionnaire and you've got to number 25 and this particular one goes to 30 and you've made exactly the same repetitive choices each time whether it's one to five and I think even with the best will in the world it's too much. You really need to fill in five at a time and then leave it.

Lucy takes the implications further, beyond whether repetitive questions are pleasurable or not, and suggests 'you don't think about them enough'. Laura replies: 'Yes that . . . It becomes an automatic knee-jerk response.' In other words it does not encourage critical reading. While the aim of this research was to differentiate English teachers' views, and to avoid generalisations about their positions, most teachers would claim to encourage a critical response to reading. The publication *Literacy Is not Enough* (Cox, 1998) – which boasts an eclectic range of authors from Valentine Cunningham and Colin MacCabe through Richard Hoggart and Sven Birketts to representatives of the National Association of the Teaching of English – illustrates the point. All the contributors demand thoughtful or critical readers. While it is not clear that all use the word 'critical' in the same way it is clear that most are using the term to imply some form of active analytical engagement. (Hoggart's use of the phrase 'critical literacy', for example, does not appear entirely to coincide with Freire and Macedo's (1987) use of the term.) All express concern at anything which, they deem, prevents this process.

Such a view is intimately connected, particularly for the NATE contributors to *Literacy Is not Enough*, with their view of assessment activities that either encourage or discourage such approach to texts. I suspected that English teachers' wariness of questionnaires might stem from an anxiety about decontextualised responses (see for example Close, Furlong and Swain, 1997, and NATE, 1998). One of the frequent complaints of English teachers over standardised reading tests is that children are being asked to read decontextualised sentences rather than interpret a whole text (see for example Barrs, 1990). In addition, the format of questionnaires is suggestive of multiple choice questions. Such a form of testing is often attacked by English teachers because it appears to reduce the complexities of an idea to a single statement that is either right or wrong, leaving little room for ambiguity or interpretation (Wiliam, 1995a; Marshall, 1997; Furlong, 1998). Both these, the decontextualisation of sentences and the reductive nature of multiple choice tests, are seen as a bar to encouraging critical readers (Cooper and Davies, 1993).

Lucy's contrast between the Rough Guide and Findlay and Goodwyn's questionnaire echoes these concerns, with the questionnaire demonstrating the shortcomings of reading tests and multiple choice questions, and the Rough Guide promoting more critical reading. For Lucy, the ideas in the Rough Guide are placed in context in a manner that encourages responses to a whole text. She comments: 'It [the Rough Guide] wasn't asking me questions that I had to tick. It felt as if it had been put together as a coherent set of ideas much more than just a single statement about English teaching.' Later she adds:

What I also think is . . . With this you read it through and then you go back to the one you agree with. With the questionnaire you immediately read a sentence and then decide your answer and so you don't get a whole view that will soften how you feel, you know, because you read it all and then you decide.

The process of reading the Rough Guide made her 'think carefully and reflect carefully'. For Laura this reflective activity, which the guide encouraged, is closer to her classroom practice. Comparing her response to the guide with that to the questionnaire, she comments:

It made me think a little bit more. Whereas with the questionnaire, if I'm really pushed for time, I can do it very quickly, and if you want to be bland about it you can tick box 3 in the middle all the time and not put yourself on any side of the fence. Whereas with that [the Rough Guide] you had to think carefully about what was being said and highlight, and that's a skill that we are using all the time in the classroom, you know, analysing what is being said. So I felt it was far more relevant to me.

Like Lucy, Laura contrasts the 'tick-box' approach with that of reflection. What is particularly interesting about this response, quite apart from the misplaced notion that question 3 is always the mid-point in the gradation of a view between 1 and 5, is her view that you do not have to think when filling in a questionnaire. Or, at least, the kind of thought it encourages is different from the sort of analysis of a text which she both seeks to encourage and is willing to practise. Again it is the familiarity of the form – and a form of which she approves – that encourages her not to skimp the reading of the Rough Guide but to give it some thought. It is possible that her sense of the validity of the research instrument may well make the results of her response both more valid and reliable.

Yet the anxiety about the form of questionnaires is not only about a desire to encourage critical reading. It taps into a broader wish to encourage a personal rather than a mechanistic response. In a sense Laura's comment on the repetitive nature of the questionnaire, as opposed to the Rough Guide, hints at this contrast.

This notion, that texts should invite personal response, is pivotal to secondary English teaching (Matthieson, 1975; St John Brooks, 1983; DES and WO, 1989; Davies, 1996). So much so that it has caused some to complain that the 'liberal humanist' position from which it arises 'is so deeply ingrained in so much English teaching . . . that its formulation can be referred to as self evident truths' (Peim, 1990: 25). As we have seen, the origins of this idea can in part be found in the nineteenth-century desire to find an alternative, almost an inoculation against the ravages of industrialism, and the utilitarianism that many believed accompanied it. Making this point in *Culture and Society*, Raymond Williams looks to Thomas Carlyle as the definer of such views. He traces the influence of Carlyle's work – in particular 'Signs of the Times' – on the Coke Town of Dickens' *Hard Times* and Arnold's *Culture and Anarchy*. In the essay 'Signs of the Times', first published in the *Edinburgh Review* in 1829, Carlyle complains that in the 'Mechanical Age' in which he lives, 'Not the external and physical alone is now managed by machinery, but the internal and spiritual also . . . Men are grown mechanical in head and in heart, as well as in hand' (cited in Williams, 1961: 86). He adds: 'To the inward world (if there be any) our only conceivable road is through the outward; that in short, what cannot be investigated and understood mechanically, cannot be investigated and understood at all' (ibid.: 87).

It is indicative of the force such metaphors have had on the thinking of English teachers at the end of the twentieth century that Lawrence, the head of department, can comment on the difference between the Rough Guide and a questionnaire in such similar terms. This teacher appears to eschew the utilitarian and atomistic nature of questionnaires, preferring an approach that is more holistic and human.

> The questionnaire is in some ways quite superficial. You become depersonalised in your answering of it and you think I'll be in one of these groups and everyone will be ticking or crossing. Whereas with this [the Rough Guide] you engage much more with [it] as a profile of a teacher.

He goes on to add:

> You might get a statement in here, in the questionnaire, that was also in the body of this [the Rough Guide]. But because of the layout of the questionnaire it seems far less personal. But when you see the same thing in the guide . . . It appears in this . . . You feel as if you've been undone in some sort of way. As if what you'd always thought about yourself had actually been found out. Whereas with a questionnaire I never feel that.

Although he does not use the terms 'internal' and 'external' Lawrence has a strong sense that mechanical activities are depersonalising. In contrast, reading a whole text can be revelatory about the self. In this way the questionnaire is external, 'superficial'; the Rough Guide gets below the surface to the internal, 'you feel as if you've been undone . . . actually been found out'. Again such views are redolent of English teaching as 'the curriculum's centrally humanising element' (Matthieson, 1975: 80).

In a sense it is the way in which the Rough Guide appears to enable this empathetic response that is the most significant factor in validating both its form and content. These two are also intimately connected when these three teachers describe their approach to the Rough Guide. Importantly for Lucy, the groups in it were not 'stereotyped' but created 'a view we could identify with'. Laura adds later: 'you are almost finding yourself in it'. Both Lucy and Lawrence describe how the Rough Guide captures an 'essence' of what they are doing, of their 'philosophy'.

Linked to this, and as important, is the confirmatory message which the readers sense the Rough Guide confers upon their work. Laura comments: 'It's very good to read something and think, "Yes I do think like that, and that sums up the motivation behind what I'm doing."' Both Laura and Lucy, to this extent, find the Rough Guide 'reassuring'.

It seems, therefore, that part of the appeal of the Rough Guide for these teachers is the positive light in which their views are represented to them. They are clearly flattered and fascinated by the way in which they see themselves portrayed. Although this was to an extent intentional, I admit to being surprised by the extent to which they are prepared to be both affirmed and, in Lawrence's words, 'undone' by the guide. As we have seen, I consciously portrayed each group in a positive light in order to attract teachers' responses. I was also aware of the compelling nature of reading one's own experience represented by another. It is an appeal to vanity. I confess to being mesmerised by Ball's analysis of London English teachers in the 1980s (1987). These teachers admit to a similar sentiment. Lucy confesses: 'It's a sort of self-analysis and I think we're all vain.'

Part of the attraction seems to lie in the entertainment value, the appeal to vanity in comparing one's own response to those of others. The guide acted almost as a piece of gossip that allowed a kind of moral oneupmanship. As Lucy again admits, 'It was quite compelling. It was interesting and I suppose you get drawn in partly out of sheer nosiness you know – "well that's what others think" and "I know who that is".' The transcript notes that all laugh at this point as if to confirm their own similar response.

Lawrence's comments, while on a more serious note, are equally telling:

> It's also quite nice, quite confirming of your own professional skills. Embedded in there is a considerable level of skill and that's quite nice. You don't get the same feeling from the Goodwyn questionnaire, that seems much more, as I said, superficial. With the guide,

you feel there's an analysis, that it's the essence of what you are doing. Even if you don't reflect on it all the time, you are doing it all the time, and that's quite ennobling.

It would seem that while the guide flatters them, the questionnaire, because of its apparent superficiality, gives the impression to the reader that it pays them less attention and so takes their views less seriously.

Yet it is not only the content but the form that conveys this impression. Laura suggests that not only does it not take her views seriously, the questionnaire almost wants to pick a fight. 'There's something quite confrontational about the questionnaire because the statements tend to get your back up as you read them.' Part of her sense of confrontation appears to lie in her dislike of the demand to disagree strongly (it was Laura who wanted to compromise by filling in the middle option in the questionnaire): 'It almost colours the whole questionnaire, I think, because it's right there in the middle of the page and you think, "Oh no I don't agree with that at all."' Part of the appeal of the Rough Guide is that you can 'agree with something in every group. The process is very different with the guide.'

As we have seen, Lucy follows this up by adding: 'With the questionnaire you immediately read a sentence and then decide your answer and so you don't get a whole view that will soften how you feel, you know because you read it all and then you decide.' Again the implication is that the questionnaire demands snap decisions that make the reader feel defensive. Lucy feels that she is being asked to make a judgement without 'a whole view'. Part of her anxiety may arise from Lawrence's perception, expressed earlier in the discussion, that 'most surveys . . . come with an agenda'. In other words, without the 'whole view' her responses may be used in a way that is beyond her control.

Evidently the very layout of the Rough Guide contributed to the way in which these teachers completed it, not simply because it was more familiar, but because it allowed them to feel more in control of the process, less manipulated, and so perhaps taken more seriously. The agenda did not lie elsewhere but was, in a way, transparent. For Lawrence, 'The good thing about this is also that it [the Rough Guide] doesn't come with an agenda, as most surveys do', to which Lucy replies 'Yeah, we know how to analyse their agenda.' Lawrence extends this comment by adding:

> Yes, whereas this one really does seem to just lay it all out for you to choose which suits you. I mean we felt we're asked to fill in lots of questionnaires and really, you know, they are not interested in the results unless they [the results] are clearly what they are angling for.

This brief dialogue betrays much distrust of questionnaires, almost as if they were part of some establishment conspiracy – 'their agenda' and 'they are not interested in the results unless they are clearly what they are angling for'. 'Angling' here connotes both a wheedling manner and a desire to trick the respondent, and suggests that the 'they' of the question-naire are not genuinely engaged with the respondents. 'They' are both anonymous and potentially dismissive. Lucy's response, however, has the resonance of a 1960s radical fighting the system. The stress of the sen-tence falls on 'their agenda'. The drawled 'yeah' at the beginning gives it an added ring of antinomian protest. Interestingly, her comment also betrays a belief in the need for some form of critical literacy. Again it is unclear quite how she might apply such a term, whether it be in Hoggart's (1998) Leavisite manner or with the more overtly political resonance of Freire and Macedo (1987), but at one level her sense is clear. Agendas need to be analysed.

Yet Lucy and Lawrence's exchange also confirms the power of writing the medium to guide the reading. The layout of the Rough Guide invited a different reading (see Kress, 1996). For although of course I did have an agenda the very layout appears to have made it transparent and, therefore, seemingly more acceptable. Nor did any of the teachers ask where I posi-tioned myself. One possible explanation is that the content, as well as the form of the Rough Guide, suggested an insider rather than an impersonal, anonymous and thus mistrusted outsider, and this was more important than any particular position I adopted. The general insider knowledge displayed in the Rough Guide encouraged the reader to believe I was on their side by appearing to be someone, who, according to Lucy, 'knew what they were talking about'. In contrast, she added, 'Often question-naires don't and you don't have specialist knowledge.' Again it may well be the form that conveys this impression, as Kate Findlay and Andrew Goodwyn do share that 'specialist knowledge'.

It may be, however, that they did not attribute the guide to a sole author. Lawrence suggests that the Rough Guide must have been pro-duced by someone who had 'had considerable experience of either the current changes and the battlefield over the last few years,' adding 'I'd be surprised if the people who wrote it had not taught English at all.' There is a hint in Lawrence's reply, in his reference to 'people', and his follow-up question 'Had they taught?' that he believes the Rough Guide to have been written by more than one person. It almost suggests that he thinks that each group was written by someone who espoused that position. This may in part explain his view that the guide has no agenda.

What is interesting about this, however, is that whereas I assumed these teachers knew I had written it, it appears that they were less clear about my role, although my part in the exercise was important. Lawrence later comments:

> We knew Bethan as well, whether that made a difference? She'd been in with us and I'd got the impression that she was, as I'm sure she is, serious about it all. So I was quite happy to say . . . You see I might have filtered a questionnaire out and never given it to the department. I mean there are loads of things that come in that I don't pass on. I'll look at them and just say this is a waste of our time. So maybe partly having known Bethan was important too. And having read it through . . . it clearly seems to know what English teaching is all about.

In a sense this comment confirms my perception that the teachers feel the need to be taken seriously. It suggests, too, that a display of insider knowledge aids this process. In addition my personal contact with the recipients also made the process seem less anonymous. That I considered the survey to be important was enough to prevent it being thrown in the bin. Yet what is curious is that there is no sense that I wrote it. It is unclear from these comments, however, whether or not this would have made a difference; whether this would have encouraged the view that I too had 'an agenda'.

Nevertheless, part of their engagement with the text and their sense that they are being taken seriously appears to arise from the perception that the form of the Rough Guide encourages dialogue. Lucy comments on the descriptions: 'They spoke to you, if that makes sense.' At another part she says: 'I felt when I read it that there were some bits in the one I identified with that I agreed with so much that I wanted to write all over it . . . I wanted to say yes, "Yes, but it's even more like this" and change the text slightly.' It is as if she feels she has something to contribute to the debate, and the form of the Rough Guide, the opportunity to modify the text, enables her to do this.

It is also possible that this sense of being taken seriously and the chance to comment on the text makes the teachers more willing to accept the more negative side of the descriptions, or at least the parts with which they feel least comfortable about identifying. The seriousness of the task makes them more prepared to be honest. Lucy goes some way to describing this process when she comments 'I'd like to be a bit more like that but I know deep down I'm not.' She adds: 'There were shades where you think I ought to be and then you think, "No, I can't fudge it whether I like it or not."' She continues: 'But you think, "No, if I'm honest, that's not me"; and with the one you are you think, "Yes, this is me. This is what I feel." And in that you can't escape the negative . . . It's a sort of self-analysis.'

Throughout this Laura punctuates Lucy's comments with 'Yes' and 'Yes definitely', confirming Lucy's approach. Yet the dialogue is revealing on a number of levels. Clearly, at one level, the notion that the predominantly affirmatory nature of the descriptions helps to offset the more critical implications of the position, works. 'You can't escape the negative.' While on the surface this appears to be personal, to be a kind of 'self-analysis' at another point, the affirmation comes from belonging to a group. The reader is prepared to identify because they are not alone in holding the position. This dialogue is framed by Laura's comments on the benefits of the guide over the questionnaire. She starts: 'You were identifying with other teachers.' Lucy adds: 'You knew their philosophies', and Laura concludes, after Lucy has made her comment on self-analysis, 'and it's also nice to know you fit into a particular group because it makes you realise there are other people like that'. In a sense both are prepared to sign up for one group because they feel that even if it has a down side, they are not alone. In part it lessens the sense of risk, which Lucy confesses to feeling later in the discussion.

> I did get a bit panicky 'cause no one else was the same one as me and then I found out that I was the same one as Lawrence and I felt enormously relieved. I thought Laura might be the same one as me and then she wasn't and I remember thinking, 'Oh no I'm out on a limb here.'

One of the central reasons for keeping the Rough Guide anonymous was to reduce teachers' anxiety that their view was isolated within the department. Even Lucy's misplaced apprehension that she was the same as Laura still enabled her to fill in the guide. What it could not prevent was teachers comparing notes. That they wished to do so, however, is another indication of their engagement with the Rough Guide.

What is less clear is why Lucy and Laura decide they are one group rather than another. One possible interpretation is that they are differentiating between their ideal and their practice. 'I'd like to be a bit more like that but I know deep down that I'm not.' To this extent the guide may be making them confront the kind of differences between their theory and practice that St John Brooks (1983) identified.

Yet at another level it suggests that the Rough Guide has made it possible for these teachers to differentiate their views from the views of others, which was its central aim. What is particularly important for the validation of the research instrument is that, for all the teachers, it includes both those aspects of their philosophy of which they seem proud, and those which they would rather hide. The Rough Guide presents no positive gloss to these teachers, rather it does seem to get to the heart of their identity.

But this is not just about the content of the descriptions. For Laura this is intrinsic to the way in which the Rough Guide was devised. She admits: 'As I read through it . . . that if I agreed with the group I put myself in – and I agreed with a lot of it – a lot of it – I thought, "Oh my god, I don't want to be like that", but I am. I am because that's how views are grouped together.' Lawrence agreed. It is linked to his later comments that the Rough Guide, unlike a questionnaire, 'really does just seem to lay it all out for you to chose which suits you'. More importantly, as we have already seen, for Lawrence, it is the form of the Rough Guide that provokes the quality of response.

Conclusion

Although these teachers are clear in their preferences and although all but three teachers were able to categorise themselves, the Rough Guide does have its limitations. Perhaps the most obvious is the way in which it does not allow you to derive any other information about the respondent other than that which they choose to give. It does not, for example, allow you to derive any sense of the academic background, age or gender of the respondents, nor does it enable you to know whether they have been teaching for long or, indeed, whether English is their main subject. Any one of these might well have been ascertained by the standard questions at the beginning of a questionnaire and may well have given a richer profile of the kinds of teachers that identify with particular groups. I would, for example, have been interested to know if there was a gender bias in the groups or if the length of time people had taught made a difference. It might also be that non-specialist teachers, or teachers who did not train as English teachers but who have nevertheless spent most of their careers teaching it, tended to belong to one group rather than another. Laura, from school L, also noted the potential limitations of the format of the Rough Guide.

> This questionnaire right on the front asks for age and years of teaching and background information, but this one didn't . . . Because I was interested to see if certain groups fit certain ages or certain levels of experience or degrees of seniority because that would be fascinating to know.

My feeling, when omitting these features from the Rough Guide, was that it was important to make its form as different from a questionnaire as possible. As these are standard features, it would have been difficult to include them without in some way undermining this purpose. Given that I was also aware that teachers may resist being categorised, or not wish others to know their views if they differed from the dominant view of the department, I wished to omit all features that might readily identify them to the head of department, who was to collate the booklets before sending them back to me. It is difficult to know to what extent the openness of many of the responses was attributable either to the anonymity of the exercise, or to the form and content. Nevertheless, such information might have been significant in understanding elements of the philosophies of English teachers. It is possible, therefore, that, given the generally favourable response to the Rough Guide, I would include a space for such information were I to use it again.

Despite these shortcomings, however, the Rough Guide to English Teachers appears to have been successful in its aim of eliciting the implicit philosophies of English teachers through a form that reflected the subject discipline. To this extent the form and the content of the Rough Guide are intimately entwined when considering the research instrument. Lawrence's comment, that 'the layout of the questionnaire . . . seems far less personal. But when you see the same thing in the guide . . . it appears in this . . . You feel as if you've been undone', suggests that the form of the Rough Guide enabled the philosophies of English teachers to be disentangled, to be unravelled in a way that a questionnaire would not. Such an observation confirms not only how I chose to delineate them – he feels 'undone' and 'found out' – but the manner in which I presented them – his reaction to a similar statement in the Rough Guide and questionnaire is not the same because the 'layout' of the latter is 'far less personal'.

It appears that the teachers in the focus group from school L felt alienated by the very nature of the questionnaire in a way that they did not by the Rough Guide. As we have seen, this response was in part dictated by the teachers' broad view of their subject: that texts should invite personal response, that questions should not be decontextualised, and that the possibility of critical reading should be promoted. Evidence that all these were possible with the Rough Guide appears to have encouraged them to respond honestly to the descriptions in it. It is also possible that it was their familiarity with such a form and the kind of response that it appeared to encourage, including a dialogue with the text and its author, that made them feel that their views were being taken more seriously. This too may have affected their approach to the quality of response they gave and made them, in turn, treat the exercise more seriously. Certainly they were prepared to complete the Rough Guide more thoroughly even though they perceived it as more time consuming.

It is probable, however, that the form in itself would not have been sufficient for teachers to take the guide seriously. The content had also to resonate with their experience. Here again, the feeling that the Rough Guide had been compiled by an insider, or insiders, appears to have aided the focus group of teachers' treatment of the booklet. More importantly, as with all but three of the 62 teachers who completed the Rough Guide (72 if we include both the teachers and the school that replied after the deadline), they were able to identify with the descriptions and recognise others in them.

This in itself would go a long way towards confirming the content of the research instrument were it not for the added feature of the teachers' annotations. As we have seen, many of the teachers responded in a language that reflected the style in which I had chosen to represent that philosophy. These I identified as academic, managerial, compromising, corrective, and theoretical with elements of dissent. These five types of response echoed my five types of English teacher: Old Grammarians, Pragmatists, Liberals, Technicians and Critical Dissenters. Features of these styles were found only in the comments of those respondents identifying with the corresponding philosophy.

In this way the form, content and language of the Rough Guide all contributed to the central aim of creating a large-scale qualitative research instrument for eliciting the implicit philosophies of English teachers. In the next chapter I will explore a possible application of the Rough Guide.

6 Marking the essay

In chapter 13 of his book *The Empty Raincoat*, Charles Handy quotes what has become known as the Macnamara Fallacy:

> The first step is to measure whatever can be easily measured. This is OK as far as it goes. The second is to disregard that which can't be easily measured or to give it arbitrary quantitative value. This is artificial and misleading. The third step is to presume that what can't be measured easily really isn't important. This is blindness. The fourth step is to say that what can't be easily measured really doesn't exist. This is suicide.
>
> (Handy, 1995: 219)

He summarises: 'What does not get counted does not count.' Given that Handy's subject is economics, he concludes 'Money is easily counted. Therefore all too soon, money becomes the measure of all things. A just society needs a new scorecard.' Now the connection between the Macnamara Fallacy and English teachers may not be immediately apparent but they are intimately connected in that most abstract and yet contentious of educational issues – assessment.

For assessment is possibly the biggest area of conflict between secondary English teachers and government, of whatever political persuasion. This is because, to a greater or lesser extent, politicians, anxious about reliability, have concentrated their attention on those aspects of the subject which are 'easily measured'. English teachers, on the other hand, have focused on the issue of validity and so have looked to ways of assessing that which is *not* 'easily measured'. This has led them to prefer predominantly course-based assessment, the politicians – timed tests. Many English teachers believe, however, that the emphasis of successive governments so distorts what is valuable about the subject that we are fast approaching the suicidal fourth step of the Macnamara Fallacy. For English teachers have claimed that an overemphasis on timed exams is invalid, while politicians have argued that coursework is unreliable.

Perhaps one of the most frequently used justifications for this latter position is the idea that English teachers themselves are not sufficiently agreed on what it means to be good at English. In other words, differing philosophies of the subject affect the way in which teachers assess (see Hayhoe, 1982). Yet work by Dylan Wiliam (1996 and 1998) suggests that this may not be so and that English teachers, while holding different views of the subject, have come to a shared understanding of how to interpret grade boundaries through what he calls 'construct referencing'.

Having established that the Rough Guide was able to capture the philosophies of English teachers, I considered putting the information derived from the survey to use. To this end I decided to find out whether or not teachers' philosophies of their subject made any difference to the way in which they assessed. Before looking, however, at how I used the Rough Guide to contribute to the debate surrounding coursework, it is worth contextualising the nature of the conflict.

The background

As we have seen, the origins of the conflict are intimately connected with the beginnings of the subject. While Arnold acknowledged the need for some form of testing, he clearly saw the dangers of high stakes exams. In some respects, however, his anxieties about testing arose from his conviction that English is an arts subject. And it is this strain of the argument that, until more recently, has predominated. From the beginning of the twentieth century, those arguing for the place of English have always used it as an opportunity to criticise what they saw as the narrowness and formulaic quality of learning encouraged by exams. Holmes, Sampson, even the Newbolt Report, all suggested that timed tests would limit the expression of creativity and response to literature.

But it was only in the 1960s that this desire to find an alternative began to be a practical reality. The Joint Matriculation Board, one of the examination boards, is a useful case study. As early as 1964 it began the first tentative steps towards coursework-based exams by establishing local consortia of ten schools who were willing to participate in the experiment. The scheme was sponsored for the first three years by the Department of Education and Science and, in its last year, by the Schools Council. At this point the new-style exam proved so popular that its scope was extended well beyond the limits of Yorkshire, where it had begun, to include the north-east and local education authorities in the Manchester, Liverpool and Birmingham areas (Rooke and Hewitt, 1970: 8). By 1977 it was introduced nationwide. What had begun as an experiment involving 479 pupils within twelve years included almost 30,000, if the JMB's 16+ exam (which combined O level and CSE), is included in the figures (Smith, 1978: 4). This exponential growth in the use of coursework represents only one board. Alongside the JMB's early experiments came similar work with the AEB (Associated Examining Board) and the introduction of CSE, which used Mode 3, a syllabus devised by the schools. Such moves also accounted for an explosion in the number of candidates being entered for 100 per cent coursework exams.

Three interim reports on the experiment were published by the JMB in 1965, 1967 and 1970. All these reports are clear about the reason for the popularity of such exams. The first argues:

> The lively interest which should be aroused by learning to read and to write English is killed, so it is asserted, by the need to prepare for writing answers to stereotyped questions on GCE language papers.
>
> (Wilson, cited in Hewitt and Gordon, 1965: 1)

While the second in 1967 comments:

> In sum among teachers co-operating with the board in this experiment the opinion is widely held that all the tests normally set in traditional English Language papers go directly counter to what they think is the proper function of teachers in secondary schools, namely 'to encourage the pupil through reading, more and more about himself and the nature of his human and physical environment, and in speech and writing to make statements about relationships that are truly interesting'.
>
> (Petch, 1967: 5)

But it is, perhaps, the comments of a paper, produced in 1978 by the board on course-assessed exams, that are the most telling and most closely echo the language of English teachers over a decade later when the opportunity to assess in this way was denied them. The report notes:

> It is more likely, however, that internal assessment is proposed because of a conviction that it is a more valid way of assessing the attributes or the skills which are involved. Increased validity could result for two reasons: first because the assessment of skills concerned may be difficult or impossible to achieve by external examination and second, because assessment on a single occasion may be a totally inadequate test of a candidate's overall competence.
>
> (Smith, 1978: 5)

Such arguments eventually won the day, and when (nine years later) the then Conservative administration introduced the GCSE, which was to abolish the difference between O level and CSE, coursework was introduced as a major component in most exams. In English the choice was between 100 per cent coursework and 50 per cent coursework. Most took the former option. But its heyday was short lived. At the risk of covering well-worn ground, it is worth briefly recapping some of the key events that we looked at in chapter 2. The wrangles surrounding National Curriculum testing absorbed GCSE into the debate. In June 1991, in an after-dinner speech to the Centre for Policy Studies, John Major effectively undid 25 years of coursework by announcing that any more than 20 per cent coursework in an examination was too much.

As we have seen, it was Kenneth Clarke, then Secretary of State for Education, who announced in November 1991 that the amount of coursework for English was to be reduced to 40 per cent in English and 30 per cent in literature. This announcement coincided with the alterations being made to the testing at key stage 3 for fourteen-year-olds. Replacing the standard assessment tasks, which had been successfully piloted by CATS (Consortium for Assessment and Testing in Schools), were to be short so-called 'pencil and paper' tests. As Mike Baker, the BBC education correspondent, points out in his book *Who Rules Our Schools?* (1994), it was the demise of 100 per cent coursework at GCSE, along with the new ruling on key stage 3, that fuelled the boycott of the tests the following year.

Protest against these moves began almost straight away. It was a Birmingham teacher, Mike Lloyd, who began the Save English Coursework Campaign. He petitioned 4000 schools (almost all the secondary schools in the country), both independent and maintained, and received an 85 per cent return. Of this 85 per cent, 95 per cent wanted no more than 20 per cent timed testing (Lloyd, 1994 and 1997). This was already required by the 100 per cent GCSE, whereby one piece of work was to be examined under controlled conditions in the classroom. As a general election loomed, the NEA (NEA, nd) lent its support to the campaign. Kathleen Tattersall, the chief executive of the JMB, attended a seminar at the beginning of February 1992 organised by Derek Fatchet, then Labour's shadow schools minister, to look into the benefits of coursework. Even the Confederation for British Industry (CBI, nd) was persuaded to lend its voice to the campaign by producing a flier that supported more course-based exams.

But with a Conservative victory, and a new Education Secretary, John Patten, the chances of altering the exam system diminished. John Patten, however, increased the chances of a boycott of the key stage 3 tests. Over the summer, he sacked the Northern Board, the exam agency who had been employed to take over from the CATS consortium, in devising new tests for key stage 3. Instead he employed the University of Cambridge Local Examination Syndicate (UCLES). UCLES had a great deal of experience in writing exams for overseas students, but little if any experience of developing tests in this country. The confusion was compounded when, at the beginning of the school year, Patten announced that certain 'set' texts were to be introduced. Pupils were to be tested the following summer on an anthology, which had yet to be collated, and one of three Shakespeare plays. In addition the test of comprehension was to include multiple choice questions.

Many London English teachers, who were opposed to the tests in principle and were just waiting for an excuse to boycott them, used Patten's mismanagement of the situation to argue against the tests. The real question was whether English teachers were prepared to break their contracts by refusing to administer the tests without the backing of the unions. It relied on what number, what critical mass of schools taking part in the action, would make it impossible for them all to be disciplined. The London Association of Teachers of English had surveyed the country and found that teachers were willing to gamble if 500 other schools joined them. A vote to boycott the tests was carried unanimously at a decisive meeting held in November 1992 at the English and Media Centre in London. This action in effect launched what became known in popular parlance as the SATs boycott, which led to the eventual resignation of John Patten, then Secretary of State for Education.

Dylan Wiliam points out in his essay (1995b) that the argument given by English teachers as the basis of the boycott, myself included, had no legal foundation. We argued that because schools had had no time to buy these texts or to prepare pupils for the new-style test, to take place the following May, they should be piloted as the maths and science tests had been the previous summer. Wiliam points out that the government had no statutory need to pilot these tests in the way the English teachers were suggesting. Yet it gave the campaign a readily understood logic that could be argued for in the media. It is a measure of the success of this strategy that Melanie Phillips, then writing for the *Guardian* and not noted for her sympathy with English teachers, supported the call for the 1993 tests to be run as a pilot (Phillips, 1993). The irony is that if the government had acquiesced to our demands it would almost certainly have been the end of the boycott.

The teacher unions did not join the campaign until some months later, and it was only in the Easter of 1993 that English teachers, now with the rest of the profession, had official backing. Paul Cooper and Chris Davies'

(1993) research, undertaken at the time of the boycott, indicates the uncertainty felt by many English teachers during this period. It shows a picture of many teachers torn between their opposition to the tests and their desire not to let the pupils down by failing to prepare them for an exam they may be forced to take.

The researchers point to the way in which the eventual union action brought by the National Association of Schoolmasters and Union of Women Teachers – which was shortly followed by all the other major unions – helped resolve this dilemma. But the objections to the tests are significant, in particular because teachers felt that teaching to the test altered their teaching. Most of the teachers surveyed viewed the effect as negative, 'A more didactic approach/More time spent on "bitesize" (superficial) responses to literature (implying a "right" answer)/Less time to develop individual responses' (Cooper and Davies, 1993: 566).

These responses echo those collated by the London Association for the Teaching of English. The first *Voices from the Classroom* was published in the first year of the boycott and arose from the comments added by teachers, from all over the country, when they were surveyed to see if they would take action. They indicate the passionate aversion to the tests that eventually led to the boycott. One head of English writes: 'KS3 English assessment arrangements and procedures for 1993 are the most dreadful things I have encountered in 33 years of teaching' (LATE, 1993: 11). Another lends Arnoldian weight to his argument: 'I've been teaching for 19 years and love the job but this latest development makes me so ANGRY at the Philistines who are mismanaging education' (ibid.: 9).

The second report, *The Real Cost of SATs*, was published in 1995, after the first year of SATs, and again the perceived affect on their teaching is evident.

> The SATs have a negative influence on the curriculum because they narrow and limit what can be done. They tend to eliminate creativity and imagination in both the teachers and the student. Instead we are told what to do, what play to read, and what scenes will be examined.
>
> (LATE, 1995: 31)

These anecdotal accounts are supported in a survey of secondary English, maths and science teachers carried out by the NUT in the summer of 1995 (Close, Furlong and Simon, 1995). The survey asked to what extent they felt the tests had altered their practice, and also to what extent they used past papers. By far the highest number to believe that their practice was being affected were English teachers. Instead of being able to encourage a wide range of responses to a text, they felt that the potential for variety posed a threat that needed to be circumscribed by close attention to the likeliest answers.

The research carried out by the Association of Teachers and Lecturers (ATL, 1996) published the following year found that nearly three quarters of English teachers felt they had been 'teaching to the test more than was reasonable' (ibid.: 16), as opposed to just over a quarter of maths teachers and almost a fifth of science teachers. In fact the figures also show that while English teachers had become increasingly frustrated with the distorting effect of the tests, science and maths teachers were accommodating more easily. The figure of dissatisfaction for English teachers stood at just over half, compared with over around two fifths of maths teachers and a fifth of science teachers. Nearly 80 per cent of English teachers felt that 'the tests [had] narrowed the curriculum' (ibid.: 12).

The criticisms and cures

The JMB

The comments of English teachers in this chapter illustrate the way in which their views of assessment are intimately bound up with a general philosophy of the subject. What these comments do not answer is the extent to which the nuanced variety in English teachers' philosophy of the subject affects the way they assess. This question fuels one of the chief objections to 100 per cent coursework, which is its perceived subjectivity. The potential criticisms of course-based exams are to be found in the very first interim report published by the JMB. In the preface, Wilson, then chairman of the board and of the standing committee on research, points to the dilemmas that have plagued discussion of coursework ever since:

> But if each teacher is to be free to teach his pupils without regard to traditional examination syllabuses and question papers, how can the examining board, whose *testamur* at the end of the course is required, be assured those pupils have benefited from this untrammelled teaching and learning to an extent which merits an O level pass in English?
>
> (Hewitt and Gordon, 1965: 1)

In essence Wilson is asking how the board can ensure standards are maintained when teachers control both the content of the syllabus and its marking. As Wiliam (1996) points out, the question of standards, particularly those surrounding public examinations, are fraught with controversy. Yet what particularly concerns those anxious about 100 per cent coursework is the lack of objectivity that may accompany it. This anxiety is often expressed in a fear about falling standards.

As Petch (1967) argues, in the second interim report, the coursework exam had to

> devise means of making school assessments which could be endorsed by the board as indicating that by the end of their Fifth form course pupils had achieved not less than O-level pass standard in their writing and understanding of English.
>
> (ibid.: 3)

By contrast, in 'the traditional examination of two and a half hours' with 'certain particular skills . . . it is generally thought to be possible to test them satisfactorily and with some degree of objectivity' (ibid.: 4). But the teachers objected to this type of test because it gave these skills 'a position of inordinate importance' (ibid.: 4).

The early scheme showed the difficulties inherent in the approach. In the final paragraph of the first interim report, Hewitt and Gordon confess,

> It must be admitted, however, that variations from school to school in standards of marking have not been countered in a way that affords complete satisfaction, and that these variations present an exceedingly difficult problem.
>
> (Hewitt and Gordon, 1965: 10)

The JMB sought to combat some of these criticisms by experimenting with ways of ensuring consistency of marking among the teachers involved. In this first account of the processes we see the beginnings of a system that is now employed by almost three quarters of the schools in England and Wales. What they instituted was a system of trial marking, now known as standardisation materials, in which teachers marked candidates' work blind and fed the grades back to the board. In addition, they located moderators by using the trial marking scores to find the most consistently accurate. As the 1978 report indicates, the process 'was gradually modified over the years' (Smith, 1978: 4) but the principle of trial marking and moderation remained the same and, as Smith points out, it was adopted by other boards and CSE examinations.

By this time the moderation procedures were elaborate. They are worth noting in full, as the results of the procedures are potentially significant in understanding the process by which English teachers assess. The JMB and its successor, the Northern Examinations and Assessment Board (NEAB), demanded that all teachers with examination classes had to assess, bi-annually, trial marking material, consisting of folders of work of candidates from the previous year. To ensure the reliability of these judgements a rigorous system of checks and double checks was introduced. All candidates were marked both by their own teacher and another member of department. Where there was any disagreement, or when the candidate was on the borderline between two grades, their folder was submitted for scrutiny by the whole department.

The whole school entry was then moderated to ensure that the candidates' work was placed in the correct rank order, from grade A to U, before sending them to the exam board. Here the work was moderated by a member of the Review Panel. This was made up of practising teachers, who had been chosen through the trial marking for the accuracy of their assessments. All Review Panel members worked with partners. When one panel member moderated a school's entry, the other checked their judgement. The Review Panel members had the power to alter a school's grades, either up or down, if they felt that they had placed more than 50 per cent of the candidates on the wrong grade. Hence a C could become a D or a B an A. (The rank order of individual candidates could be changed only when the Review Panel members felt that an individual candidate had been wrongly graded by at least two complete grades.) The work of the vast majority of candidates was, therefore, read by at least five different English teachers before a final grade was awarded. One final check was built into the system. A sample of the cohort was sent to an Inter School Assessor. This teacher marked the entry blind and then sent their grades to the Review Panel. Again if there was any serious discrepancy between the assessors' grades and the school's, the panel members would moderate the school's entry.

The exam boards returned all coursework to the schools, after they had been externally moderated, with comments both on any adjustments that had been made and on the quality of the work. In this way a national network began to develop where the teachers were firmly in charge, but learning constantly from the dialogues that were created by the process.

James Britton

While the JMB and other exam boards were experimenting with course-based exams, in the 1960s James Britton at the Institute of Education in London was also considering ways of increasing the validity and reliability of the assessment of written English. In research funded by the Schools Council he looked at what later became known as double impression marking. The results of his early pilot studies were included in the Lockwood Committee (DES, 1964), which was set up to investigate the

O level examination. Writing in 1989 he summarises the research by saying: 'The upshot of the experiment was to indicate that parcelling out scripts to examiners is a considerably less reliable process than parcelling them out to teams of three rapid impression markers' (Britton and Martin, 1989: 2). They also found it more accurate than the traditional 'very careful analytic marking system' (ibid.: 2–3).

Construct referencing

Britton's research begs an important question, however. For while it worked it did not explain where the 'impression' came from. This is where the work of Dylan Wiliam is particularly helpful. In a conference paper (Wiliam, 1998) he points out that the two main classical forms of assessment, norm referencing and criterion referencing, have not sufficiently explained what teachers actually do. He argues that their day-to-day practice is much closer to what he describes as 'construct referencing'. (see also Wiliam, 1994 and 1996)

Part of his argument rests on the contention that the validity of the assessment of a pupil's ability lies less in the nature of the task and more in the interpretation of the evidence arising. Coursework-based assessments are often open to criticism because the range of evidence to be assessed may vary considerably. Anxiety about assessing that range, and still ensuring that the standard remains the same, lies behind the comments made by Hewitt and Gordon in 1965. Wiliam, however, refers to such assessments as 'authentic' because they are less prone to teaching-to-the-test and the kind of hoop jumping that we have seen English teachers so object to. Hayhoe (1982) points to the way in which the question of reliability and validity are intimately connected among English practitioners. To this extent course-based assessments ensure the validity of the domain being assessed and avoid the narrowing of concentration on those elements of the subject which are easily examinable in timed test form.

The question that then arises is how to arrive at some kind of uniformity of interpretation of the evidence to ensure that the assessment made of the performance is both valid and reliable. Britton's evidence seemed to indicate that impression marking was reliable. Wiliam's notion of 'construct referencing' reinforces this reliability and helps us to understand its contribution to the validity of the assessment also. To illustrate his notion of 'construct referencing' he turns to English teachers in England and Wales. He explains:

> The innovative feature of such assessment is that no attempt is made to prescribe learning outcomes. In that it is defined at all, it is defined

simply as the consensus of the teachers making the assessments. The assessment is not objective, in that there are no objective criteria for a student to satisfy . . . the assessment system relies on the existence of a construct (of what it means to be competent in a particular domain) being shared by a community of interpreters.

(Wiliam, 1998: 6)

Wiliam argues that the procedures instituted by the examination boards may go some of the way to explaining how that community of interpreters arises. As early as 1970 Rooke and Hewitt note (1970: 14): 'Experience has shown that it is essential for groups to meet together to discuss the results of trial marking and procedures for assessment.' They go on to recommend that, on the extension of the scheme, 'Provision must therefore be made for groups to meet for discussion' (ibid.).

Trial marking, along with the network of local consortia, meant that teachers were engaged in a constant debate, with other practitioners from a variety of different schools, about levels of achievement in pupils' work. In this way a professional discourse began to emerge. The annual moderation of candidates' folders meant that lessons learned in the abstract, through trial marking, were applied to the pupils in the teacher's own school. What had emerged from the apparently mundane activity of marking was a shared meaning among a community of interpreters.

Neither norm referencing, nor criterion referencing in its strictest sense, construct referencing has elements of both and something else besides. It took a notion that English teachers had always understood – impression marking – one stage further. In essence, when English teachers award a grade to a piece of work, or a folder, they are using a construct of what they think that grade looks like, based on their previous encounters with work of a similar standard. While not referring to 'construct referencing' Protherough, Atkinson and Fawcett (1989) describe this process, concluding 'In the end, grade descriptions for English have to be matters of judgement and not of objective fact, and developing this judgement is one of the skills that young English teachers have to acquire' (ibid.: 31).

Wiliam argues that teachers' understanding of that construct has been honed by considering and discussing borderline cases. Deciding the characteristics of a bird is better done by asking why a bat is not a bird rather than why a cow is not. Anyone who has done trial marking will know that it becomes easy to spot the C/D borderlines; the question that always has to be answered is which grade it is. Such a decision has to be made collectively by the department and then at local level, and so the community of interpreters emerges. Although there is an inherent danger that such a community may also become conservative in its judgements, it is nevertheless more flexible and open to modification than one which is centrally and bureaucratically imposed (see Mabry, 1999, for a discussion on the limits of such a system).

The research

The design

This then is the background to the research question I wished to pose. How robust was the construct that teachers used? Or, to put it another way, was the construct likely to be influenced by the teachers' philosophy of the subject? Having validated the Rough Guide as a research instrument I used this as my indicator of teachers' subject philosophies. My next problem was to find a way of seeing how they assessed. To this end I turned once more to the Northern Board. Since the introduction of the latest GCSE syllabus in 1996, the NEAB has became the largest single examiner of GCSE English and English literature, its share of the market being just under 75 per cent.

This being so it was likely that a high percentage of the schools I had used in my original survey would use the NEAB syllabus and thus its standardisation materials. If they did, this would allow me to correlate teachers' philosophies against the grades that they award the candidates in the standardising materials. To this end I decided to use all twenty schools, on the basis that some of those who had not returned the original Rough Guides might still have copies and be able to use them before sending me their grades.

Until recently, teachers assessed these papers using grades alone, using a three-point scale within any given grade. Candidates could, for example receive a + or − on any grade as well as the grade score itself, resulting in a 27-point scale for the entire range from U to A*. From the 1997 standardisation meetings onwards, each point on the previous scale has been subdivided in two, resulting in a 54-point scale, summarised in Table 6.

My experience of this kind of marking led me to believe that teachers still preferred to think in terms of literal grades, even if they subsequently turned them into numerical marks. Indeed, my sense was that the construct was in part formed through an understanding of what a particular grade looked like and that the sense of the grade governed the mark awarded.

The standardisation materials required that teachers assessed the work of four candidates. Each candidate had five pieces of work. Three of these pieces of work were to be assessed for EN2 (reading), including a wider reading assignment, a media assignment and a Shakespeare assignment;

Table 6 The relationship of points to GCSE grades

Grade	U	G	F	E	D	C	B	A	A*
Points range	1–6	7–12	13–18	19–24	25–30	31–36	37–42	43–48	49–54

two for EN3 (writing), including an original piece of writing and the media assignment. English literature was also assessed through the Shakespeare assignment, the wider reading assignment and an assignment on twentieth-century drama. The EN2 and EN3 marks would eventually be combined to give an overall grade for English. For literature, teachers were asked to give an additional mark out of three for spelling, punctuation and grammar. Each teacher has to award their own marks. A school grade is arrived at by a standardisation meeting, usually held after school. The school grades are then submitted to the board at a local consortium meeting.

I contacted all the schools involved in the original survey and asked them to send me both the subject philosophy of each teacher and the grades they had awarded each candidate. This gave me all the scores in numerical form for EN2, EN3, literature and spelling, punctuation and grammar, along with the subject philosophy.

My sense, however, that this was not how teachers actually approached the task of grading, was borne out by the second strand of this research. I was also interested in finding out how teachers talked about what they were doing; if there was any indication, in the way in which they discussed the candidates' work, to suggest that they were using constructs of grades rather than the criteria set out by the board at the beginning of the standardisation materials.

To this end I attended two school-based standardising meetings, one at school C and the other at school E, as well as a consortium meeting, which included a representative from school E. As we have seen, both these schools had a spread of different kinds of teachers: the only kind of teacher who was unrepresented in either school was an Old Grammarian. I used a tape recorder as well as taking notes in school C and at the consortium meeting. In school E I only took notes, as one of the members of department objected to being recorded. Three main issues arose from these meetings, all of which could and should be developed in further research.

The first was the way in which they were having difficulties in adjusting to the new assessment system. The new syllabus had been introduced in 1996 to reflect the changes to the National Curriculum. Changes had already been made to the assessment system in 1993 to reduce the amount of coursework. The 1996 syllabus was, then, the third incarnation of

GCSE English in nine years, two of the changes having been made in the last three.

All the teachers involved, however, felt that this latest version was by far the most exacting in the way it demanded certain criteria should be met. The experienced head of department in school C confessed at the start of the meeting that she had 'never looked at the criteria so closely'. Later, however, the department discussed the extent to which work set should be manufactured to match the exam criteria. This prompted several comments. The former head of department, now a senior teacher, complained that the criteria were 'stupid'. The deputy head, also a member of the department and an experienced NEAB moderator, in a manner redolent of those teachers that the JMB research cited, believed that to arrange assignments around the exam criteria would 'distort teaching'. The senior teacher replied that it 'already was'. She believed that they were 'forcing' her to teach in a particular way.

Problems with the criteria appear like a leitmotif throughout the discussions in both schools. Nevertheless, teachers do refer to them in order to support their judgements. The most typical pattern involves one teacher reading aloud a section of a candidate's work and then referring to the criteria to which they think this applies. These interjections are, however, frequently countermanded by another teacher repeating the process with another piece of text and the relevant criterion to refute the first teacher's assertion. To this extent these discussions are clear evidence of the way in which, as Wiliam's (1998) paper suggests, it is the interpretation of evidence that is crucial rather than the criterion descriptors themselves. It is also a possible explanation of why Britton and Martin (1989) found that simply furnishing examiners with mark schemes was a less than satisfactory way of ensuring reliability.

A similar process was witnessed at the consortium meeting, but these meetings have an additional function. They act, in part, as a forum for schools to raise anxieties about the assessment procedures; these, in turn, are fed back to the board. While the comments of the consortium convenor are not representative of the board's own position, the convenor, as an experienced and serving moderator, is there to guide teachers through the whole process. Their comments are, therefore, likely to indicate how many of the board's moderators are interpreting the procedures. So this convenor's comments provide an interesting glimpse of the way in which moderators view the criteria.

Arguments were raised over the awarding of an A* to candidate 1. The convenor agreed that the criteria for this award were 'nebulous'. Later he encouraged them not to 'get bogged down in looking at the assessment criteria', adding 'Just look what they've done. Don't use a check list to see what they haven't done.' One of the most contentious issues was to the extent to which candidates were to be penalised for failing to meet the 'social and historical context' requirement in the wider reading assignment. Because it was the first year teachers had entered candidates for this exam, there was a reluctance to take risks. The convenor, however, was quite clear: 'Moderators won't be bogged down in criteria.'

What was more interesting, however, was how both he and certain members of the meeting attempted to encourage people to take risks, and it was this debate that provided the clearest evidence of Wiliam's 'construct referencing' (see Wiliam, 1994, 1996 and 1998). An exchange between the convenor and an experienced female head of English is particularly revealing.

Convenor: Candidate 4 doesn't comment at all on the socio-historical . . . but I instinctively know what it is and adjusted the marks accordingly. This screams D.

Pam: Have you felt more dominated by the criteria, though, because we do mark subjectively . . . and we've done it by years of experience.

Convenor: Yes, I take Harry's [another teacher present] point, we are being asked to mark differently now.

Pam: Should we penalise the candidate if they are not fulfilling the criteria?

Convenor: No, I think we give leeway . . . This candidate screams D.

Several things are interesting in this exchange. The first is the way in which both speakers acknowledge the subjectivity of their response as being a better way of validating the assessment. The convenor knows the grade 'instinctively', the teacher says she marks 'subjectively'. According to the teacher her confidence in this approach has arisen from 'years of experience'. More importantly, the convenor encourages this subjective sense of the value of the work as a better way of awarding the grade than the criteria. It 'screams D'. On this basis he is prepared not only to 'give leeway' but to 'adjust the marks accordingly'. In this way he is encouraging the teacher to trust her instincts rather than the criteria and to subordinate the criteria to the grade 'construct'. To this extent the convenor is suggesting that only the use of the construct will provide a valid assessment of the pupil's work.

Another head of department (George) also complained that the new system was taking him away from the method of assessment he understood. This prompted an exchange with two other teachers and the convenor. Again, discussing candidate 4, the convenor comments:

Convenor:	If you get bogged down in looking at the assessment criteria, just read what they've done. Don't use it as a check list to see what they haven't done.
George:	I had an understanding of what a D was. I've marked scripts. But I simply don't see it . . . The only way we can do it is to relate it to the criteria.
Harry:	An historical note. In the past the people who were looking to reward 'making meanings' came out on top and we all internalised those judgements. At the moment some people are running scared. We should stick to our judgements . . . Where our hunch is we should stick to it. Stick to the old system if you're experienced.
Convenor:	because moderators won't be bogged down in criteria . . . surely you're not suggesting tick-boxes.
Harry:	Schools are going this way and it's a mistake.
Mary:	This is a political exercise and we're not playing by the rules of the game . . .
Convenor:	It is a game but we will overcome.

And that was how the meeting ended. Several issues arise from this exchange. Again the use of the construct is clear. George 'had an understanding of what a D was'. Harry talks of the way in which they have 'internalised judgements' and tells teachers to 'stick to our judgements' and to trust 'our hunch'. The convenor claims 'Moderators won't be bogged down in criteria'. He contrasts this method with 'tick-boxes', adding emphasis to his comments with the disdainful 'surely you're not . . .'. Again, also, an assumption is made that construct referencing will allow for more valid assessments, but this time the validity lies in the type of work to be assessed rather than in a judgement of the pupil's performance. Harry was looking to reward ' "making meanings" '.

What is as interesting, however, is how they view their use of the construct as transgressive, an act of defiance against a growing orthodoxy which they are desirous to resist. While all the teachers feel they are being pushed by the exam criteria into making certain decisions, they see this as something to be resisted. Mary identifies this struggle as 'a political exercise' and that she is not 'playing by the rules of the game'. Harry believes that people who comply are 'running scared', and the convenor wraps up the meeting in the language of 1960s rebellion: 'It is a game but we will overcome.' Only George, the least experienced of the teachers, seems more reluctant to fight but even he proffers his comments in the spirit of annoyance at the constraints of the new system.

Perhaps this exchange is as much a manifestation of English teachers' perception that their methods are different and better than anyone else's (see Matthieson, 1975 and Protherough and Atkinson, 1991) as it is of Woods, Jeffrey, Troman and Boyle's (1997) observation on the 'constraints' teachers feel. But the way they use 'construct referencing' to articulate their frustration makes it particularly interesting. While I do not know the view of English taken by the convenor, Harry, George and Mary were Critical Dissenters. This clearly affects the way in which they choose to interpret the intention of the changes being made, but an understanding of the construct is not confined to these three. For what is important is that they use 'construct referencing' as part of their appeal to the rest of the group at the consortium meeting, many of whom are not Critical Dissenters, precisely because they believe it to be generally understood. That 'construct referencing' is understood and practised beyond the Critical Dissenters is evident in the first exchange between the convenor, whose view is unknown, and Pam, who is not a Critical Dissenter.

The results

The question still remained, however, as to the extent to which the construct withstood the interpretation of the subject philosophies. In order to investigate this, the teachers' scores (on the 1–54 scale) were entered onto a computer and analysed using the DataDesk statistics software package. The data therefore consisted of a record, for each of the teachers, of their scores for En2, En3, Literature and SPG for each of the four candidates, together with the teachers' subject philosophy. A composite scale for English was then constructed by adding the En2 and En3 scores; this composite scale and the Literature scores were then analysed to see whether there were any significant differences in the scores given by teachers with different subject philosophies.

As would be expected, the differences in the scores allocated to the different candidates were significant ($p < 0.001$), and there were significant differences between teachers, some being more lenient than others ($p < 0.001$). However, there were no statistically significant differences between schools nor between subject philosophies for the scoring of either Literature or English. In other words a teacher's philosophy of the subject does not influence the way in which she or he assesses.

Conclusion

These findings, along with the evidence from the standardising meetings, would appear to support Dylan Wiliam's assertion that English teachers not only use 'construct referencing' as a means of assessing pupils' work but that this method is both valid and reliable. Clearly their predisposition to this form of assessment is intimately connected with a general and historical view of the subject, which is to a large extent shared by the majority of English teachers. In a somewhat circular fashion this view of the subject appears to lead them to want a form of assessment which mirrors it – that of a subjective impression given meaning by a community of interpreters.

This work urgently needs further research if the persistent call of English teachers to change the current forms of examining pupils is to be heard. For their desire has always looked feebly subjective beside those who have argued for the apparent rigour that objectivity affords. Even the language in which English teachers have described the process by which they assess – impression marking – has seemed wiffling and insubstantial, the educational equivalent of floaty dresses and crystals against the scientific rigour of cloze procedures and tightly controlled mark schemes.

At present these results are not generalisable but they do point very clearly to a language and theory that English teachers might employ to lend rigour to their argument. Were further research to be undertaken, again using the Rough Guide and standardising materials, English teachers would have objective evidence that their subjective means of assessing works. Whether this in itself would be enough to persuade policy makers of the virtue of the English teachers' case is hard to determine, but it would make their cause that much harder to refute.

Conclusion

The process of writing this book has had much in common with that of a first person narrative. While the parallels are imprecise they act as a useful metaphor for the relationship I have with the material described and the characters involved. Nick Carraway, the narrator in Fitzgerald's *The Great Gatsby*, best illustrates the point. At one point in his tale Carraway describes his position as being both 'within and without' (Fitzgerald, 1991: 40). While he elaborates on the ambivalence of his perspective by confessing that he was 'simultaneously enchanted and repelled by the inexhaustible variety of life' (ibid.: 40) it is the way he locates himself within the narrative that provides both his strength and weakness as a commentator on the events he describes.

He is not an unreliable narrator as such, merely one whose critical gaze has become enmeshed in the story he seeks to explore and explain. His own part cannot be neatly extricated from the characters involved. Yet as the tragedy unfolds he has a distance from events that all the other players lack. This outsider perspective arises partly from his social position and partly because he has deliberately chosen the role of observer. 'I'm inclined to reserve all judgements' (ibid.: 5), he confesses at the beginning of the story. At the end, however, when he begins truly to see what has happened, to see Jay Gatz and Daisy Buchanan for who they really are, he uses his insider knowledge, their common heritage – they are all midwesterners – to interpret and understand events. He writes: 'I see now that this has been a story of the Wes, after all – Tom and Gatsby, Daisy and Jordan and I, were all Westerners, and perhaps we shared some deficiency in common which made us subtly unadaptable to Eastern life' (ibid.: 184).

But this perspective, that of one who is both within and without, does not only come from his part in the events. In the best ethnographic tradition he can only see what has happened because the sojourn of all these midwestern characters on the east coast has made the familiar strange (see Todorov, 1988). The compulsion of the narrative is in part dependent on the complex interplay between the insider and outsider roles Carraway inhabits. Even though it is only ever Carraway's point of view, for his account to ring true the insider's account has to have an outsider's perspective and vice versa. The one is symbiotically dependent on the other.

The same is true of this research. Undoubtedly the content and form of the Rough Guide arose from my experience of working both with English teachers and as one myself. To this extent it has been very much an insider's account. Without this perspective I doubt very much whether my attempt to develop a research instrument to capture the philosophies of English teachers would have emerged in the manner in which it did.

Although it went through several stages of refinement, the final form of the Rough Guide emerged at the point when, fairly early on in the process, I was asked how I would validate the English subject philosophies I had identified. The idea of presenting it as a close reading exercise of sorts came directly out of my experience as an English teacher. It was an activity which I had often used and practised. But the relationship between the form and content of the Rough Guide and my experience as an English teacher worked at a more instinctive level. Before I ever faced the question of developing a research instrument I knew and shared English teachers' misgivings about tick-boxes and the suspicion of anything that smacked of the reductive nature of the psychometric. To produce something that resembled such a test went against the grain, and these two processes were at work when I began to develop a means of validating the philosophies I had identified.

But another element also played a part and this, too, was connected with my perception of the subject discipline: the notion of considering audience response, of questioning the way in which the form of the survey might affect its reception. Both experience and instinct told me that I was unlikely to get at English teachers' philosophies unless I developed an audience-sensitive research instrument. In order to work the measuring stick had to be as much a product of what was measured as a means of measuring it.

Yet this research has not simply been the account of an insider and, therefore, an unreliable narrator of sorts. For although I am part of the English teaching community my own subject philosophy is not shared by all those who teach English. As with Nick Carraway, the narrative has been constructed by someone who has been a participant in the story told and yet separate from it. It too has been written by one who is both 'within and without'. But it is not only that I describe the Old Grammarians, for example, or the Technicians, from an outsider's perspective. I was an English teacher but now work in a university department. For the last nine years I have had the leisure of one removed from the hurly burly of the classroom and have been able to observe others' reactions to events as they unfold, and to frame this in the light of the subject's contested history. The benefits of this critical distance cannot be underestimated in the construction of the Rough Guide. Both the job and the events of the 1990s have made me stand back and ask questions about where I and others are coming from in relationship to the subject known as English. And, as I suggested in the introduction, part of the process of writing this book has been to unravel or disentangle these competing views from each other and from my own position.

But before we move on to consider what we have learned about English teachers, one last point about the methodology chosen to capture their views is worth making. Many of the arguments that revolve around the validity and reliability of educational research are not dissimilar to those to that rage over assessment. As we have seen, these too involve debates about objectivity and subjectivity, which are often crudely linked with quantitative and qualitative research respectively, the timed exam and coursework equivalents of the research world. Chris Woodhead's attacks on the research establishment, for example (see Woodhead, 1998 and 1999), almost always entail some form of accusation about the political bias of the latter while extolling the virtues of the former.

My own desire to problematise such perceptions almost certainly arises from my position both 'within and without' the research community. For, as I suggested in the introduction, this research has been about what happens when you mix disciplines; about the processes involved when you ask someone with an English degree to undertake research in the social sciences. Just as this research has begun to suggest that teachers' subjective responses may well be a more reliable way of achieving a valid assessment of a pupil's achievement, so the Rough Guide, as a research instrument, has problematised the simple equation about the reliability and validity of certain forms of data collection. Although the findings are only indicative, they do appear to suggest that it is not enough to assume that an apparently objective form, that of the questionnaire, will elicit objective evidence. The teachers in the focus group, in particular, found such an instrument alienating. This in turn led at least one of them to complete Findlay and Goodwyn's questionnaire in a manner which was likely to distort the results, namely by filling in nothing but the middle option. Such findings need to be the beginning of a debate about other ways of eliciting the views of those involved in education and about breaking down some of the rigid divides that people perceive between quantitative and qualitative research.

There are of course many shortcomings to the Rough Guide. In its current form it tells us nothing of the gender, experience or educational background of the respondents, information that would undoubtedly enrich our understanding of their position. More importantly, it provides only a snapshot of teachers' views. Both Lacey's (1977) and Stephen Ball's work (Ball and Lacey, 1980) indicate that the philosophies of teachers are a complex amalgam of the bias of the subject discipline and the way in which they are socialised professionally. Work that I have already begun, following PGCE students into their first two years of teaching, suggests that teachers define and redefine their positions (Marshall, Turvey and Brindley, 2000).

What this research does tell us, however, is that the views of English teachers are infinitely more complex and well developed than any screaming *Daily Mail* headline or education minister's invective might suggest. When David Almond, teacher and award-winning author of the children's book *Skellig*, suggested (1999) that teachers should be allowed to encourage pupils' creativity in writing and reading, he was met with a violent response from the Secretary of State for Education David Blunkett. While not actually mentioning Almond by name (few doubted to whom he was referring, given that the article appeared only days after Almond's speech) Blunkett wrote in the *Daily Mail*:

> I still encounter those in the education world who would prefer the quiet life of the past, where education was 'progressive' and where the failure of half our pupils was taken for granted. There are even those who suggest that learning to read properly threatens creativity. Can they really be taken seriously? Are they actually claiming that to be illiterate helps you to become a better artist? . . .
>
> I suspect the real reason why these critics say this stifles creativity is that it ends the ill disciplined 'anything goes' philosophy which did so much damage to a generation.
>
> (Blunkett, 1999)

The Rough Guide to English Teachers presents a very different picture. All are committed to encouraging 'critical readers' though their definition of the term may differ. Not one suggests an 'anything goes' philosophy. Yet, arguably, the vast majority of the teachers surveyed take a broadly 'progressive' view of education, where the child's learning is central to the process of teaching.

But the sterile rhetoric of press and politicians has done much to debase the language in which we discuss education. English, central as always to the debate, has suffered particularly in the process. For this rhetoric has ironed out the subtle but significant differences that exist within the subject and reduced genuine intellectual enquiry to the binary world of soundbites – you are either on or off message, for or against the reforms. This has left little or no room for carefully nuanced argument and, more importantly, robbed English teachers of vocabulary in which they can describe their professional activity. For if every time an individual puts forwards the notion of English as an arts subject, of the inexhaustible power of words to move, transport or persuade, they are accused of 'claiming that to be illiterate helps you to become a better artist': then we are in trouble indeed.

Like so many of the teachers in this book my first real love is language – its rhythms and cadences, its capacity to create meaning for the author and audience alike. It is why I became an English teacher. How such a love is to be taught, however, is quite another matter – it requires rigour and thought. It needs Dewey's 'high organisation based upon ideas' (Dewey 1966: 28–9). There is never room for complacency.

That is why we should worry when a *Guardian* leader can announce the death of educational debate. The writer's contribution follows the pattern of all media coverage of the issues for the last three decades. Commenting on the introduction of the new National Curriculum for initial teacher training, they claimed: 'The culmination of the move away from child centred learning came yesterday with the publication of a new compulsory National Curriculum for teacher training courses.' The message was clear. 'All major political parties *are now agreed* [my emphasis] that there has to be more focus on "tried and tested" teaching methods' (*Guardian*, 1997).

But believing that the answers to our educational future lie somewhere in the past, and that all we have to do is to follow the prescribed remedy, stifles innovation. The art of English teaching has been refined and developed precisely because it has not stood still. The hope must be that English teachers will continue to discover, and fight for, those ever harder to find spaces in which to develop the voices of the children they teach.

References

ATL (1996) *Level Best Revisited: An evaluation of the statutory assessment in 1996*, London, ATL Publications.

Abbs, P. (1982) *English within the Arts: A radical alternative for English and the Arts in the curriculum*, London, Hodder and Stoughton.

Abbs, P. (1989a) *A Is for Aesthetic: essays on creative and aesthetic education*, London, Falmer.

Abbs, P. (ed.) (1989b) *The Symbolic Order: A contemporary reader on the arts debate*, London, Falmer.

Adams, A. (ed.) (1982) *New Directions in English Teaching*, London, Falmer.

Adams, A. (1997) Introduction. In S. Tweddle and A. Adams (eds) *English for Tomorrow*, Buckingham, Open University Press.

Almond, D. (1999) Leave Time for Imaginations, *Independent* 15 July.

Appleyard, B. (1994) The Loose Canons of Academe, *Independent* 16 March.

Arnold, M. (1948) *Culture and Anarchy*, J. Dover Wilson (ed.), Cambridge, Cambridge University Press.

Arnold, M. (1979) *Selected Poetry and Prose*, D. Thompson (ed.), London, Heinemann.

Ashton, P. and Simons, M., with Denaro, D. and Raleigh, M. (1979) *Our Lives: Young Peoples' Autobiographies*, London, English Centre.

Bain, R., Bibby, B. and Walton, S. (1989) *The National Curriculum: Summary and commentary on the proposals of the Cox Committee*, Sheffield, NATE.

Baker, M. (1994) *Who Rules Our Schools?*, London, Hodder and Stoughton.

Ball, S. J. (1984) Conflict, Panic and Inertia: Mother tongue teaching in England 1970–1983. In W. Herlitz (ed.) *Mother Tongue Education in Europe, Studies in Mother Tongue Education 1, International Mother Tongue Education Network*, Enschede, Netherlands, National Institute for Curriculum Development.

Ball, S. J. (1985) English for the English since 1906. In I. Goodson (ed.) *Social Histories of the Secondary Curriculum: Subjects for study*, London, Falmer.

Ball, S. J. (1987) English Teaching, the State and Forms of Literacy. In S. Kroon and J. Sturm (eds) *Research on Mother Tongue Education in an International Perspective, Studies in Mother Tongue Education 3, International Mother Tongue Education Network*, Enschede, Netherlands, The Advisory Committee for Curriculum Development.

Appendix

The following pages show four teachers' responses to the Rough Guide. In each case the language and type of annotation the teacher has used is broadly representative of the group they have chosen.

Group A

⊂⊃ = influenced decision to choose this

This group are Arnoldian in their view of the subject. They believe in the improving and civilising qualities of literature. It is less, however, about books correcting behaviour than (literature unlocking other worlds) other possibilities; a form of escape. And perhaps most importantly they are about developing an aesthetic sensibility.

This means that the literature they choose will have two purposes. The idea of the reading habit is fostered because, unlike television, it gives more (scope for the imagination to roam.) While there is an overtone of the Protestant work ethic – books are harder – there is also the sense that they allow more freedom than a television drama, where many decisions have already been made. In this sense there is a curious tension between moralistic aims – of hard work and improvement – and at the same time a kind of aesthetic hedonism – you read for pleasure. The former justifies the latter.

more than this – it's to do with admiration of the difficulty and the pleasure to be derived from intellectual challenge

The tension is there in Matthew Arnold's writing, particularly on education. He posits many of his theories on poetry and reading against that which he views as Philistine utilitarianism and yet feels compelled to argue that there is a point to literature. He cannot argue art for art's sake, where his arguments tend. Books must have worth and value.

Leavis is the most obvious inheritor of this tradition, but his work focused the tradition more narrowly on the canonical value of texts. It is his legacy, however, that has made some uneasy that this tradition is in effect a rejection of working class culture. For literature is both an escape of the mind – the light in a dark place – and, through education, a route out of the slums. His emphasis on high and low culture reinforces this, but it is more tellingly worked out in the books of writers like Richard Hoggart, and evident in the biography of Brian Cox.

Literature, then, is intimately tied in with their view of what education is for – it is reformatory at the level of the individual; it is about *it's also teaching people to thi...*

Personally, I'm with John Donne and other metaphysical poets in their understanding of the almost sensual pleasure in intellectual activity – "the felt thought".

personal growth, about personal fulfilment, both emotionally and in terms of life chances. This can lead to endorsing some form of selection as a means of enhancing the chances of those who will benefit from education the most. It is possible that many of this group will not 'set' in the early secondary years as they wish to provide every opportunity for latent qualities to emerge but they will probably introduce some form of setting, however broad, for exam classes. It is most likely to result in the creation of a top set with broad ability groups for the majority and then a bottom set. Some, however, will set that middle group more rigidly.

This is because at a certain significant point they do not believe that you can teach all children in the same way. And most importantly because you may hold back those who can escape or blossom. Their views lead them to concentrate their attention on the most able, with whom they have a rapport and a mission, and the least able, who have clearly identifiable needs. Even though they are concerned by literacy levels at the bottom end, they are unlikely to take a rigidly phonetic approach because they view reading as more than a mechanistic skill.

While such views are not clearly party political, and they take the class system as a given that can only be ameliorated at a personal level, their views on literature brought them into conflict with the Conservative government. This group seeks to foster empathy, the imagination and enlightenment in the students they teach. While they are not averse to the idea that some literature is better than others, they cannot have that choice imposed because teaching is about finding the book that will create the spark. It is about inspiration, which almost by definition cannot be produced by government diktat.

On the whole this group is also in favour of 100 per cent coursework because it avoids the reductive nature of timed tests. It is hard to produce inspiration to order. Similarly they are deeply suspicious of criterion-referencing because it is hard to predict originality. As this is one of the chief virtues they are trying to foster, criteria seem to miss the point, not least because they are perceived as bureaucratic. They view the current exams, and KS3 tests in particular, as reducing literature to the accumulation of facts rather than an opportunity to develop a personal response. In the pupils' own writing they will place a strong emphasis on flair and originality. *and honesty.*

In addition, because they prefer impromptu ways of working to what they see as more formulaic methods, English departments run by this group often find themselves at variance with the senior management in their schools, who want 'checklist' assessment policies or rigid schemes of work. As teachers they are unashamedly teacher-centred because the teacher is the conduit of inspiration. Entitlement for the children lies less in the curriculum they follow, therefore, than in their access to good teaching. GCSE and the National Curriculum encouraged them to enter all sets for literature because the courses allowed for the possibility of finding appropriate texts and learning for all pupils.

The other way in which the National Curriculum influenced this group was in their views on Standard English. They are interested in the study of the grammar of English which relates to their position on Standard English. They would describe this in terms of command rather than ownership or empowerment. Yet their interest in grammar leads them away from any simple definitions of correctness towards the notion of a facility with language. Their emphasis on creativity resists the notion of the formulaic. The 'knowledge about language' strand in the National Curriculum gave them a diverse way of studying the language away from the old primers without necessarily involving them in discourse analysis or critical language awareness which takes a more oppositional stance to the language of power.

As with Leavis, *Hard Times* is a seminal text which defines their opposing views. They are with the circus people – the realm of the imagination. The Gradgrinds of this world are the enemy.

Not been an emphasis on class & routes out of the working class.

You've overemphasised this group's attachment to empathy in studying literature (~~or is it my?~~)

I think it values analysis, argument & 'rigour'.

Group B

This group is significant because of the way in which they attempt to manage educational change, both within the school and at national level, and in particular the way in which they <u>confront those changes</u> which most <u>impinge upon their beliefs and practice as English teachers</u>. Many in this group, though by no means all, will have entered the teaching profession from the mid-eighties onwards so that their degrees may have been influenced by some form of literary theory and their training will have emphasised the rationale behind mixed-ability teaching as well as the benefits of coursework.

Many will never have taught O-level or CSE, a significant number will either not have taught long before the National Curriculum was introduced or never known a time when it was not there. The most recent entrants to the profession will not have had the opportunity to teach 100 per cent coursework. While some of these will have experienced its benefits as pupils, many will have just missed it both at school and then as a teacher. They will, to a person, say, however, that they <u>oppose government reforms</u> in terms of both the content and the assessment of the English curriculum.

Nevertheless they will <u>place the emphasis on preparing pupils for what is in store for them</u>. Some, though by no means all, will, for example, want to see the new grammar tests and perhaps pilot them because it is important to be ready for whatever is coming. <u>Advanced knowledge may allow damage limitation</u>. They are also keen to implement new initiatives and will set up <u>working parties</u> around issues such as boys and English, whole-school language and reading policies and the like. Their departmental policy documents will reflect <u>clear positions</u> on <u>equal opportunities</u> including gender, race and often class. They have adopted a systematic approach to assessment policies, schemes of work and statements of aims partly from a desire to democratise the pupils' entitlement and partly from a belief that management systems will enhance the quality control and <u>monitoring of the department</u>.

[Handwritten margin notes, left side:]
e tmth
re –
t I do
t place
much
gy
I could
my
thons
the,
se.

– we
st work
n what
have,
nsure
child
ers an
mination
repared.

[Handwritten note, right of paragraph:] DO NOT LIKE GRAMMAR TESTS.

[Handwritten note, right margin:] I do feel akin to this

[Handwritten note, right margin:] Very valuable – cross-curricular working parties.

[Handwritten note, bottom left:]
sclnated by these reports.
ish I had more time
– spend analysing exam
sults, etc.

[Handwritten note, bottom centre:]
Vital, i.e. positive comments
to each other – professional
development.

For them, the English curriculum allows for the possibility of <u>em-powering pupils</u> by giving them the ability to <u>analyse critically the society in which they live</u>. Again they are keen to equip and prepare pupils with the critical tools that they need to analyse any text. This view informs both their approach to literature and the study of language and has led them to consider the importance of the role of the media. Texts are chosen which highlight issues and critical possibilities. Teachers are likely to emphasise the social context in which they were produced. When considering the issue of Standard English they would be likely to look at the power relationships implied in the phrase and do work on dialect and regional variety. In pupils' writing they <u>reward flair and originality</u> as well as <u>thoroughness and attention to detail</u>.

[margin: Definitely.]
[margin: Media and IT part of this.]
[margin: ✓✓]
[margin: Yes — although literature is an escape, (English is also survival tool for the C21]

Mixed-ability grouping is a problem area for this group. While it is an end devoutly to be <u>wished,</u> they argue, it <u>is not always possible</u>. They look to two sources of external pressure that have brought about their dilemma.

The first and most immediate pressure often comes from the senior management within the school. Many heads themselves claim to be sympathetic to the cause of mixed-ability teaching but place the blame on market forces. Parents, they claim, prefer setting and they have to give them what they want to maintain school rolls.

The second is connected. Government reforms, in particular the tiering of tests at KS3 and <u>GCSE exams, have made mixed-ability teaching harder to organise</u>. This has meant that the issue of setting has now affected lower school classes as well as GCSE groups.

This group accommodates these pressures into their view of pupil grouping. While they rarely allow, if in the position of head of department, more than a '<u>top-set and the rest</u>' in year 9, and the possible inclusion of a <u>bottom set at GCSE</u> for those likely to be entered for the foundation tier, they will still argue that they are implementing mixed-ability grouping. They describe it, however, as a 'broad-banding' policy that maintains the spirit, if not the letter, of mixed-ability teaching.

[margin: Do value the 'small' bottom set.]

Again they would share the belief that English is difficult to assess under the current arrangements, not least because acts of the imagination are hard to produce to order, and <u>set books may dampen enthusiasm</u>. But they believe <u>it is possible to accommodate their ideas within the framework</u> – that <u>it is possible to make the best of a bad job</u>. This group believes that the subject is being altered by external pressures and for the worse but continues to look for evidence of their view of <u>English teaching,</u> as a <u>space to analyse and explore</u> texts within the National Curriculum and its assessment arrangements.

[margin: Yes.]

[margin: This in itself is an exciting challenge]

VALUE OF 'TEAM' SKILLS

Combination of some of the thoughts in 'E' – i.e. exploration of group dynamics in the classroom (part of classroom management). Encourage a range of working situations for students, i.e. never work with the same person twice – aim – mixed pairs. Develop team work! Few jobs expect their employees to work alone and early experience of working with a wide range of people will enable young people to foster effective working relationships quickly. – Keen to ask the students to evaluate their team – to be self-critical – to offer constructive advice.

Group D

The chief characteristic of this group is their desire to <u>focus on the skills necessary to be good at English.</u> They are likely to encourage pupils to study spelling, punctuation and grammar so that they can become confident users of the language. They are also <u>keen to develop creative writing</u> in order to <u>encourage a more imaginative response to language</u> because they believe that English is the only area in the curriculum where this can be done.

They may well, however, stress the importance of language in every day use, for example, writing letters or instructions, in order to ensure that pupils become competent in these forms. Teaching Standard English is important in this endeavour because it will increase pupils' command of the English language and their ability to communicate effectively and accurately.

<u>In reading they are concerned to know how much pupils have under-stood of what they have read and to develop their reading skills.</u> Com-prehension is likely, therefore, to be an important teaching strategy, both as a means of assessing the pupils' understanding and as a means of increasing their reading skills. They believe that it is important that children read and are likely to commend it as an activity over computer games and watching television. Study of the media is not, therefore, a high priority in their classrooms, as they would prefer pupils to exercise their critical skills on more traditional texts.

<u>They believe strongly that it is important for children to be taught appropriately according to their needs and that teachers should be able to focus on addressing the weaknesses of the pupils, particularly the technical and linguistic.</u> They may well consider that not all pupils are capable of studying certain writers and that while it is important to stretch and challenge the most able, by presenting them with demand-ing literature, it is often preferable to give the 'less-able' books that are more relevant to them, or abridged versions so that they can appreciate

the story. They are particularly aware that many less able children find poetry difficult.

This view of the appropriate needs of the pupils leads them to favour setting and they may well be sympathetic to the notion of selection. In a non-selective school, they are more likely to implement a system that is finely-tuned rather than broad-banding, because they believe it will allow them to concentrate more fully on each group's particular needs and set appropriate work.

They acknowledge the need for coursework because it offers more opportunity for creative writing but they are likely to argue for the discipline that exam work provides. For this reason they often opted for the 50 per cent exam/coursework divide when GCSE allowed such a choice, though they were more likely to take this option with literature, because it more obviously presented a body of knowledge to be tested. Given the importance of exams, they believe it is important to prepare children thoroughly for them. When assessing pupils' work they are likely to give priority to those pupils who are accurate and controlled users of English.

They are, however, not necessarily in favour of many of the education reforms because they believe that it has reduced their ability to control the curriculum and choose work that is appropriate for the pupils. They dislike the sense of something being externally imposed on them that will interfere with their ways of working, even if they are broadly sympathetic to some of the National Curriculum's aims. They are keenly aware of the workload implications. Initiatives such as OFSTED inspections or teacher appraisal may also be seen as an unnecessary imposition that detracts from the business of teaching. As a head of department, they are likely to value efficiency and like to see things well-run and organised with clear, definable aims.

I have underlined all that is accurate; there is nothing here which is actually wrong — merely some issues on which I am neutral, or not actively engaged in.

Group E

I stand

Not overture what I actually. More e linguistics,

This group have been described as 'cultural theorists' or interested in
critical literacy, but in many ways they form a broader spectrum than
this because not everyone who may be classified under this heading is
as interested in critical or, more especially, linguistic, theory as this
description suggests. They form a spectrum of opinion that is coloured
by the degree of emphasis placed on literature. At one end can be
found those influenced by linguistic theories which emphasise the notion of critical literacy arising out of theorists like Gramsci. At the
other end are those influenced by a literary model of cultural dissent,
which emphasises the political context and connotations of all literature and the need to challenge received norms.

I think this is me.

Many teachers gravitate towards the middle of the spectrum, or
modify their opinion depending on the area being discussed, so they
do not form two distinct groups. As a group these teachers are marked
chiefly by the rigour of their perception of culture and the way this
impacts on their view of the subject, pedagogy and classroom organisation. As a group they are, of necessity, clearly to the left of centre.

Yes

This group sees personal growth in terms of empowerment. This has
manifested itself in various ways over the last twenty years and may
still change, depending on the position in the spectrum, but the aim is
always similar. In the late sixties and early seventies much of the emphasis lay in discovering a personal voice. Spearheaded by teachers
like Chris Searle in Hackney, and later through publications such as
Our Lives, published by the English and Media Centre, this movement sought to empower pupils by allowing them freedom of expression. It was a way of breaking free of the dead weight of the Leavisite
canon.

But this emphasis appears to have been amalgamated, in the late
seventies and early eighties, with literary theory which allowed students to deconstruct texts, knowingly to debunk the canon and find

alternative texts that had been omitted. It also led to the rise of media studies and the examination of popular culture. Some have, however, been dissatisfied with the cultural relativism which this position implies and so have sought to explore more the idea of radical readings of canonical texts as well as suggesting alternatives to that canon.

The notion of discovering a personal voice has been maintained but refined. While the significance of non-standard variants is passionately defended, a new orthodoxy has emerged, namely that pupils are disenfranchised if they are not given access to standard forms of English, provided that these are discussed within the context of notions of the language of power and that notions of appropriateness are debated within the idea of critical language awareness. In some quarters, in fact, there is a hint of a movement away from the pre-eminence of literature within the English curriculum, and towards reconsidering language as an area of study. The emergence of knowledge about language in the Cox curriculum facilitated this development.

This flux in the ways of discussing empowerment is symptomatic of the mind-set of this group. Their position must constantly be reappraised and so its manifestations will continue to alter and this means, to an extent, that their classroom practice may alter also. They are likely to be influenced by ideas on learning theory as there is no rigid divide between theory and practice. Many will have been influenced by theorists such as Vygotsky, but they are likely to experiment with new ideas and theories within the classroom. While they pay lip service to the idea of teacher as facilitator, they are in fact highly directional in the way in which they teach.

Nevertheless, they are totally committed to mixed-ability teaching. This is mainly to do with their notion of democratic entitlement, not only in the desire not to treat one group differently by labelling them, but also to do with the idea that all children should have access to the same texts and ideas. Both these connect under the more general heading of equal opportunities. It is not, as has been suggested, saying all children are the same, but is insisting on the idea that all should have the same opportunities.

This insistence on mixed-ability teaching does, however, influence pedagogy, for while the teacher is highly directional they use the pupils to facilitate the learning. This is where the role of oracy and Britton's interpretation of Vygotsky is so significant. Group work and discussion are essential to the way in which the subject is delivered because it allows all pupils access to challenging texts. So, too, is coursework because it allows pupils to explore the same text in a far greater variety of ways than the terminal exam and allows for more scope in the way

yes

in which the pupils' work is approached. This emphasis may well lead them to value originality when assessing pupils' work.

All this has brought this group into direct conflict with government reform and it was this group that spearheaded the opposition to testing and the new curriculum. They have come round to the notion of a more prescribed curriculum and schemes of work through the notion of an entitlement curriculum as a form of equal opportunities, but are opposed to the way in which this currently manifests itself in legislation.

True – I am for entitlement but clearly this should be left in the hands of people who 'know'.

Ball, S. J. and Lacey, C. (1980) Subject Disciplines as the Opportunity for Group Action: A measured critique of subject sub-cultures. In P. Woods (ed.) *Teacher Strategies in the Sociology of the School*, London, Croom Helm.

Ball, S. J., Kenny, A. and Gardiner, D. (1990) Literacy Policy and the Teaching of English. In I. Goodson and P. Medway (eds) *Bringing English to Order*, London, Falmer.

Barnes, A. (1997) An English Curriculum for the 21st Century, *Education Review* 11(2): 35–9.

Barnes, A. (1998) Reading at Ages 14–16. In B. Cox (ed.) *Literacy Is not Enough: Essays on the importance of reading*, Manchester, Manchester University Press.

Barnes, D., Barnes, D. and Clarke, S. (1984) *Versions of English*, London, Heinemann Educational Books.

Barnes, D., Britton, J. and Rosen, H. (1972) *Language, the Learner and the School*, Harmondsworth, Penguin Books.

Barrs, M. (1990) *Words not Numbers: Assessment in English*, Sheffield, NATE.

Batsleer, J. (1985) *Re-writing English: Cultural politics of gender and class*, London, Methuen.

Berelson, B. R. and Steiner, G. A. (1964) *Human Behaviour: An inventory of scientific findings*, New York, Harcourt.

Bergonzi, B. (1990) *Exploding English: Criticism, theory, culture*, Oxford, Clarendon.

Black, P. J. and Wiliam, D. (1998a) Assessment and Classroom Learning, *Assessment in Education: Principles, Policy and Practice* 5(1): 7–74.

Black, P. J. and Wiliam, D. (1998b) Inside the Black Box: Raising standards through classroom assessment, *Phi Delta Kappan* 80(2): 139–48.

Blunkett, D. (1999) Commentary: Moaners who are cheating your children, *Daily Mail* 19 July.

Boaler, J. (1997) *Experiencing School Mathematics: Teaching styles, sex and setting*, Buckingham, Open University Press.

Bousted, M. (1993) When Will They Ever Learn?, *English in Education* 27(3): 33–41.

Britton, J. (1974) *Language and Learning*, Harmondsworth, Penguin Books.

Britton, J. and Martin, N. (1989) English Teaching – Is It a Profession? *English in Education* 23(2): 1–8.

Britton, J. and Squires, J. (1975) Foreword. In J. Dixon *Growth through English*, Oxford, Oxford University Press.

Brumfit, C. (1992) *The Oxford Companion to the English Language*, Oxford, Oxford University Press.

Burgess, A. (1996) A Different Angle: English teaching and its narratives, *Changing English* 3(1): 57–77.

CBI (nd) *Coursework*, London, CBI.

Callaghan, J. (1996) The Ruskin College Speech. In J. Ahier, B. Cosin and M. Hales (eds) *Diversity and Change: Education, policy and selection*, London, Routledge.

Carter, R. (ed.) (1991) *Language in the National Curriculum: The LINC reader*, London, Hodder and Stoughton.

Carter, R. (ed.) (1992) *Language in the National Curriculum: Materials for professional development*, Nottingham, Nottingham University Department of English.

Chubb, J. and Moe, T. (1990) *Politics, Markets, and American Schools*, Washington DC, The Brookings Institution.

Clark, U. (1994) Bringing English to Order: A personal account of the NCC English Evaluation Project, *English in Education* 28(1): 33–8.

Close, G., Furlong, T. and Simon, S. (1995) *The Impact and Effect of KS3 Tasks and Tests on the Curriculum, Teaching and Learning and Teachers' Assessments: A report from King's College London University, commissioned by the NUT*, London, NUT.

Close, G., Furlong, T. and Swain, J. (1997) *The Validity of the 1996 Key Stage 2 Tests in English Maths and Science: A report commissioned by the Association of Teachers and Lecturers*, London, King's College London School of Education.

Coe, R. (1999) The Effect of Feedback on Teachers' Attitudes: Difficulties of measurement. Paper presented at British Educational Research Association 25th annual conference held at University of Sussex.

Cooper, P. and Davies, C. (1993) The Impact of National Curriculum Assessment Arrangements on English Teachers' Thinking and Classroom Practice in Secondary English Schools, *Teaching and Teacher Education* 9(5/6): 559–70.

Cox, B. (1991) *Cox on Cox: An English Curriculum for the 1990s*, London, Hodder and Stoughton.

Cox, B. (1992) *The Great Betrayal: Memoirs of a life in education*, London, Hodder and Stoughton.

Cox, B. (1995) *Cox on the Battle for the English Curriculum*, London, Hodder and Stoughton.

Cox, B. (ed.) (1998) *Literacy Is not Enough: Essays on the importance of reading*, Manchester, Manchester University Press.

Cox, B. and Boyson, R. (eds) (1975) *Black Paper 1975: The Fight for Education*, London, Dent.

Cox, B. and Boyson, R. (eds) (1977) *Black Paper 1977*, London, Temple Smith.

Cox, B. and Dyson, A. E. (eds) (1969) *Fight for Education: A black paper*, London, Critical Quarterly Society.

Cox, B. and Dyson, A. E. (eds) (1970a) *Black Paper Two: The crisis in education.* London, Critical Quarterly Society.

Cox, B. and Dyson, A. E. (eds) (1970b) *Black Paper Three: Goodbye Mr Shore.* London, Critical Quarterly Society.

Creber, P. (1990) *Thinking through English*, Buckingham, Open University Press.

DES [Department of Education and Science] (1964) *Lockwood Committee: Report of a working party on the school curriculum and examinations*, London, HMSO.

DES (1975) *A Language for Life: Report of the committee of inquiry appointed by the secretary of state for science and education under the chairmanship of Sir Alan Bullock* [Bullock Report], London, HMSO.

DES and WO [Department and Education and Science and Welsh Office] (1967) *Children and Their Primary Schooling: The Plowden Report of the Central Advisory Council for England and Wales* [Plowden Report], London, HMSO.

DES and WO (1988) *A Report of the Committee of Inquiry into the Teaching of English* [Kingman Report], London, HMSO.

DES and WO (1989) *English for Ages 5–16* [Cox Report], London, HMSO.

DES and WO (1990) *English in the National Curriculum*, London, HMSO.

DfE [Department for Education] and WO (1993) *English for Ages 5–16* [Pascall curriculum], London, HMSO.

DfEE [Department for Education and Employment] and WO (1995) *English in the National Curriculum* [Dearing curriculum], London, HMSO.

DfEE (1997) *Excellence in Schools*, London, HMSO.

DfEE (1998) *The National Literacy Strategy*, London, HMSO.

DfEE (1999a) *English: The national curriculum for England*, London, HMSO.

DfEE (1999b) *The National Curriculum: Handbook for secondary teachers in England* [Curriculum 2000], London, HMSO.

DfEE (2000) *Draft Proposals for KS3 Literacy Framework*, Unpublished.

Davies, C. (1991) The Future of English, *English in Education* 25(3): 28–32.

Davies, C. (1992) English Teacher Ideologies: An empirical study, *British Educational Research Journal* 18(2): 193–207.

Davies C. (1996) *What Is English Teaching?*, Buckingham, Open University Press.

Davies, C. and Benton, P. (1991) What is Secondary English For? In R. Protherough and J. Atkinson (eds) *The Making of English Teachers*, Buckingham, Open University Press.

Departmental Committtee of the Board of Education (1921) *The Teaching of English in England: Being the report of the departmental committee appointed by the President of the Board of Education to inquire into the position of English in the educational system of England* [Newbolt Report], London, HMSO.

Dewey, J. (1916) *Democracy and Education*, New York, Macmillan.

Dewey, J. (1966) *Experience and Education*, London, Collier Books.

Dickens, C. (1980) *Hard Times*, Harmondsworth, Penguin Books.

Dixon, J. (1975) *Growth through English*, Oxford, Oxford University Press.

Dixon, J. (1994) Categories to Frame an English Curriculum, *English in Education* 28(1): 3–9.

Dover Wilson, J. (1948) Introduction. In M. Arnold, *Culture and Anarchy*, J. Dover Wilson (ed.), Cambridge, Cambridge University Press.

Doyle, B. (1989) *English and Englishness*, London, Routledge.

Eagleton, T. (1991) The Enemy Within, *English in Education* 25(3): 3–10.

Eliot, T. S. (1973) The Wasteland. In *The Wasteland and Other Poems*, London, Faber and Faber.

Eliot, T. S. (1975) Notes Towards a Definition of Culture. In F. Kermode (ed.) *Selected Prose of T. S. Eliot*, London, Faber and Faber.

English and Media Centre (nd) *English Curriculum: Gender: materials for discussion*, London, English and Media Centre.

Findlay, K. and Goodwyn, A. (1999) The Cox Models Revisited: English teachers' views of their subject and the national curriculum, *English in Education* 33(2): 19–31.

Fitz-Gibbon, C. T. (1996) *Monitoring Education: Indicators, quality and effectiveness*, London, Cassell.

Fitzgerald, F. S. (1991) *The Great Gatsby*, Cambridge, Cambridge University Press.

Freire, P. and Macedo, D. (1987) *Literacy: Reading the word and the world*, London, Routledge.

Furlong, T. (1998) Reading in the Primary School. In B. Cox (ed.) *Literacy Is not Enough*, Manchester, Manchester University Press.

Gerwirtz, S., Ball, S. and Bowe, R. (1995) *Markets, Choice and Equity*, Buckingham, Open University Press.

Goodson, I. and Medway, P. (eds) (1990) *Bringing English to Order*, London, Falmer.

Goodwyn, A. (1992) English Teachers and the Cox Models, *English in Education* 26(3): 4–11.

Graddol, D., Maybin J., Mercer, N. and Swann, J. (eds) (1991) *Talk and Learning 5–16: An inservice pack on the oracy for teachers*, Buckingham, Open University Press.

Graham, D. (1996) *The Education Racket: Who cares about the children?* Glasgow, Neil Wilson Publishing.

Griffiths, P. (1992) *English at the Core*, Buckingham, Open University Press.

Guardian (1997) Editorial, *Guardian* 27 June.

Hall, N. (1997) Going Forward into the Past. In N. McLelland (ed.) *Building a Literate Nation: The strategic agenda for literacy over the next five years*, Stoke on Trent, Trentham Books.

Handy, C. (1995) *The Empty Raincoat: Making sense of the future*, London, Arrow Books.

Hargreaves, A. (1994) *Changing Teachers, Changing Times: Teachers' work and culture in the postmodern age*, London, Cassell.

Harlen, W. and Macolm, H. (1997) *Setting and Streaming: A research review*, Scottish Council for Educational Research.

Hayhoe, M. (1982) A Historical View of Essay Marking. In A. Adams (ed.) *New Directions in English Teaching*, Lewes, Falmer Press.

Hewitt, E. A. and Gordon, D. I. (1965) *English Language: An experiment in school assessing (first interim report)*, Manchester, Joint Matriculation Board.

Hitchens, C. (1988) *Prepared for the Worst: Selected essays and minority reports*, London, Chatto and Windus.

Hoggart, R. (1998) Critical Literacy and Creative Reading. In B. Cox (ed.) *Literacy Is not Enough: Essays on the importance of reading*, Manchester, Manchester University Press.

Holbrook, D. (1961) *English for Maturity*, Cambridge, Cambridge University Press.

Holbrook, D. (1964) *English for the Rejected*, Cambridge, Cambridge University Press.

Holmes, E. (1911) *What Is and What Might Be*, London, Constable.

Honey, J. (1997) *Language Is Power*, London, Faber and Faber.

Jones, K. (1991) Revolution and Restoration, *English and Media Magazine* 25: 4–7.

Jones, K. (ed.) (1992) *English in the National Curriculum: Cox's Revolution*, London, Bedford Way Paper, Kogan Page.

Kress, G. (1995) *Writing the Future: English and the making of a culture of innovation*, Sheffield, NATE Papers in Education.

Kress, G. (1996) Internalisation and Globalisation: Rethinking a curriculum of communication, *Comparative Education* 32(2): 185–96.

Kress, G. (1997) *Before Writing*, London, Routledge.

LATE (1993) *KS3: Voices from the Classroom*, London, LATE.

LATE (1995) *The Real Cost of SATs: A report from the London Association for the Teaching of English*, London, LATE.

Lacey, C. (1977) *The Socialization of Teachers*, London, Methuen.

Leavis, F. R. (1993) *The Great Tradition: George Eliot, Henry James, Joseph Conrad*, Harmondsworth, Penguin Books.

Likert, R. (1931) A Technique for the Measurement of Attitudes. In *Archives of Psychology*, New York, Columbia University Press.

Lloyd, M. (1994) *Save English Coursework: Coursework in GCSE English*, Sheffield, NATE.

Lloyd, M. (1997) Dark before Dawn on Coursework? *NATE News*.

Mabry, J. (1999) Writing to the Rubric: Lingering effects of traditional standardised testing on direct writing assessment, *Phi Delta Kappan* 80(9): 673–9.

MacCabe, C. (1990) Language, Literature, Identity: Reflections on the Cox Report, *Critical Quarterly* 32(4): 7–33.

MacDiarmid, H. (1985) A Drunk Man Looks at the Thistle. In *The Complete Poems of Hugh MacDiarmid Vol. 2*, M. Grieve and W. R. Aitken (eds), Harmondsworth, Penguin.

McLelland, N. (ed.) (1997) *Building a Literate Nation: The strategic agenda for literacy over the next five years*, Stoke on Trent, Trentham Books.

Marenbon, J. (1987) *English Our English*, London, Centre for Policy Studies.

Marenbon, J. (1994) English, the Government and the Curriculum. In M. Hayhoe and S. Parker (eds) *Who Owns English?* Buckingham, Open University Press.

Marshall, B. (1996a) Whose Canon Is it Anyway? *Critical Quarterly* 38(4): 97–102.

Marshall, B. (1996b) No More Tiers, *British Journal of Curriculum and Assessment* 6(2): 18–19.

Marshall, B. (1997) Assessment – a Community of Interpreters, *Critical Quarterly* 39(2): 101–9.

Marshall, B. (1998) English Teachers and the Third Way. In B. Cox (ed.) *Literacy Is not Enough: Essays on the importance of reading*, Manchester, Manchester University Press.

Marshall, B. (1999) The Development and Validation of a Large-scale Qualitative Research Instrument for Eliciting the Implicit Philosophies of English Teachers. Unpublished University of London PhD thesis.

Marshall, B. and Brindley S. (1998) Cross-phase or Just a Lack of Communication: Models of English at key stages 2 and 3 and their possible effect on pupil transfer, *Changing English* 5(2): 123–34.

Marshall, B., Turvey, A. and Brindley, S. (2000) English Teachers – Born or Made: A longitudinal study on the socialisation of English teachers. Paper presented at the 26th annual conference of the British Educational Research Association held at the University of Cardiff.

Marshall, B., Reay, D. and Wiliam, D. (1999) 'I found it confrontational': Rethinking Questionnaires as a Large-scale Research Instrument. Paper presented at British Educational Research Association 25th annual conference held at University of Sussex.

Marum, E. (ed.) (1995) *Towards 2000: The future of childhood, literacy and schooling*, London, Falmer.

Matthieson, M. (1975) *Preachers of Culture*, London, Allen and Unwin.

Meek, M. and Miller, J. (eds) (1984) *Changing English: Essays for Harold Rosen*, London, Heinemann Educational Books for the Institute of Education.

Medway, P. (1990) Into the Sixties: English and English society at a time of change. In I. Goodson and P. Medway (eds) *Bringing English to Order*, London, Falmer.

Medway, P. (1996) Technology and English: Language and practical applications. In M. Simons (ed.) *Where We've Been: Articles from the English and Media Magazine*, London, English and Media Centre.

Milton, J. (1977) Areopagitica. In *Complete English Poems, Of Education, Areopagitica*, G. Campbell (ed.), London, J. M. Dent.

Morgan, D. L. (1988) *Focus Groups as Qualitative Research*, Newbury Park CA, Sage.

Morgan, D. L. (1995) *Successful Focus Groups: Advancing the state of the art*, Newbury Park, CA, Sage.

Motion, A. (1998) *Keats*, London, Faber and Faber.

NATE (nd) *The Redbridge Handbook*, Sheffield, NATE.

NATE (1992) *Made Tongue Tied by Authority: New orders for English? A response by the National Association for the Teaching of English to the review of the statutory order for English*, Sheffield, NATE.

NATE (1998) *Position Paper: Coursework assessment in GCSE and 'A' level English and English literature*, Sheffield, NATE.

NEA (nd) *Course Work in GCSE*, Manchester, NEA.

NCC (1992) *National Curriculum English: The case for revising the order*, York, NCC.

National Writing Project (1989a) *Writing and Learning*, Walton-on-Thames, Thomas Nelson.

National Writing Project (1989b) *Audiences for Writing*, Walton-on-Thames, Thomas Nelson.

National Writing Project (1990) *Writing Partnerships 1: Home school and community*, Walton-on-Thames, Thomas Nelson.

O'Connell, J., Davidson, J. and Layder, D. (1994) *Methods, Sex and Madness*, London, Routledge.

Paine, T. (1994) *The Rights of Man* and *Common Sense*, London, D. Campbell.

Paulin, T. (ed.) (1986) *The Faber Book of Political Verse*, London, Faber and Faber.

Paulin, T. (ed.) (1990) *The Faber Book of Vernacular Verse*, London, Faber and Faber.

Paulin, T. (1996a) Undesirable, *London Review of Books* 9 May.

Paulin, T. (1996b) Serbonian Bog and Wild Gas: A note and a pamphlet. In J. Uglow (ed.) *Cultural Babbage*, London, Faber and Faber.

Paulin, T. (1998) *The Day Star of Liberty*, London, Faber and Faber.

Peim, N. (1990) NATE and the Politics of English, *English in Education* 24(2): 20–30.

Petch, J. A. (1967) *English Language: An experiment in assessing, second interim report*, Manchester, Joint Matriculation Board.

Phillips, M. (1992a) The Closing of a Teacher's Mind, *Guardian* 16 October.

Phillips, M. (1992b) English as She Is Tort, *Guardian* 9 October.

Phillips, M. (1993) Muddling through English, *Guardian* 22 January.

Phillips, M. (1994) Education's Guerrillas Prepare for War, *Guardian* 3 January.

Phillips, M. (1997) *All Must Have Prizes*, London, Little, Brown and Co.

Phillips, M. (1998) Question: Why Is Teaching Grammar Still Taboo? Answer: Because Teachers Don't Understand It, *Observer* 10 May.

Poulson, L. (1998) *The English Curriculum in Schools*, London, Cassell.

Protherough, R. (1995) Introduction: Whose curriculum? In R. Protherough and P. King (eds) *The Challenge of English in the National Curriculum*, London, Routledge.

Protherough, R. and Atkinson, J. (eds) (1991) *The Making of English Teachers*, Buckingham, Open University Press.

Protherough, R. and Atkinson, J. (1994) Shaping the Image of an English Teacher. In S. Brindley (ed.) *Teaching English*, London, Routledge.

Protherough, R., Atkinson, J. and Fawcett, J. (1989) *The Effective Teaching of English*, London, Longman.

QCA (1998) *The Grammar Papers: Perspectives on the teaching of grammar in the national curriculum*, London, QCA Publishing.

QCA (1999a) Key Stage 3 Schemes of Work, unpublished.

QCA (1999b) *Not Whether but How: Teaching grammar at key stages 3 and 4*, London, QCA Publishing.

QCA (1999c) *Improving Writing at Key Stages 3 and 4*, London, QCA Publishing.

Raban-Brisby, B. (1995) The State of English in the State of England. In B. Raban with G. Brooks and S. Wolfendale (eds) *Developing Language and Literacy*, Stoke on Trent, Trentham Books.

Raban, B., Clark, U. and McIntyre, J. (1994) *Evaluation of the Implementation of English in the National Curriculum at Key Stages 1, 2 and 3*, London, SCAA.

Raleigh, M., Richmond, J. and Simons, M. (ed.) (nd) *The English Curriculum: Race: materials for discussion*, London, English and Media Centre.

Richmond, J. (1991) What Do We Mean by Knowledge about Language? In R. Carter (ed.) *The National Curriculum: The LINC reader*, London, Hodder and Stoughton.

Rooke, H. M. and Hewitt, E. A. (1970) *An Experimental Scheme of School Assessment in Ordinary Level English Language: Third report*, Manchester, Joint Matriculation Board.

SCAA (1996) *Promoting Continuity between Key Stage 2 and Key Stage 3*, Hayes, SCAA Publishing.

Said, E. (1993) *Culture and Imperialism*, London, Chatto and Windus.

St John Brooks, C. (1983) English: A curriculum for personal development? In M. Hammersley and A. Hargreaves (eds) *Curriculum Practice*, Lewes, Falmer.

Sammons, O., Hillman, J. and Mortimore, P. (1995) *Key Characteristics of Effective Schools*, London, Institute of Education, International School of Effectiveness and Improvement Centre.

Sampson, G. (1952) *English for the English*, Cambridge, Cambridge University Press.

Savva, H. (1991) The Rights of Bilingual Children. In R. Carter (ed.) *Knowledge about Language: The LINC Reader*, London, Hodder and Stoughton.

Sayer, A. (1993) *Method in Social Science: a realist approach*, London: Routledge.

Searle, C. (ed.) (1972) *Fireworks*, London, Jonathan Cape.

Simons, M. (ed.) (1996a) *English and Media Magazine* 34.

Simons, M. (ed.) (1996b) Where We've Been: A brief history of English teaching 1920–1970. In M. Simons (ed.) *Where We've Been: Articles from the English and Media Magazine*, London, English and Media Centre.

Smith, G. A. (1978) *JMB Experience of the Moderation of Internal Assessments*, Manchester, Joint Matriculation Board.

Snow, J. (1991) On the Subject of English, *English in Education* 25(3): 18–28.

Street, B. (1996) Academic Literacies. In D. Baker, J. Clay and C. Fox (eds) *Challenging Ways of Knowing*, London, Falmer.

Street, B. (1997) The Implications of the New Literacy Studies for Literacy Education, *English in Education* 31(3): 44–55.

Stronach, I. and MacLure, M. (1998) *Educational Research Undone: The postmodern embrace*, Buckingham, Open University Press.

Sukhnanden, L. with Lee, B. (1998) *Streaming, Setting and Grouping by Ability: A review of the literature*, Slough, NFER.

Tate, N. (1996) Why Learn? Keynote address to the Association of Teachers and Lecturers, June.

Tate, N. (1998) What Is Education For? The Fifth Annual Education Lecture, King's College London, London.

Todorov, T. (1988) Knowledge in Social Anthropology: Distancing and universality, *Anthropology Today* 4(2): 2–5.

Traves, P. (1996) The Entitlement to Be 'Properly Literate'. In M. Simons (ed.) *Where We've Been: Articles from the English and Media Magazine*, London, English and Media Centre.

Tweddle, S. (1995) A Curriculum for the Future: A curriculum built for change, *English in Education* 29(2): 3–11.

Tweddle, S. and Adams, A. (eds) (1997) *English for Tomorrow*, Buckingham, Open University Press.

Unger, R. K. (1983) Through the Looking Glass: No wonderland yet! (The reciprocal relationship between methodology and modes of reality), *Psychology of Women's Quarterly* 8: 9–32.

Viswanathan, G. (1989) *Masks of Conquests: Literary study and British rule in India*, London, Faber and Faber.

Vygotsky, L. S. (1984) *Mind in Society*, Cambridge MA, Harvard University Press.

Vygotsky, L. S. (1986) *Thought and Language*, Cambridge MA, Harvard University Press.

West, A. (1995) The Centrality of Literature in Teaching English. In S. Brindley (ed.) *Teaching English*, London, Routledge.

Whitehead, F. (1966) *The Disappearing Dais: A study in the principles and practice of English teaching*, London, Chatto and Windus.

Wiliam, D. (1994) Assessing Authentic Tasks: Alternatives to mark-schemes, *Nordic Studies in Mathematics Education* 2(1): 48–68.

Wiliam, D. (1995a) It'll All End in Tiers, *British Journal of Curriculum and Assessment* 6(1): 21–4.

Wiliam, D. (1995b) The Development of National Curriculum Assessment in England and Wales. In T. Oakland and R. K. Hambleton (eds) *International Perspectives on Academic Assessment*, Boston, Kluwer Academic Publishers.

Wiliam, D. (1996) Standards in Education: A matter of trust, *The Curriculum Journal* 7(3): 293–306.

Wiliam, D. (1998) The Validity of Teachers' Assessments. Paper presented at the 22nd annual conference of the International Group for the Psychology of Mathematics Education, Stellenbosch, South Africa.

Wilkes, J. (1998) Reading for Pupils Age 11–14. In B. Cox (ed.) *Literacy Is not Enough: Essays on the importance of reading*, Manchester, Manchester University Press.

Williams, R. (1961) *Culture and Society*, Harmondsworth, Penguin.

Wilson, A. (1965) Foreword. In E. A. Hewitt and D. I. Gordon *English Language: An experiment in school assessing (first interim report)*, Manchester, Joint Matriculation Board.

Wittig, M. (1985) Metatheoretical Dilemmas in the Psychology of Gender, *American Psychologist* 40: 800–12.

Woods, P., Jeffrey, B., Troman, G. and Boyle, M. (1997) *Restructuring Schools, Restructuring Teachers: Responding to change in the primary classroom*, Buckingham, Open University Press.

Woodhead, C. (1998) Academia Gone to Seed, *The New Statesman* 20 March.

Woodhead, C. (1999) The Annual Lecture of Her Majesty's Chief Inspector, London, OFSTED.

Wordsworth, W. (1969) The Solitary Reaper. In *Wordsworth: Poetry and prose*, W. M. Marchent (ed.), London, Rupert Hart Davis.

Index